THE RESONANCE OF EMPTINESS

This book presents an exploration of Buddhist philosophy and practice as a potential resource for an approach to psychotherapy which is responsive to the needs of time and context, and attempts to open up a three-way dialogue between Buddhism, psychotherapy and contemporary discourse to reveal a meaningful theory and practice for a contemporary psychotherapy.

What is unique about this book is that it raises the question of what it is in Buddhism itself that provides such a rich resource for psychotherapy. Gay Watson firmly places her exploration of these themes within the context of contemporary life and thought, as a response to the pathologies, physical and intellectual, of our time.

Organized according to the traditional Tibetan plan of Ground, Path and Fruition, the book first presents a brief survey of Western psychotherapies followed by an introduction to Buddhist views, with particular reference to those most relevant to psychotherapy. Path considers the two major branches of the Buddhist way, ethics and meditation, in the context of contemporary life and psychotherapy. Fruition compares the goals of Buddhism and psychotherapy and subsequently explores the implications of adopting Buddhist influence in the light of contemporary discourse and of the experienced domains of body, speech and mind. Finally, the lineaments of a contemporary Buddhist-inspired psychotherapy are suggested.

Gay Watson is a writer, teacher and psychotherapist.

General Editors:

Charles S. Prebish and Damien Keown

The Curzon Critical Studies in Buddhism Series is a comprehensive study of the Buddhist tradition. The series explores this complex and extensive tradition from a variety of perspectives, using a range of different methodologies.

The Series is diverse in its focus, including historical studies, textual translations and commentaries, sociological investigations, bibliographic studies, and considerations of religious practice as an expression of Buddhism's integral religiosity. It also presents materials on modern intellectual historical studies, including the role of Buddhist thought and scholarship in a contemporary, critical context and in the light of current social issues. The series is expansive and imaginative in scope, spanning more than two and a half millennia of Buddhist history. It is receptive to all research works that inform and advance our knowledge and understanding of the Buddhist tradition.

THE REFLEXIVE NATURE OF AWARENESS
Paul Williams

BUDDHISM AND HUMAN RIGHTS
Edited by Damien Keown, Charles Prebish, Wayne Husted

ALTRUISM AND REALITY
Paul Williams

WOMEN IN THE FOOTSTEPS OF THE BUDDHA
Kathryn R. Blackstone

THE RESONANCE OF EMPTINESS
Gay Watson

IMAGING WISDOM
Jacob N. Kinnard

AMERICAN BUDDHISM
Edited by Duncan Ryuken Williams and Christopher Queen

PAIN AND ITS ENDING
Carol S. Anderson

THE SOUND OF LIBERATING TRUTH
Edited by Sallie B. King and Paul O. Ingram

BUDDHIST THEOLOGY
Edited by Roger R. Jackson and John J. Makransky

EMPTINESS APPRAISED
David F. Burton

THE GLORIOUS DEEDS OF PŪRṆA
Joel Tatelman

CONTEMPORARY BUDDHIST ETHICS
Edited by Damien Keown

INNOVATIVE BUDDHIST WOMEN
Edited by Karma Lekshe Tsomo

TEACHING BUDDHISM IN THE WEST
Edited by V.S. Hori, R.P. Hayes and J.M. Shields

EMPTY VISION
David L. McMahan

SELF, REALITY AND REASON IN TIBETAN PHILOSOPHY
Thupten Jinpa

BUDDHIST PHEMENOLOGY
Dan Lusthaus

THE RESONANCE OF EMPTINESS

A Buddhist Inspiration for a Contemporary Psychotherapy

Gay Watson

First published 1998 by Curzon Press

First published in paperback 2002
by RoutledgeCurzon
11 New Fetter Lane, London EC4P 4EE

Simultaneously published in the USA and Canada
by RoutledgeCurzon
29 West 35th Street, New York, NY 10001

RoutledgeCurzon is an imprint of the Taylor & Francis Group

Typeset in Sabon by LaserScript Ltd, Mitcham, Surrey
Printed and bound in Great Britain by
TJ International, Padstow, Cornwall

British Library Cataloguing in Publication Data
A catalogue record of this book is available from the British Library

Library of Congress Cataloguing in Publication Data
A catalogue record for this book has been requested

ISBN 0-7007-1057-4 (Hbk)
ISBN 0-7007-1566-5 (Pbk)

CONTENTS

ACKNOWLEDGEMENTS

This work had its beginnings in a doctoral thesis, and I would therefore like to express my gratitude firstly to my supervisors: from the side of Buddhist Studies, Dr Tadeusz Skorupski, School of Oriental and African Studies, University of London, and from the side of psychology, Fr Brendan Callaghan S.J., Principal, Heythrop College, University of London. Each most generously gave of their specialist knowledge in their own area and acted as non specialist intelligent reader in the other. I am grateful to them both. For my training as a psychotherapist I would like to thank Maura Sills of the Karuna Institute in Devon, and Karen Kissel Wegela and the staff of the Naropa Institute's Maitri Intensive training for a brief but invaluable introduction to Contemplative Psychology in the summer of 1993. For a bursary which enabled me to travel to Colorado to attend this, I am indebted to the Irwin Fund of the University of London. I would also like to thank Stephen Batchelor who, in the ostensible guise of teaching me Tibetan, has generously shared with me his deep and extensive knowledge of Buddhism over the past years. Without the many and varied discussions we have had, this work would be incomparably the poorer. I thank him too for permission to use his powerful and poetic translation of Nāgārjuna's Mūlamadhyamikakārikā, which is as yet unpublished. I would also like to thank Dr. Maria Phyllactou for her constant encouragement, friendship and help, and also Professor Guy Claxton. My thanks also go to all my psychotherapy clients and supervisees, and to the first students, the 'guinea pigs' of the Sharpham College. Finally my thanks to my husband David, for his constant support, and to him and my children my thanks for their patience during the time I have been engaged on this work.

I am grateful to the following authors and publishers for permission to reproduce quotations and diagrams: (1) Shambhala Publications Inc. and Ken Wilber for the diagram of Spectrum of Consciousness from *No Boundary* by Ken Wilber © 1979 by Ken Wilber. Reprinted by arrangement with Shambhala Publications, Inc. (2) Faber & Faber, Ltd. and Harcourt Brace & Co., for excerpts from "The Dry Salvages" and "East Coker" by T.S. Eliot from *Four Quartets*. (3) Mainstream Publishing Co., and Kenneth White for "In the Great Monotony" by Kenneth White from *Handbook for the Diamond Country* by Kenneth White published by Mainstream Publishing (Edinburgh) Ltd., 1990. (4) University Press of New England and Jane Hirshfield for excerpts from "Lullabye" from *Of Gravity and Angels* © 1988 by Jane Hirshfield, Wesleyan University Press by permission of University Press of new England.

CHAPTER ONE

Introduction

"Our life is a faint tracing on the surface of mystery."[1]

Buddhism and Psychotherapy

Just over one hundred years ago in 1893 the World's Parliament of Religions was held during the Exposition in Chicago. This was, perhaps, the starting point for the popular and not merely scholastic dissemination of Buddhism and Hinduism in the West. Following this conference a disciple of the Rinzai Zen Buddhist representative Shaku Soen came to America to work as an assistant to the scholar and publisher Paul Carus. This disciple was D.T. Suzuki, whose work was not only influential in introducing Zen to the West, but who may be said to have forged the first of many strong links between Buddhism and psychology by his interest in and openness to this then new field.[2] Since that time, not only Zen, but many different forms of Buddhism have, at some stage in their reception in the West, been associated with aspects of psychology. Reading "many different forms of Buddhism" in association with "aspects of psychology", one realises that the first step in this work needs to be definition. For there are, indeed, many forms of psychology, more of psychotherapy, and also many "Buddhisms". Throughout my emphasis will be general rather than specific. According to the Oxford Dictionary, *psychology* is "(a) the science of the nature, function, and phenomenon of the human soul or mind; (b) A treatise on, or system of psychology." *Psychotherapeutic* is "of or pertaining to the treatment of mental or psychic disease."

In this study I shall generally use *psychology* to denote the theory of mind, and *psychotherapy*, praxis relating to healing of disease or to healthful expansion of the potential of the mind of the individual. However, I am aware that at times there is some overlap. When speaking of Buddhism, I am attempting, as far as possible, to give an overall view, explicating those doctrines which are central to Buddhism in general, rather than restricted to any particular school. Views from specific schools and outlooks will be credited as such. However, I acknowledge that the balance is weighted towards the views of Mahāyāna in general and Tibetan Buddhism in particular. I would also agree with David Loy, one of the more interesting participants in the dialogue between Buddhism and contemporary thought, in his suggestion that we should distinguish between Buddhism as a path of liberation and Buddhism as an institution. My concern is pre-eminently with the former. While I hope to show that the philosophy and praxis of Buddhism as a path of liberation may be interpreted as almost uncannily in tune with the contemporary horizon of ideas, this is not the interpretation of any of the more culturally crystallised forms of institutional Buddhism as religion, though partaking of aspects of all of them. Let us now return to history.

In 1923 Mrs. Rhys Davids entitled her translation of one of the books of the Theravāda Abhidhamma, *A Buddhist Manual of Psychological Ethics,* and wrote: "Buddhism from a quite early stage of its development set itself to analyse and classify mental processes with remarkable insight and sagacity. And on the results of that psychological analysis it sought to base the whole rationale of its practical doctrine and discipline. From studying the processes of attention, and the nature of 'sensation', the range and depth of feeling and the plasticity of the will in desire and in control, it organised its system of personal self-culture."[3]

In the 1930s Carl Jung published psychological commentaries to accompany German translations of two major Tibetan works, *The Tibetan Book of the Dead* and *The Tibetan Book of the Great Liberation*. In 1939 he also wrote an introduction to a German translation of D.T. Suzuki's *Introduction to Zen*

Buddhism and in 1943 he delivered a lecture on *The Psychology of Eastern Meditation.* Although Jung was always extremely wary of what he saw as the dangers and illusory promises of Eastern texts and ways for Westerners, and felt that a direct transplantation of Zen or Tibetan Buddhism was neither possible nor commendable, he could not fail to be impressed by the seriousness of their enterprise and its relevance for therapists, writing of Zen that, "the psychotherapist who is seriously concerned with the question of the aim of his therapy cannot remain unmoved when he sees the end towards which this Eastern method of psychic 'healing' – i.e., 'making whole' – is striving. As we know, this question has occupied the most adventurous minds of the East for more than two thousand years, and in this respect methods and philosophical doctrines have been developed which simply put all Western attempts along those lines into the shade."[4]

In 1957 D.T. Suzuki was the guest of honour at a conference on Psychoanalysis and Zen Buddhism at the National University of Mexico which resulted in an important publication containing works by himself and by Erich Fromm and others.[5] In 1961 Alan Watts, who wrote many works popularising Buddhism and Taoism, published *Psychotherapy East and West* stating: "The main resemblance between the Eastern ways of life and Western psychotherapy is in the concern of both with bringing about changes of consciousness, changes in our ways of feeling our own existence and our relations to human society and the natural world."[6] Since the 1960s the dialogue between Buddhism and psychology has expanded exponentially. At that time Watts claimed to have read everything written in the field. Today that would hardly be possible, such has been the explosion of texts concerned with the subject, particularly after events in 1959 initiated the dissemination of Tibetan Buddhism in the West. Nor has the emphasis been entirely one way. When some Tibetan centres in the West were founded, certain teachers such as Chogyam Trungpa and Tarthang Tulku gave their teachings a specifically psychological slant, and directed them towards an audience of psychotherapists and healers.[7]

Why have there been historically and do there continue to be, these strong links between Buddhism and the world of psychology? I would argue that there are several reasons: some that come from the very nature of Buddhism and of psychology, and some that come from the specific relevance of Buddhist ideas now to the contemporary scene in the West. Of the former the most important is an overwhelming shared concern with experience. This is at the heart of Buddhism, the very foundation of Buddhist philosophy.[8] Indeed Buddhism has, from a Western perspective, been described as a psychological religion, for its "entire philosophy and the medical system which adjoins it, is based on the analysis of mind ... the Dharma is not a rigid theology, but a support for the search for the real meaning in life, and for the attempt to comprehend oneself, one's mind and the nature of one's experience."[9] Using terminology more frequently found in the realms of psychotherapy and counselling Sue Hamilton has recently described Buddhism, perhaps uniquely among the world's major religions, as "notably person-centred."[10] Although Buddhist teachings are deeply rooted in philosophical and cosmological considerations, their principal aim is concerned with understanding the human condition. Liberation from the suffering of ordinary life is achieved through understanding its nature. In line with this, I would agree also with Richard Gombrich's assertion that Buddhism is not pre-eminently concerned with ontology, with what exists, but is concerned rather with *how* things exist, with existence and our experience of it rather than essence.[11]

And the method of considering experience is through analysis of the mind. Concern with mind is central to Buddhism. As the *Dhammapada* begins:

> We are what we think
> All that we are arises with our thoughts.
> With our thoughts we make the world.
> Speak or act with an impure mind
> And trouble will follow you
> As the wheel follows the ox that draws the cart.

We are what we think
All that we are arises with our thoughts.
With our thoughts we make the world.
Speak or act with a pure mind
And happiness will follow you
As your shadow, unshakeable.[12]

Following on from recognition of the importance of mind, Buddhism provides over two thousand years of experience of the systematic and phenomenological study of the mind, and of methods of cultivation of desirable mental processes based on this. Such practices of cultivation of mind arise hand in hand with the philosophical theories which underwrite them, something which is quite alien to Western philosophy which almost entirely separates itself from questions of practice and of embodied experience.[13] In the East personal cultivation is an integral part of traditional philosophy. Knowledge is not divorced from usage, from practical questions of personal salvation, behaviour and ethics to the extent that has occurred in the West where philosophy has become increasingly an endangered species in the everyday world, to be found only in the protected and high-walled pastures of the academy. True knowledge according to Buddhism, is considered not to be the result of mere theoretical thinking but a realisation that involves one's total mind and body. Buddhist theory and practice is equally concerned with cognitive and affective processes and with the understanding that both are embodied. Thus learning is not seen as separate from body as it has been in accordance with dualistic Western views since Descartes. In Buddhist thought material and immaterial components are part of the process that comprises a human being and learning becomes cultivation of the body/mind and not the brain alone, as evidenced by the Buddhist trilogy of morality, meditation and wisdom, and the equal importance of wisdom and compassion or skill in means in the Mahāyāna.

Like Buddhism, psychotherapy is a process whereby through the initial application of language and analysis, a deeper level of experience is sought, a realisation through which change and transformation may occur. Although the first psychotherapy, psychoanalysis, was popularly called "the talking cure", to effect lasting benefit an affective embodied realisation needs to be experienced. Rational analytic understanding alone will not suffice to bring about transformation.

Even etymologically there are links between therapy and Buddhism. Archetypal psychologist James Hillman notes "the Greek word *therapeia* refers also to care, the root is *dher*, which means 'carry, support, hold,' and is related to *dharma*, the Sanskrit meaning 'habit' and 'custom' as 'carrier.' The therapist is one who carries and takes care as does a servant (Greek = *theraps, therapon*)."[14] A Tibetan lama also points to dharma as the carrier of truth, which can be thought of as an antidote, a remedy or cure to promote change and transformation.[15] The therapist is one who carries and takes care.

Psychotherapy is a practical and purposeful enterprise for relieving suffering and expanding potential. Can the thousands of years of Buddhist exploration of this field be of assistance to this relatively young Western discourse? This is the problematic of this work, and its exploration of this is particularly concerned with the contemporary context, the current field of ideas, knowledge and experience which we inhabit today, which is already a significantly different context from that in which psychology and psychotherapy had their beginnings.

Buddhism and the Contemporary Horizon

Thus, it is the question of the relevance of Buddhism to the contemporary situation which may be most compelling and most important. For Western views would seem to be in the process of experiencing a paradigm shift.[16] Nietzsche proclaimed the death of God; Heidegger saw the end of metaphysics in forgetfulness of Being; Derrida has undertaken the deconstruction of logocentric philosophy. The atom has been split unleashing the potential for vast destruction; the principle of relativity and the principle of uncertainty have been discovered. New views coming from philosophy, literature and science seriously unsettle ancient beliefs and certainties, even those of earlier science itself. Speaking in general terms they show a concern for difference rather than identity, for process rather than for substance and for relativity, contingency and specificity rather than for absolute overarching and unchanging truths and systems. Such views challenge and undermine the traditional dualities of earlier Western philosophies, but can, I will suggest, engage in dialogue more easily with ancient Buddhist views, particularly those of the Madhyamaka school.[17] A Christian, albeit radical, theologian Don Cupitt recently suggested that we are getting ourselves "into a rather Buddhist cultural condition", and named it "a post Buddhism of the sign."[18]

First it is necessary to attempt some description of the contemporary cultural condition often called the postmodern, a description rather than a definition which would surely in itself be a contradiction in terms for something open-ended, unbounded and in process of becoming. I use the word postmodern with caution, aware of the aura (both of avocation and disagreement) which hangs over it, as a useful term to embrace the multifarious array of concepts and characteristics of that contemporary discourse which has followed the *modern*.[19] The postmodern begins with a sense that the world we inherited, upheld by the foundations of philosophic and scientific theories, is crumbling.[20] The main theme of the postmodern is Lyotard's oft-quoted "incredulity towards meta-narratives,"[21] those unquestioned foundations which give legitimacy to our beliefs and actions. The resultant difficulty of legitimation may be the cause for the neo-pragmatism that is another of the major aspects of the postmodern.[22] If legitimation is not to be found in a conceptual abstraction (God or Truth or Reality) outside the system it legitimises, an immanent and pragmatic legitimation in action may be sought instead; a legitimation in action occurring in a context of embodiment and shared linguistic and cultural practice.

Other major themes are those of difference, decentralisation and new views of self, in which the earlier modern view of the decontextualised individual is both fragmented and re-inserted into the social and cultural context. There is a simultaneous loss of naive realism, belief in the objective world; human knowledge is no longer considered as representation, a mirror of an externally existing reality, but is seen as a construction, a mutual "enaction"[23] which arises from cognitive and embodied interactions with the world. Through all of these themes weaves a most important thread of interaction and interdependence. If modern discourse was monologic and closed, postmodern discourse is open and in process. If the modern world was a representation of externally existing reality which accorded with transcendental rules, the postmodern world is conditioned, contingent, outsideless, immanent in itself with no external guarantees, and is a function of the meaning with which we imbue it, and is tied to the context of society, language and history within which it is embedded. And it is unfinished, unfinalizable, in process of becoming. In short, the postmodern world view, like the Buddhist one, carries the marks of impermanence, unsatisfactoriness and selflesness.

Buddhism as an Inspiration for a Contemporary Psychotherapy

Thus, it is in this postmodern climate that I suggest that Buddhist teachings may resonate clearly for us in the West today.[24] Firstly the view given by Buddhism has always been essentially different from that of the 'modern' West from which we too today are forcefully growing estranged. Buddhism emphasises process rather than substance in a seemingly contemporary manner. At the foundation of Buddhist philosophy is a view of interdependent origination of all phenomena which is quite distinct from the linear causality espoused by the West. Underlying this network of interdependent origination is emptiness, the transparency or lack of essential, unchanging essence in all phenomena, including persons. These views of the contingency, impermanence and dependence of all phenomena including persons, hand in hand with an understanding of the way suffering arises in everyday human life when they are ignored, constitute the Buddhist view. The descriptions and models of causality and of the human being are undertaken in order to show how things occur rather than what they consist of. Through understanding of how the world is, how its processes work and how we perceive them, liberation from ignorance and suffering may be gained. Those metaphysical questions concerned with ontology are the questions that the Buddha refused to answer. The outlook and practices which rest upon such non-substantial foundations display a middle path, a centred understanding, free of the major dualities which structure our very thought in the West, the hierarchy of distinctions of our essentially dualistic mode of thinking. Subjective/objective, inner/outer, self/world, mind/body, life/death become interrelated and interdependent rather than contradictory, in a logic of complementarity rather than of exclusion.[25]

Secondly, I would point to the holistic view presented by Buddhism in which philosophy, religion, psychology, morality and even medicine are inextricably interlinked. In the history of western psychology, with the striking early exception of William James with his works on psychology, philosophy and religious experience, all these disciplines have become increasingly independent and isolated from one another. As an American psychologist wrote recently; "We have lost sight of the deeper roots of our discipline in philosophy, and in turn of philosophy in religion."[26] Medard Boss, instigator of *Daseinsanalyse*, an existential approach to psychoanalysis based on the philosophy of Martin Heidegger also regretted this lack of consciousness of interdependence: "Western psychology tells us absolutely nothing about the subjectivity of the subject, the personality of the person and the consciousness of the mind in a manner that would enable us to understand the connection between these, the environment and our real selves."[27] Such a concern for the nature of the world and the relation between man and world is vital, and "its adequacy in regard to the particular way of mans' existence will always be of first importance for their practical therapeutic actions as well."[28]

In the West itself, the changes in view mentioned above have led recently to a more interactive understanding, and new hybrid disciplines such as Cognitive Science and Systems Theory have arisen which partake of many previously separate areas of study. It is here that some of the most exciting Western studies in the field of Mind are taking place, some of which have themselves given rise to comparisons with Buddhist views.[29] It has even been suggested that the discipline of scientific psychology itself is pre-eminently a child of modernity that in the postmodern era is out of touch with contemporary discourse; that indeed the terms "psychology" and "postmodernity" may be incompatible, and that the main tasks for a postmodern psychology, those of cultural critique and the construction of new worlds may be better carried out by anthropology and literary theory.[30] Only some trends in practical psychology are seen as being closer to postmodern conceptions displaying a shift in the focus of theorising away from both the interiority of the individual and the metanarratives of natural science towards relationship with society and communities of practice. However, here too the findings of current research and ideas are only just being acknowledged. Their effects upon psychotherapy are hard to find.

Even in western terms, the very word *psyche* has suffered a constriction of meaning. "Psyche was for the Greeks an unbreakable relationship between men, gods and nature which even encompassed death."[31] The contemporary western view considers mind alone as the exclusive locus of concepts, values and feelings, so that it alone is seen as psychic and is separated from body and from world. Obviously such a belief narrows the field of psychotherapy. It has been suggested that this separation with its accompanying move towards interiority is a consequence of progression from an oral to a literary culture, and from the participatory view of an "ontic logos", world conceived as a self manifesting reality, to a disengaged stance towards a mechanistic universe.[32] Such separation is a loss, and it is symptomatic of many separations found in the western view. The contemporary western individual has, perhaps, become more isolated in his or her individuality than at any other time. Links with family, with land, with tradition and society are increasingly rarely honoured or studied. In some ways it may be argued that psychotherapy itself, both in its theories and its practices, has unwittingly contributed to, and exacerbated this isolation, due to its emphasis on individuality and interiority, and its exclusion of the cultural and political horizons of the individual life.

Traditionally, as we have seen, western views have been dualistic, and the non-dualistic view of Buddhism may offer a new and helpful perspective to those in the West who are now suffering from alienation and the reactionary narcissism which has arisen from our separation of man and world, following in the wake of the collapse of many traditional religious beliefs. Such a view may helpfully enter into dialogue with those western voices which have attempted to find new ways of seeing unconfined by traditional "common-sense" or traditional philosophical distinctions.

Contentions and Intentions

Thus it is the contention of this work that Buddhism has much to offer Western psychotherapy at this time. Firstly because of its long history of familiarity with, and exploration of, such views as interdependence and emptiness. Secondly, and more importantly, because, unlike the separate intellectual disciplines of the West, it is not merely analytical or descriptive, but is a 'way', containing methods of practice and cultivation of awareness which may link theory with experience, instantiate views in praxis and offer a legitimation and escape from relativism in practice and in non-egocentrism. All of which may enable an alternative view of psychology which, as Kvale suggests, may enable it to move out of "the archaeology of the psyche and into the cultural landscape of the present world, entering a postmodern discourse."[33]

This work sets out from these links between Buddhism and psychotherapy, with a desire to place them in the context of contemporary discourse which, questioning its own western precursors, is frequently found to resonate with Buddhist concepts. From the Buddhist perspective, engaged as I am with the specifically human experiential realm of psychotherapy, my concern, as I have stated, is not so much with the transcendental and religious dimensions of Buddhism as an institution, as with those aspects and ideas which provide theoretical expositions and concrete methods for the attainment and retention of mentally and emotionally healthy living; that is with Buddhism as a path of liberation. From the Western perspective it is influenced by many thinkers whose work has led to, or constitutes, the postmodern view with its questioning of the previously unquestioned divisions of mind/body and individual/world. It is particularly influenced by those within the postmodern view who have attempted or are attempting to reach beyond the aporias and nihilism inherent in such questioning; that is those writers and scientists who are phenomenologically grounded in embodied human reality and in an interconnective view of world. Pre-eminent amongst these are Europeans such as Heidegger, Levinas, Merleau-Ponty, Derrida and Lacan, also Americans, Rorty, Lakoff and Johnson; and from the realms of cognitive science, the work of Francisco Varela and his colleagues. It is influenced also by the dialogical approach of Mikhail Bakhtin. The principle of dialogue is that all meaning is relative, a result of the relation between at least two bodies. Every dialogue consists of an utterance, a response and the relation between them. It is a model neither of monism nor of dualism but of multiplicity or polyphony. No word or self is virgin and isolated, "every word is directed towards an *answer* and cannot escape the profound influence of the answering word that it anticipates."[34] The fundamental a priori of the dialogical approach is "that nothing *is* in itself. Existence is *sobytie sobytiya*, the event of co-being; it is a vast web of interconnections each and all of which are linked as participants in an event whose totality is so immense that no single one of us can ever know it."[35] A description which might be that of the Buddhist notion of dependent origination.

From Bakhtin's history of sociocultural periods anthropologist Stan Mumford has extrapolated a model of three layers of temporal identity which I find to be useful.[36] The first period which Bakhtin calls the ancient matrix or folkloric period is that in which the life of man and nature is fused, time is perceived as cyclical, spatial and concrete, containing all elements in equal validity. The experience of primitive man in this layer was seen as an aspect of life itself, not as a function of his abstract thought processes or consciousness. From this ancient matrix arises the second layer of the individual life sequence in which the embedded realities of the matrix are dissociated from one another, and undergo internal splitting and a hierarchical reinterpretation, and become impoverished within the boundaries of individual life narratives. In the transition to the third layer of historical becoming, the boundaries of individuals and ideologies become questioned and doubted, subjected to mockery and irony, and the bounded individual is recontextualised, as images of the ancient matrix return in a reflexive manner, the result of dialogue between many interpenetrating voices of cultural and ideological exchange. This tripartite sequence will be found relevant to many processes described throughout this work. It can be found in the evolution of the postmodern from the modern and premodern. It may also be used to describe aspects of the development of Buddhist philosophy, the development and transcendence of the individual self, and aspects of the development of Western psychology. Psychotherapy has predominantly considered itself only in terms of the middle, individualistic period of this model. Perhaps an almost unconscious realisation of the impoverishment of this lies behind an increasing contemporary interest in shamanism, myth and folklore.

This idea of the relationship and interconnectedness presented by Bakhtin and by the Buddhist doctrines of dependent origination and emptiness is most fully expressed by the school of Hua Yen Buddhism with its image of the net of Indra. This symbol, used to explain the cosmos and the manner in which things exist in mutual identity and intercausality, portrays an image of a cosmic web extending infinitely in time and space, whose every intersection contains a jewel in whose polished surface every other jewel and its reflections are reflected. Furthermore each of the jewels reflected in this one jewel is also reflecting all the others, so there is an infinite reflecting process occurring.[37] This is the guiding image which lies behind the approach of this work, which is an attempt to carry on dialogue between several different discourses. It is an attempt to explore conversation between Buddhism and contemporary postmodern discourse. For in terms of Richard Rorty's distinction between philosophy that is systematic, providing grounds for present customs and that whose "aim is to edify – to help their readers – or society as a whole, break free from outworn vocabularies and attitudes", Buddhism has always presented an "edifying" philosophy, which strangely may appear more in tune today than the systematic philosophies of the more recent western past.[38] It is also an attempt to situate psychotherapy, both in the context of this contemporary discourse from philosophy, science and literary theory and in the context of the contemporary pathologies with which it is faced, some of which may be seen to be resultant from a disability to live with these very views.[39] It is finally and pre-eminently an attempt to explore and illuminate the dialogue between Buddhist views and practices and a psychotherapy for the current time, in the hope that similarities of view, and the long Buddhist tradition of mind training may give rise to an approach arising from the meeting between Buddhism, psychotherapy and contemporary discourse which may be of value in the training of therapists.

Thus, it is one intention to present psychotherapy as part of the postmodern world of historical becoming, inserted within a many-voiced dialogue. That there are major differences between Buddhism, postmodernism and psychotherapy may be not an impasse but a source of possibility for dialogue. For the intention is not to weld them together into a new metanarrative or to reach the closure of a coherent totality, but to encourage open-ended dialogue, wherein acceptance of difference leads to new insights and continuing conversation. Contemporary discourse stresses the "between". It is from the spaces, the relationship, the intervals, that new dialogue emerges.[40] Furthermore as Rorty suggests: "Edifying philosophers want to keep space open for the sense of wonder which poets can sometimes cause – wonder that there is something new under the sun, something which is not an accurate representation of what was already there, something which (at least for the moment) cannot be explained and can barely be described."[41]

The middle way of Buddhism with its reliance on interdependence and emptiness exemplifies this attempt to keep dialogue open, the attempt to evade both the closure of the monologic and the lack of differentiation of the folkloric. Such a middle way mediates between the major Western distinctions of individual and world, subject and object, and mind and body. The search for such an approach is a recurring theme in contemporary discourse, a search for a "between" that escapes the unsatisfactory dualism of subject/object, body/mind and self/world. Echoes of such a project are heard in many different fields; in Heidegger's "*Dasein*, Polanyi's "indwelling", Merleau-Ponty's "flesh", Geoffrey Samuel's "multimodal framework" and in Gregory Bateson's "the pattern that connects", and his reference to patterns of relatedness as "the ecology of mind". If the image of the individualistic modern age was the hierarchical tree, the image for the postmodern or the dialogic is surely the aforementioned net of Indra. Another image is that of the rhizome, a many-centred, interconnecting underground network.[42] Each image encompasses many centres, many perspectives, none with overriding hierarchical dominance, just as, according to Rorty there is no longer *a* human essence, only a conversation of many voices. A contemporary psychotherapy must be in touch with what Samuel calls "the flow of relatedness" and imbued with such images.[43] If Buddhism is already a philosophy of the between – between asceticism and sensuality, between eternalism and nihilism – the dialogue we are about to enter is doubly between. It is, I suggest, in the very process of this constant betweenness, which refuses to weld itself into an objectified totality but remains responsive to shifting, impermanent and interdependent processes and boundaries, that its value lies.

In the past three decades, as I have mentioned, a great amount has been written about the meeting of Buddhism and psychology or psychotherapy, but such works have usually approached this wide topic from a point of comparison between one particular school of therapy and one particular school of Buddhism, or have focused on a single aspect such as meditation.[44] They have also most frequently been written by psychotherapists who are Buddhist followers of one or another specific tradition, and they have mostly concentrated on the practical aspects of incorporating Buddhist models of mind and awareness techniques into Western psychotherapies, without fully exploring the theoretical and moral aspects which underlie such models and practices.[45]

Two Buddhist influenced professional trainings for psychotherapists exist, and at the time of writing two more are coming into being.[46] However none of these have as yet produced any comprehensive written account covering both their theoretical approach and practical training, or explicated the interrelationship between the Buddhist and the Western components of the training[47]. Thus, it seems timely to step back from close discussion of the manner in which specific Buddhist theories or practices compare with or assist specific types of psychotherapies, to consider the wider view. To consider what it is in Buddhism, in its generally shared theories and practices, which is attractive and valuable to the psychotherapeutic project.

This study then, is an attempt to provide an overview; an attempt to explicate the underlying theories of Buddhism in relation to psychotherapy and to contemporary discourse, as well as their instantiation in practice. Coming from academic familiarity with the field of Buddhist studies and practical experience as a trained psychotherapist, I will attempt to explore issues within Buddhist philosophy and praxis which, I argue, may provide inspiration for a good contemporary psychotherapy which is aware of its position vis-à-vis other contemporary discourse, and the pathologies with which it is faced. I will also try to situate those theories, models and practices which a Buddhist-influenced psychotherapy might use within the context of the central tenets of Buddhist thought. This last issue is addressed in reply to the critique that to take randomly from Buddhism only what is useful in another context is not only unjustifiable but weakening to Buddhism itself. It arises also from some disquiet concerning the lack of consideration given to contextualising those theories and practices taught in the context of psychotherapy within the sphere of Buddhist thought. The importance of hermeneutic awareness of contextuality is central within this work.

To cover all these areas in detail would obviously require several books, and I am aware that advocates of particular schools and approaches in psychotherapy with which I am less familiar or sympathetic, will inevitably feel their own fields have been inadequately explored. I can only offer my apologies. It is my intention to delineate the territory, introduce the participants and suggest the dialogue. More detailed and carefully selected perspectives have been and will continue to be explored, but what has not appeared heretofore is a broadly-based discussion on the topic of Buddhist inspiration for a psychotherapy which is aware of and responsive to the horizons of contemporary Western thought and research. This is a question of Buddhist philosophy and praxis as an inspiration for an integrative psychotherapy; it is not advocacy of Buddhism *as* a therapy.

There will also be more emphasis on the training of therapists than on clinical experience. For as Jung wrote, "the attitude of the therapist is infinitely more important than the theories and methods of psychotherapy."[48] Such observations regarding the prime importance of attitudes and personality of therapist and client, rather than the centrality of technique or theory have been confirmed in subsequent studies.[49] The views and practices influenced by Buddhism will inform the work of the therapist as an *approach*; to become implicit in the *way* she works rather than to act as an overt offering or theoretical framework for the client. Thus there is no necessity for the client to espouse Buddhist ideals and beliefs themselves, or even to be made aware of the Buddhist inspiration behind the therapeutic practice.[50] Nor is it necessary for the therapists to become practising and committed Buddhists, though for the therapists a positive attitude towards the philosophy of Buddhism and the ideals of mindfulness would be necessary.[51]

Perhaps the ambivalent results of research into the process and results of psychotherapy to date are a reflection of how little is really understood about the process of therapy itself. As a therapist wrote recently: "Our understanding of the human psyche is considerably more solid than is our understanding of psychotherapeutic work."[52] In 1964 R.D. Laing stated that: "Psychotherapy must remain an obstinate attempt of two people to recover the wholeness of being human through the relationship between them."[53] It may, perhaps, be seen as a paradigm of human interaction. What occurs in the therapeutic encounter is a meeting of two or more individuals, their energies, relationships and world views; body, speech and mind. For the therapist, at least, some explicit understanding of their own philosophy is necessary. As the existential psychiatrist Medard Boss wrote: "It is not necessary that the patient himself learn to recognize thematically the ontological existential structure of human being-in-the-world. His insight need not extend beyond the limits of his individual, directly perceptible ontic ways of relating to the therapist. But it is the duty of the latter to become thoroughly acquainted with, and clearly aware of the ontological nature of being together."[54] Elsewhere Boss has written: "what our psychotherapy needs above all is a change in the psychotherapists. If our science of mental health is to become more effective, psychotherapists will have to balance their knowledge of psychological concepts and techniques with a contemplative awareness."[55] Boss wrote this after his foundational attempt to provide an new existential grounding for psychoanalysis in the philosophy of Martin Heidegger, since he believed that the scientific view embraced by Freud was no longer adequate on its own as a basis for a contemporary psychotherapy.

It is the contention of this study that a dialogue with Buddhism may provide both the philosophical orientation and the pragmatic awareness practices that may effect change both in the theory of psychotherapy and in psychotherapists themselves, which may bring both more into harmony with current scientific and philosophical discourse and with the presenting problems of contemporary clients. I am uneasily aware that this attempt holds a double paradox. Not only am I attempting to describe theory which can give inspiration and validity to a profoundly practical enterprise, but also I am trying to ground this practice in a theory which insists it is no-theory, a ground which is no-ground, a view written in invisible ink. But I hope to show that this perhaps is indeed suitable for an age whose focus of attention has shifted towards difference rather than identity, wave rather than particle, where the only certainty is that of change and impermanence.

The structure of my exploration, based upon traditional Tibetan Buddhist method, is divided into the three parts of Ground, Path and Fruition. These are presented in Western terms as Theoretical Considerations, Methodological Considerations and Goals and Implications. Before considering the ground of the views either of Western Psychotherapies or of Buddhism, I will begin with a preamble, a consideration of experience and meaning which underlie and relate to both. Experience is the raw material of both Buddhism and psychotherapy and the aim of both, I would suggest, is to understand or reveal the meaning of that experience. Therefore the section of Ground will start with a brief exploration of the ground of the ground, that is, experience and meaning and the relation between them. Then I will review Western psychotherapies, grouped under the four major schools, the Analytic, Behaviourist, Humanistic and Existential, and Transpersonal, with a brief account of the history and outlook of the major individual therapies, with their own views of themselves in relation to the problems and possibilities they address. Then I will turn to Buddhism, with a particular emphasis on those philosophical and psychological views which, I contend, peculiarly fit it as a source of meaning and practice for contemporary psychotherapy in the light of some current Western discourse. Finally, since both Buddhism and psychotherapy are concerned with the liberation from suffering of the human being, and as the Dalai Lama has recently pointed out that view refers "either to the consciousness that views, or the object that is viewed,"[56] I will look at concepts of Self in Buddhism and in contemporary thought. This will be the longest section, as my orientation is primarily, though not exclusively, theoretical; that is, an examination of ideas which could support the practice of an integrative Buddhist psychotherapy.

Path will look at the instantiation of the Buddhist view in practice; at those aspects of the eightfold Buddhist path of ethics, meditation and wisdom which may be of special relevance to the therapeutic journey, again with particular reference to the training of therapists. Three factors, those of right speech, right action and right livelihood constitute ethics; three factors, right effort, right mindfulness and right meditation pertain to meditation; and two factors, right thought and right understanding constitute the wisdom aspect of the path which is the fourth noble truth for Buddhists. The foundation for wisdom, right thought leading to its achievement in right understanding will, I hope, have been adequately explicated in Part One and in this section I will concentrate on ethics and meditation. Ethical considerations are commonly noticeable by their absence from any psychotherapeutic discourse, except in terms of the ethics of the therapeutic relationship itself. Discussion of any form of natural ethics as part of a healthy, responsive and responsible relationship to others and world has largely been ignored, which is perhaps why much of contemporary psychotherapy has been considered by outsiders (and some insiders) and by the media as narcissistic. As contemporary postmodern trends, as we have mentioned, are concerned with increasing contextualisation, dialogue and widening horizons, this section will look at morality in terms of responsibility, both from the perspective of Buddhist ethics and from that of some recent trends in Cognitive Science and western philosophy.

In contrast to morality, meditation has been one of the most explored areas within the dialogue between Eastern thought and psychotherapy. However, most scientific research has been carried out with Transcendental Meditation, and it is the different and specifically Buddhist practice of *vipassanā* meditation and mindfulness with which this section will be predominantly concerned. Meditation and mindfulness will be considered from the perspective of the therapist and their training, the experience of the client, and the therapeutic relationship itself.

The first part of "Fruition" will attempt to compare and contrast the goals of both Buddhism and psychotherapy, suggesting a qualitative similarity and quantitative disparity. Then I will consider some implications of the engagement of the Buddhist theories and practices discussed earlier in psychotherapeutic training; how they can be of value, and how they "fit" with contemporary discourse. I shall conduct such an exploration in terms of Body, Speech and Mind, the traditional Buddhist divisions of experience which may provide a useful framework within which to position the different layers of experience, intra, inter and trans personal. Embodiment will consider our embodied experience from the perspective of Buddhism and from the contemporary discourse discussed previously. It will consider a revaluing of embodiment, not as a poor relation of mind, but as the foundation of our lived experience. Speech will encompass a wider frame than that perhaps normally considered in terms of speech, including language, imagination and metaphor, and will emphasise the embodied prelinguistic foundations of speech. Mind will look at the wider horizon of our relationship with world, discussing it particularly in relation to the themes of interdependence, non-egocentrism and a remedy for nihilism.

Finally, in the light of all the foregoing I will attempt to bring the discussion to a temporary or empty closure, reviewing some earlier arguments and attempting to establish if it is possible in their light to delineate any of the particular features for an integrated Buddhist psychotherapy.

This presents a somewhat linear exposition of a problematic which, I have suggested, may be better presented as a layered network of relationship. Indeed, in Buddhist discourse the goal is often described as the instantiation of the view or ground through the means of the path. In terms of this thesis, the ground is that Buddhist philosophy and practice can be both compatible with, and helpful to, contemporary Western discourse, and that much psychotherapy is often out of step with such discourse. The path is an exploration of different psychotherapies, of some trends in contemporary thought, and of the Buddhist ideas and practices. The goal is a model of a integrative psychotherapy inspired by Buddhist theories and practices which would be responsive to the horizons of contemporary experience.

Part One

Ground

Theoretical Considerations

PREAMBLE

Experience and Meaning

"We had the experience but missed the meaning."[1]

"There is, it seems to us,
At best, only a limited value
In the knowledge derived from experience,
The knowledge imposes a pattern, and falsifies,
For the pattern is new in every moment
And every moment is a new and shocking
Valuation of all we have been."[2]

Psychotherapy has often been considered as a search for meaning. Carl Jung believed: "Psychoneurosis must be understood, ultimately, as the suffering of a soul which has not discovered its meaning"[3] and that: "It is only meaning which liberates."[4] Victor Frankl, the creator of Logotherapy, also considered that man is "primarily motivated by the search for meaning to his existence, by the striving to fulfil this meaning and thereby to actualize as many value potentialities as possible. In short man is motivated by the will to meaning."[5] Those unimpressed by the endeavours of artificial intelligence critique its foundation upon a primary currency of information rather than meaning. Such meaning, however, is no longer an object to be received, but must be created. In earlier times, the great Truths of philosophy and religions stood like megaliths in the landscape, clear to sight. Today tremendous changes of view both in science and in philosophy have caused these to collapse until only fragments and ruins of the once grand structures remain. For the most common problems of those presenting to psychotherapy are no longer the common problems which confronted Freud. Clients suffering hysterical disorders are now generally outnumbered by those complaining of depression, sense of meaninglessness, lack of purpose and loss of self esteem. Such complaints are personal to individual histories, but are also symptoms of metaphysical malaise, loss of meaning and alienation from experience. Many people, today, entering therapy do so bringing issues of depression and lack and problems of personal relationships overburdened by carrying so much that once belonged elsewhere. When such relationships crack under the strain and collapse, they leave apparent the lack and absence they alone were expected to cover up.[6]

Today perhaps more than ever before we are required to create and live our meanings. A strong trend within both psychology, philosophy and literary theory has turned to narrative rather than to revealed truth to create coherence as a source for meaning. But what is the relation between experience and meaning? T.S. Eliot wrote: "We had the experience but missed the meaning,"[7] and much of psychotherapeutic work is indeed concerned with the attempt to make sense of, or find the meaning within experience. Yet there is another way of approaching this – from the opposite pole. Sometimes it seems we have so many theoretical meanings (especially in psychotherapy), which have lost their grounding in experience, that we are in danger of losing the experience itself. We may be so busy narrating that we forget to experience. As Joseph Campbell said: "We let the concept swallow up the percept ... thus defending ourselves from experience."[8] For what is meaning? According to one perspective, it is a fixed relation between objective reality and a representation of it. According to other, newer views, it is an enactment, a dynamic interactive event of understanding, and what we normally consider as fixed meanings are merely those most recurrent and stabilised patterns of our understanding. If we lose appreciation of the dynamic lived quality of understanding and meaning, we become alienated from our experience, living in a secondary world of theory and representation.

In times of change and threat to received views, when sources of certainty and previous meaning are deconstructed, there is a tendency to cling nonetheless to the theories and forms as a defence against the felt uncertainty of experience. If externally authorised meanings are gone then activities and experience must themselves become autotelic; the state that Mihalyi Csikzentmihalyi calls "flow" which we will discuss in chapter six. This concerns a return to experience for its own sake. Earlier this century, the poet Rainer Maria Rilke mourned the loss of living connection with experience and with the objects of experience: "just as language has no longer anything in common with the things it names, so the movements of most of the people who live in cities have lost their connection with the earth, they hang, as it were, in the air, hover in all directions, and find no place where they can settle."[9] Ultimately, as Campbell suggests, what we are seeking is not meaning but experience itself: "People say that what we're all seeking is a meaning for life. I don't think that's what we're really seeking. I think that what we're seeking is an experience of being alive, so that our life experiences on the purely physical plane will have resonance within our own innermost being and reality, so that we actually feel the rapture of being alive."[10] Perhaps to experience this is to experience openness to being, to experience things as they are, in Buddhist terms, *tathatā*. As Chogyam Trungpa described it: "Enlightenment is ... an honest relationship with ourselves. That is why it is connected with the truth – *being* true rather than truth as something external you are relating to. Just being."[11]

It is my contention that Buddhism may help to supply views which uphold meaning acceptable in the contemporary world and experiential praxes which instantiate such views; may, in short unite meaning and experience. And this is certainly the field of psychotherapy. I would state of psychotherapy what Campbell states of art: "The function ... is to render a *sense of existence*, not an *assurance of some meaning*."[12] Exploring both meaning and experience reveals their interdependence; how our expectations and conceptual frameworks frame and constrain our experience until sometimes the direct and immediate flavour and feel of the experience is overwhelmed by the conceptual wrappings of memory and expectation. It is the task of psychotherapy to explore mindfully this very process. Ron Kurtz the founder of Hakomi Therapy has given a wonderfully precise description of this:

> "The whole point of therapy is change, change in the meaning we give to experience. So we go for meaning in order to discover how we are creating it, what we are making out of what is given to us and to gain control of that process in order to give new meanings and create new experiences from them ... The point is to access and change the symbolic world that shapes all experiences. Of course the long range goal of this pursuit of meaning is to recover the capacity to have full feelings and experiences without interrupting them, even to search for meaning. In the long term, the meaning and the experience are one and are sensed as such."[13]

Such a sense of existence as Campbell describes must be one that can find its balance within the uncertainties of the contemporary world. For as he says: "The circle has been broken – the mandala of truth."[14] Our circle today, he likens to that whose circumference is nowhere, and whose centre is everywhere, for no fixed terms of reference can be drawn. It is the circle of the postmodern which may bear comparison with the maṇḍala of the emptiness of Nāgārjuna. It holds both threat and promise. If we cannot cling to theory, can we find ourselves in the lived experience?[15] Can we directly contact that experience? What we need to connect with is the direct presentation of experience not its representation within the frameworks of expectation, differentiation, emotion and language. In the context of meditation we will see such projects in Gendlin's "Focusing", Czikzentmihalyi's "Flow" and in the context of philosophy, in Heidegger's, Derrida's and Levinas' different attempts to evade the egological, the logocentric and the theoretical. For over two thousand years in its views and above all in its methods of contemplation Buddhism has undertaken this task. In Buddhist terms as we will discuss below, ignorance or nescience is that which takes the thought coverings as real, wisdom is that which discovers *śūnyatā*, emptiness or transparency, that is without conceptual diffusion. Buddhism sets out a path whereby one's conceptualisation of reality is discovered, contemplated, and ultimately let go of. It has much to offer psychotherapy which is a contemplative journey in which one's personal process, the way in which one creates one's own conceptualised reality and the meaning of one's experience is discovered, reflected upon, and considered in terms of change and alternative, if not of ultimately letting go to the same degree.

CHAPTER TWO

Western Psychotherapies

"O the mind, mind has mountains; cliffs of fall
Frightful, sheer, no-man-fathomed. Hold them cheap
May who ne'er hung there."[1]

"My mother loves me.
I feel good.
I feel good because she loves me.

I am good because I feel good.
I feel good because I am good.
My mother loves me because I am good.

My mother does not love me.
I feel bad.
I feel bad because she does not love me.
I am bad because I feel bad."[2]

Before considering Buddhist philosophy and practice in the light of resources for psychological health in the contemporary world, I would like to consider the approaches of different schools of Western psychotherapy. This is too large and diffuse a subject to give anything more than an orientation towards the current state of psychotherapy. However, the now vast number of different psychotherapies may, I believe, reasonably be gathered under the headings of the four major schools, Psychoanalytic, Behavioural and Cognitive, Humanistic and most recently Transpersonal. In practice today, as will be discussed later, such distinctions have often become blurred in the mushrooming growth of myriad different forms of psychotherapy. However, while noting that the map is not the territory, this map of the development of four major schools or groupings may still provide a helpful outline.

Psychoanalysis

Psychoanalysis was historically the first significant school of psychotherapy, and is the one against which almost all subsequent theories have defined themselves. It was founded and is still centred upon the work of Sigmund Freud who, as much as any one man, has changed the climate of thought in this century, presenting both a theory of the human mind and a curative practice. Freud intended psychoanalysis to be a scientific enterprise, an attempt to place psychology within a scientific and materialistic framework. He put forward a dynamic theory, arising from the existence and function of the unconscious, which spoke of the interplay of forces within the mind, arising from the tensions developing when instinctual drives confront external necessity. His theory posited an "economic" description of pleasure and pain arising from increasing and decreasing disturbance following stimuli received from this interaction of body and external world. He also described the mind first topographically, as being divided into conscious, preconscious and unconscious, and in a later model structurally, as having three distinct agencies; the id, relating to the instinctual drives, particularly the erotic libido; the ego, which is developed out of this as a mediator between the drives and the world; and superego, representing social and parental influences brought to bear upon the drives.[3] A famous, though later considered erroneous translation of one of Freud's aims reads "Where id was, there shall ego be"[4] On the whole Freud considered life a difficult business, his aim in Psychoanalysis was to enable the ego to achieve as stable a conquest as possible over the id, to replace uncontrolled neurosis with "ordinary neurosis", a level of accommodation, or acceptable repression of the drives.

In Freud's view, neurosis was caused by the inappropriate return of repressed wishes in the form of symptoms. The agents of repression are the ego and in particular the superego when they are threatened by instinctual demands which are unacceptable by the standards of the external world. What he termed the repression of the "pleasure principle" by the "reality principle" serves to keep the guilt-laden wishes out of consciousness. The ego is protected from being overwhelmed by defensive strategies such as denial, displacement, projection, introjection and sublimation. Psychoanalysis is the process of retrieval of repressed material from the unconscious by a skilled analyst and the "talking cure", using the techniques of free-association, and dream analysis, which loosen the hold of the conscious rational mind which represses buried memories. Through uncovering the repressed causes of the neurosis the patient is relieved of the conflict and the resultant symptoms are dissolved. Therapy is usually long term and frequent, and verbally rather than somatically centred.

Two important pillars of Freudian theory are the Oedipus Complex and Transference. The Oedipus complex is part of Freud's delineation of psychosocial and psychosexual development which takes place in successive stages. These stages take their names from the predominant erogenous zone of each developmental step. First is the oral stage centred upon the mouth and the breast of the mother, followed by the anal stage between one and three years old, the phallic stage, approximately three to six years, then a period of latency leading up to the genital phase starting at puberty. Healthy personality development depends on successful resolution and integration of these stages of psychosexual development, faulty development from unsuccessful resolution. The Oedipal experience occurs for males in the phallic phase wherein craving for the attention of mother, and antagonism for father as a rival gives rise to phantasies of the killing of the father and possession of the mother. This incestuous desire is abandoned in the face of father's perceived threat of castration, (having seen mother as "castrated"). A boy then moves from his love for his mother to identification with the father. The female path is more complex and reverse, the castration complex precedes the Oedipus complex, interpreting the lack of a penis as failure on the part of the mother, and turning away from the mother in hostility, towards the father who could give her a child. However Freud has been much and increasingly criticised for the inadequacy of his view of the feminine.[5]

Transference is the way in which during analysis the analysand projects onto the analyst the psychic conflicts which he suffers. Awareness and use of this transference to uncover the hidden is a central tenet of Psychoanalysis. Counter transference in turn is the analyst's uncontrolled and unconscious response to the analysand's transference. Transference within the analytic relationship exposes the projections which the analysand habitually imposes on the other participants in his life, and in this particular setting allows for them to be interpreted and addressed. Since the transference is considered so important, being the place where interpretation and healing lie, classically the relationship between analyst and patient was relatively distant, the analyst's anonymity permitting space for the analysand to project upon them themes from their own past.

From Freud's foundation there have been many splits and developments. Early on Rank and Adler broke away, and most importantly, Freud's chosen successor, Carl Jung. Jung enlarged the field of exploration into the transpersonal realms with his concept of the collective unconscious, and for this reason I would like to consider his contribution to the history of psychotherapy under that heading. Within the field of Psychoanalysis itself historical developments show a similar pattern to that we see in the history of the development of the different schools, with an increasing widening of the field of interest, from the intrapersonal to the interpersonal to the transpersonal. There are two main trends in Freud's work, that of the instincts and that of personal development. After Freud the development of his ideas turned away from psychobiology towards personality theory. Under the title of Object Relations in England and Interpersonal Relations Theory in the United States, the stages of development were delineated less in terms of biological or system ego and of instinctual maturation than in terms of the personal ego's experience with objects of relationship. Such relationship with the environment has a part to play in development; if the environment does not satisfy needs of understanding and supporting, this development will be arrested or distorted. Once the proposition of libidinal and aggressive drives regulated by a developing ego is supplanted by "the concept of a psychosomatic whole with ego-potential, developing primarily libidinally in object relations, but also aggressively if thwarted, then the ego is the whole psychic person, the psychic aspect of the basic psychosomatic whole being. This person ego has its own energy or life-drive, and develops a structural identity and individual characteristics by organising its experiences as it goes along."[6] This movement from system ego to person-ego was carried forward in different ways, by the work of Horney, Fromm, Klein, and Erikson, and came to fruition in England with Mahler, Fairbairn, Guntrip and especially Winnicott working in the field of child therapy.

Winnicott is particularly interesting and important for his work on the early relationship between mothers and children and for his concept of the "transitional object" and "transitional space". In his work as a paediatrician Winnicott drew important conclusions about the function of the "good enough mother", her "holding" of the child, and facilitation of the emergence of the individual from an early state of fusion. Following on the work of Jacques Lacan entitled *The Mirror Stage*[7] Winnicott believed "the precursor of the mirror is the mother's face."[8] In the early states of infant development a vital part is played by the environment which is not yet separated out from the infant by the infant. This environmental function involves "holding", "handling" and "object presenting".[9] As development progresses the mother separates out as an objectively perceived feature of the environment and the child forms a self in response to this reflection by the mother. In Winnicott's words:

> "When I look I am seen, so I exist,
> I can now afford to look and see."[10]

In fact Winnicott believed that "psychotherapy is not making clever and apt interpretations; by and large it is a long-term giving the patient back what the patient brings. It is a complex derivative of the face that reflects what is there to be seen."[11]

He used the terms "transitional object" and "transitional phenomenon" to designate an intermediate area of experience, between me and not-me, between early fusion experience of thumb sucking and true object relationship. In the life of an infant this may be displayed first by a teddy bear or security blanket, being the use of objects that are not part of their own body, but which are not yet recognised as belonging to external reality. Between the inner reality of the individual and the outer reality of the world, Winnicott posits another area "the third part of the life of a human being, a part that we cannot ignore, is an intermediate area of *experiencing*, to which inner reality and external life both contribute."[12] Since no human being is ever free from the tension of relating inner and outer, relief from this strain is provided by the intermediate area which is analogous to that third area of potential space between mother and baby. It is the space of play, of culture and of religion. Winnicott believed that only in play can an individual, child or adult, be creative, and that it is only in being creative that the individual discovers the true self. Whether the infant is able to learn to live creatively is a result of the early environment. Playing is the natural way of development taking place in that potential space between mother and child, when a satisfactory relationship of reliability on the mother's side and confidence on the infant's has grown up. He suggested that psychoanalysis is a highly specialised form of play in the service of communication after the failure of the natural. He suggested that "psychotherapy is done in the overlap of the two play areas, that of the patient and that of the therapist,"[13] for in that transitional space the patient may learn to play, to be creative in that unintegrated state of the personality, which when reflected back by the therapist, may become part of the organised personality, having been seen. Winnicott was adamant that the paradox involved in this transitional space between inner and outer, between conception and perception is one that must be accepted but not resolved.

In contrast, members of the Ego Psychology school which developed the work of Freud following his daughter Anna Freud first in Europe, then in the United States, retained a more scientific orientation towards the system ego rather than the personal ego. They based their theory and therapy around the development, strengthening and adaptive function of the ego. Latterly, the school has been strongly critiqued for its lack of hermeneutic awareness that these adaptive norms were themselves social constructions.[14] Lack of such awareness led to conformation and unquestioning acceptance of the status quo.

A further development within the American Analytic school is the Self Psychology of Heinz Kohut, which also marks a shift away from a biological drive-oriented description of man towards a fuller more humanistic picture "centred on the primacy of the ambitions and ideals of the cohesive self",[15] to which the drives are secondary. Self Psychology is a psychology that "deals with the formations and functions of the self, and with its break-up and re-integration."[16] Kohut found that the classical Freudian framework of psychoanalysis was suitable to explain the structural neuroses, particularly hysteria which presented with great frequency at the turn of the century, but not suitable for disorders of the self; malfunctioning arising from damage to central structures of personality which he believe required "more broadly based scientific objectivity than that of the nineteenth century scientist – an objectivity that includes the introspective-empathetic observation and theoretical conceptualization of the participating self."[17] Kohut defines the self as an abstraction derived from clinical observation and "as a potentially observable content of the mind."[18] He describes it in the narrow sense as a specific structure in the mental apparatus, and more broadly as the centre of the individual's psychological universe. There may be many different selves, conscious, unconscious and preconscious, in ego, id and superego, but he believes there is one most resistant to change – the nuclear self, which has a particular structure. This nuclear self develops from the primary self or initial given and a matrix of empathic selfobjects necessary for its development. It is composed of derivatives of the grandiose self, the self-assertive goals and ambitions which push it forwards, and of derivatives of the idealised parental imago which pull it. A functioning self is that in which "ambitions, skills and ideals form an unbroken continuum that permits joyful creative activity."[19] Narcissism, rather than being a pejorative term always relating to incomplete development or regression is reinstated in Self Psychology as valuable and important in the development of the nuclear self. It is its transformation rather than suppression or outgrowing which is necessary for mature fulfilment. Indeed Kohut saw empathy, humour, acceptance of impermanence and wisdom as transformations of narcissism involving expansion of the self, a cosmic narcissism which has transcended the bounds of the individual. Just as the primary empathy of the child with the mother is the blueprint for the empathy of the adult, so primary identity with mother is also "the precursor of an expansion of the self, late in life, when the finiteness of individual existence is acknowledged."[20] This approach, together with an emphasis on the importance of empathy and introspection, the centrality of the observation of inner experience rather than preoccupation with established theory, leads to a psychology that is far from the reductionism of Freud, particularly in its discussion of the humanities and religion. However a critique of Self Psychology has been directed at its reification of the self at the expense of a more healthy dynamic view from the perspective of process.[21]

The spread of psychoanalysis in France occurred later than in other nations. It was not until the second half of this century that psychoanalytic discourse emerged as an important factor in French cultural life. Since then its influence on intellectual life and culture has been enormous. However this is a changed psychoanalysis, uniting developments within analysis itself, with influences from Marxism and other political theory, surrealism, existentialism and linguistic theory, far more strongly involved in social philosophical and cultural issues than is the case elsewhere.

The key figure in this development was Jacques Lacan, whose writings are difficult, intriguing and influential. Lacan claimed to return to the core meaning of Freud's work (particularly in opposition to developments such as Ego Psychology which he considered to be a castration of the real intention in the unquestioned interests of social conformity) and to reinterpret such theories in symbolic and linguistic terms in the light of structuralist and post-structuralist ideas. Objecting to the totalising ambition of philosophy and its pretensions to tell the whole truth, and to the desire of the American Ego psychologists for adaptation to cultural norms, Lacan stressed that above all psychoanalysis is about the unconscious. Yet even this concept is rewritten in the light of relationship to language. Perhaps his best-known statement is that the unconscious is structured like a language. His view of language is close to that of Heidegger – "Man acts as though *he* were the shaper and master of language, while in fact *language* remains the master of man"[22] Thus although Lacan does not see man as the victim of uncontrollable drives, yet with more sociological and linguistic influences, he sees man as submitting to processes which transcend him, rather than as being an autonomous subject.

Lacan stresses the role of language and of desire. When the child acquires the capacity for language, she becomes a subject. However in language we can never completely express our meaning, thus language is linked with desire. And for Lacan, "Desire is a fundamental lack, a hole in being. . ."[23] It is an effect of "primordial absence." The subject, according to Lacan is inevitably caught in a exclusive either/or between meaning and being, that which is there beneath the meaning, adherence to either necessitating a loss or fading. If one chooses meaning, meaning survives only deprived of that inevitable part of non-meaning which is, for Lacan, the unconscious. If one chooses being, the subject disappears, falling into non-meaning.[24]

Desire is part of a triad of need-demand-desire. Need can be defined in basically biological terms of the satisfaction of basic wants, but for Lacan a transformation occurs when the child's pleas for satisfaction become expressible in language, since the request is now accompanied by a plea for recognition as the subject of the need. This he calls demand. Out of this process emerges desire: "that which goes beyond demand and conveys the subject's wish for totality. It can never be fulfilled"[25]. Again, "...the drama of the subject in language is the experience of its lack in being, and that experience is a movement of desire. Desire is a relation of being to lack."[26] And from Lacan himself; "I always find my desire outside of me because what I desire is always something that I lack, that is other to me."[27]

This definition of desire as lack of being arises developmentally. Lacan mapped his model of development onto Freud's concept of Oedipal process interpreted symbolically and linguistically rather than biologically. From an Imaginary stage which is presymbolic identification with an imago, primarily of the mother, the child passes into the symbolic world of recognition of the Father's name and law; from a body-based material relationship to one based on language, culture and social exchange. The turning point is what he called the Mirror Phase, a period at which the infant still without mastery of his own body first imagines himself through seeing his image in a mirror, as coherent and self governing. At this stage the child sees his own reflection, and sees someone else *as* someone else, recognising his discreet separation from an Other. In this way "the Other warrants the existence of the child, certifies the difference between self and other. This is the action upon which all subjectivity is based, the moment in which the human individual is born."[28] Lacan writes of this stage:

> "The *mirror stage* is a drama whose internal thrust is precipitated from insufficiency to anticipation – and which manufactures for the subject, caught up in the lure of spatial identification, the succession of phantasies that extends from a fragmented body-image to a form of its totality that I shall call orthopaedic – and lastly, to the assumption of the armour of an alienating identity, which will mark with its rigid structure the subject's entire mental development."[29]

The child has obtained an identity which is really an identification, an anticipated orthopaedic image rather than the actual fragmented insufficiency. The ego is born from this identity which is already alienating. The infant despite his imperfect control of his body, sees a coherent united image in the mirror, thus the image in which we first recognise ourselves is a misrecognition. That the subject is constituted through an image that alienates it, and thus potentially confronts it, explains for Lacan the close relationship which he sees between narcissism and aggression. Thus for Lacan, the ego is constituted by an identification with an other, a projection, an idealisation. This first alienated relationship of the self to its own image constitutes what Lacan calls the domain of the Imaginary. "This is the world, the register, of *images,* conscious or unconscious, perceived or imagined. It is the pre-linguistic, pre-Oedipal domain in which the specular image traps the subject in an illusory ideal of completeness."[30] It is to be understood as both a developmental stage, and a permanent level of the human psyche.

The Imaginary is the first of Lacan's three orders or registers. The second is the Symbolic, the linguistic universe into which the child is initiated with language, thereby in an interpretation of the Oedipal project, taking on the "name-of-the-father", and the phallus which is a metaphor for the privileged signifier. In the later works of Lacan the Symbolic becomes an autonomous structure in which the lack of being which we have already encountered is intensified in a signifying chain which excludes the human subject and offers no ultimate correspondence between words and things. The third order the Real is not a successive stage, and has little relation to any assumptions about the nature of the world, but refers to that which is outside the imaginary and the symbolic, which is inexpressible. According to Madan Sarup: "It serves to remind human subjects that their Symbolic and Imaginary constructions take place in a world which exceeds them."[31]

The Lacanian development is a study of loss or lack. The first loss occurs before birth with the sexual differentiation of the foetus. In terms of the androgynous whole, the sexually differentiated subject is lacking as fabled by Aristophanes in

Plato's *Symposium*.[32] The second occurs after birth, but prior to the acquisition of language. This is the loss incurred by the restriction of undifferentiated or "global" libido into culturally established channels. Once the subject has entered the symbolic order her organic needs pass through the channels of signification and further loss occurs as she is subordinated to the symbolic order which will determine identity and desire. Finally Lacan sees subjectivity as "entirely relational; it only comes into play through the principle of difference, by the opposition of the 'other' or the 'you' to the 'I'. In other words subjectivity is not an essence but a set of relationships."[33]

I have taken time and space to attempt to delineate, with the help of Madan Sarup's clear exposition, the difficult views of Lacan, since they are of particular interest from the point of view of a Buddhist outlook. Alone among psychoanalysts, Lacan believed that the function of the ego is a *méconnaissance*; that it is constituted by an alienating identification, and that the human search for imaginary wholeness and unity is a futile project, as the ego seeks endless substitutes for the object of lost desire, the Real which is buried in the unconscious and beyond language. Lacan retranslates Freud's famous statement "*Wo Es war, soll Ich werden*", usually, as we have seen, approvingly translated "Where *id* was, there shall ego be" as "Where it was, there must I come to be" or "Where it was, there ought I to become", and contends in these reformulations that the realm of unconscious energy, far from being in need of ever firmer control from the ego, is a source of value.

Lacan has been enormously influential in the world of European psychology and philosophy. Among the strongest responses to his work have been those from the perspective of the feminine. Lacan has made clear the power of gender in the creation of identity. In his presentation the "phallus" symbolises both the wholeness which we lack, those things the subject has lost during the stages of its constitution, and the cultural values which adhere to the symbolic order, which is a patriarchy – the "name of the father." Thus "the feminine is erased in the assumption of identity achievable only by entering into what

Lacan calls the realm of the symbolic, the realm of conventional meaning."[34] Whether this is read as descriptive or prescriptive, from a feminine point of view it would seem unsatisfactory. In different ways three French women in particular, have addressed this problem.

Julia Kristeva alters the emphasis of the Lacanian framework, perhaps restoring the feminine balance, by replacing language at the centre of the edifice with affect, going beyond his theory of linguistic representation to give more emphasis to "pre and trans-linguistic modalities of psychic inscription which we call, 'semiotic'",[35] the early experience of maternal non-separation, the non-symbolic originary experience which may be seen as hostile to ego subjectivity and linguistic control. This allows her to classify the heterogeneous nature of conscious and non-conscious representations in a manner which still allows for meaning in the eclipse of signification, giving three levels of analytic discourse – representation of words, representation of things, and semiotic traces of emotions. "*Signifiance*" is made up of the two levels of the symbolic and the semiotic. Inherent in discussion of *chora* as she terms the pre-symbolic experience, are a mixture of feelings of fear and revulsion which she calls "abjection." Kristeva states that the cause of abjection is "what disturbs identity, system order. What does not respect borders, positions, rules. The in-between, the ambiguous, the composite."[36] The emptiness of separation from mother, from the chora, underlies the formation of the subject – "the representational contrivances that cause us to speak, elaborate or believe rest upon emptiness."[37] Again: "If Narcissism is a defence against the emptiness of separation, then the whole contrivance of imagery, representation, identification and projections that accompany it on the way towards strengthening the Ego and the Subject is a means for exorcising that emptiness."[38] With the first understanding both that identity with the mother is shattered and that mother too is not complete in herself, psychic transfer to the imaginary "father", symbolic of language and symbolisation itself, is correlative with the establishment of the mother as "abjected."

Kristeva is aware of the paradoxical nature of subjectivity which is only revealed in face of the "other" and thus reveals and is revealed by lack. This discovery discloses "that I myself, at the deepest level of my wants and desires, am unsure, centerless, and divided."[39] However understanding provided by analysis can show us that we are "subjects in process" and restore a provisional unity in the subjects, and "the resumption of transitory ludic illusions. Fantasy returns to our psychic life, but no longer as cause for complaint or source of dogma. Now it provides the energy for a kind of artifice, for the art of living."[40]

Hélène Cixous and Luce Irigary are also influenced by Lacanian analysis, with particular interest in the constitution of subjectivity in relation to gender. Hélène Cixous is opposed to all forms of dualistic thinking based on hierarchies and oppositions such as head/heart, form/matter, speaking/writing, and relates these to the opposition man/woman. She argues that in each dualism one term is privileged, from which conflict ensues. Within a patriarchal society woman is represented as the Other, whose necessity for the constitution and recognition of identity we have seen in the work of Lacan and Winnicott. This other is necessary but also threatening. Cixous rejects both the Freudian and the Lacanian models of sexual difference which she sees as condemning women to inferiority and negativity. She argues for the possibility of bisexuality, and the recognition of plurality and the simultaneous presence of masculinity and femininity. She contends that writing is a privileged space for the exploration of such non-hierarchically based plurality, and calls for a specifically feminine practice of writing. Such writing rejects the principle of individual subjectivity as united and stable, and is concerned with subjectivities that are plural and shifting. She argues for an alternative economy of the feminine centred on the concept of the "gift"; a concept I would consider more in tune with the Buddhist perfection of giving with its lack of essential difference between self and other, than with what she considers the masculine western concept of giving in terms of mechanisms of exchange.

Luce Irigary too, critiques the psychoanalysis of Freud and Lacan in terms of gender bias. Her critique underlines the historical determination of psychoanalysis, which, she argues, is unacknowledged by psychoanalysis itself. Thus its historically determined patriarchal bias is unexamined and taken as normative. She suggests that the underlying phantasies of psychoanalysis are also unacknowledged and uninterpreted, and argues that representations of the mother support male phantasies, but are themselves unrepresented. The result of this is that "instead of remaining a different gender, the feminine has become, in our languages, the non-masculine, that is to say an abstract nonexistent reality."[41] Other views concerning the feminine in relation both to Buddhism and to contemporary discourse will be discussed later.[42]

Cognitive Behavioural Psychotherapy

This is the branch of psychotherapy most closely linked to scientific and experimental psychology. Behavioural therapy originated in the 1950s and early 60s as a reaction to the dominant psychoanalytic perspective within therapy. It began as an application of the principles of classical and operant conditioning to the treatment of problem behaviours, founded on the belief that changing behaviour may produce change in cognition. Originally founded on theories that stated behaviour was the result of learning through conditioning and stimulus-response mechanisms, the resultant therapy displayed no concern with conscious memory and subjective processes of mind. Since the 1970s however strict behaviourism has succumbed to the cognitive challenge, which contended that intelligence lay, not merely in stimulus and response, but in an organism's ability to mentally represent aspects of the world, and then to operate on these mental representations rather than on the world itself. Thus subjective experience became a legitimate area of concern. In recent years, Cognitive Behaviour Therapies have accepted cognitions as major determinants of feelings and actions which can be modified, thus effecting behaviour change through taking into account beliefs, expectations and interpretations.

Cognitive Behavioural psychotherapy consists of approaches that attempt to address psychological distress and disfunction primarily by identifying the distortions in the thinking of the client, formulating alternative ways of viewing their situation, before testing the implications in action. Behavioural and Cognitive therapies are usually concerned with current problems and present experience rather than with historical development and are seek overt behaviour change. They tend to be shorter-term and more goal-specific than those of the other schools. Goals are stated in objective and concrete terms and outcomes closely evaluated. Actual therapy is often concerned with step by step procedures; identifying problematic beliefs and behaviours; determining assets and resources which can motivate and maintain change; considering the context of the problem, noting antecedents and consequences of chosen behaviours; setting up treatment goals and designing strategies for achieving these in small incremental steps. As can be seen the stance of the therapist is educative and directive. As well as dealing with individual therapy, cognitive and behavioural methods are important in self-directed programmes teaching people skills they need in order to manage their own lives, such as relaxation techniques, assertiveness training, desensitization and the wide field of Twelve Step programmes addressing addiction.

Within this field important individual approaches include the Multi-Modal Psychotherapy of Arnold Lazarus, a comprehensive approach uniting techniques from the three major branches, classical, operant conditioning and cognitive, Kelly's Construct Theory, Beck's Cognitive Therapy, and Ellis' Rational Emotive Therapy. RET is one of, if not the, parent of cognitive-behavioural therapies. Ellis, asked in an interview how he would like to be remembered replied: "In the field of psychotherapy, I would like them to say that I was the main pioneering cognitive and cognitive-behavioural theorist and therapist, and I fought very hard to get cognition accepted in psychotherapy . . ".[43] The basic hypothesis of RET is that emotions stem from beliefs and interpretations, and its strategy is to identify and vitiate irrational beliefs, replacing them with rational and effective cognitions which will result in a changed emotional reaction to situations and thus to positively changed behaviour. RET works with cognition and action rather than with introspection or expression of feeling, but does encourage the application of its principles to ongoing life situations rather than only to specific presenting problems. It acts on an ABC theory; A is the activating event or fact, B is the belief about this event which causes C, the emotional and behavioural consequence or reaction. During therapy ABC are followed by D which stands for *disputation* or challenging of beliefs, *detection* of irrational beliefs particularly absolutist 'musts' and 'shoulds' and self denigration and *discrimination* between irrational and rational beliefs. D will lead to a change in C and ultimately to E standing for *effects*, both inaction and hopefully more widely in philosophy, leading to F, a new set of *feelings*.

Contemporary behavioural and cognitive therapies are concerned both with the subjective factors and with the interplay between the individual and their environment. Behavioural techniques are also now used for what might earlier have been considered humanistic ends. Similarly as short term psychotherapy becomes both more usual and more desirable, cognitive and behavioural therapies have much to offer other schools.

Existential and Humanistic Psychotherapies

Existential and Humanistic Psychotherapies represent perhaps the largest and most heterogeneous of all the schools, and thus are difficult to describe in terms that both are simple and do justice to the differences of approach. There is a great deal of overlap between the Existential and the Humanistic approaches, and often the Existential is subsumed within the label of the Humanistic or Third Force School. Perhaps the major philosophic difference between this outlook and that of the Analytic school is the shift from the medical and scientifically-oriented point of view to the phenomenological, from the instincts to individually experienced existence. It displays a shift from the intrapsychic to the interpersonal, and a holistic understanding of mind and body, and individual and world. Previous models and tendencies are seen as too intellectual and technological, emphasising the cognitive at the expense of sensation and emotion. Therapeutic approaches are designed as corrective experiential procedures to remedy this dehumanisation, disembodiment and alienation. However it is important to note that all this is a reaction to, and development from, the initial formulations of psychoanalysis. An important central belief of Humanistic Psychology is the individual's natural tendency towards health and growth or self-actualisation.

One of the most theoretically thorough approaches is that of Existential psychology arising from the philosophy of Existentialism. Ludwig Binswanger and Medard Boss are the most important European names connected with the inception of this movement. Boss' "*Psychoanalysis and Daseinsanalyse*" was an attempt to unite what he felt was of inestimable value in the view and practice of Sigmund Freud, with the very different ground of the philosophy of Martin Heidegger. In this work and in *Existential Foundations of Medicine and Psychiatry*, Boss attempted to set out a philosophical foundation for therapy springing from a different world view, with a different meaning and values from that of Freud and his followers. Although *Daseinsanalyse* retained the practical approach of psychoanalysis, its theoretical base is undoubtedly existential, which is why I consider it amongst the later division.

Boss' approach was set out with the direct involvement of Heidegger, who annually for nearly twenty years taught the Zollikon seminars for Boss' students. Interestingly, according to Boss, Heidegger had answered the first letter that Boss ever sent to him in 1946, despite the amount of his correspondence and the fact the Boss was entirely unknown to him, because "he had hoped that through me – a physician and psychotherapist – his thinking would escape the confines of the philosopher's study and become of benefit to wide circles, in particular to a large number of suffering human beings."[44] Boss' desire was to map the Freudian discoveries onto the Heideggerian conception of Being-in-the-world, which, he felt, provided "an adequately human foundation for medicine." Being-in-the-world is a relationship to the world "that is prior to all exact natural scientific conceptualisation, prior to all emotional enthusiastic experience, and the foundation for both of these. It is the fundamental relatedness of human beings to what is, our inherent worldly relationship of being-in-the-world."[45] Within this, self and world are not two divided entities, like subject and object, but form the basic determination of *Dasein* itself in the unified structure of being-in-the-world. This kind of being presupposes a special openness of man's existence, in the light of which the traditional situation seen as a mind distinct from objects which it observes, and/or acts upon, is considered a deficient mode of being-in-the-world. "Being essentially self-interpreting, Dasein has no nature. Yet Dasein always understands itself as having some specific essential nature, and feels at home in belonging to a certain nation or a certain race. Thus Dasein's everyday pre-ontological understanding of its own being necessarily involves a pre-ontological misunderstanding. Understanding itself thus as an object with a fixed essence covers up Dasein's unsettledness and calms the anxiety occasioned by recognising that Dasein is interpretation all the way down."[46] Forgetfulness of being, lack of what Heidegger terms "resoluteness", which in German is also a pun on unclosedness and is thus openness to Being, leads to the rise of the subject forgetful of the actual co-emergence of subject and object, and of the ecologically wilful project of fortifying that subject. This can sound familiar to Buddhist ears ... "no matter how many times I say 'I' there is still no actual psychic agency involved. What *is* involved is my ecstatic being-in-the-world to the extent that I have made its potentialities my own. 'I' refers to the most concrete of all beings, the *Da-sein* in its having grown as one with the world. By contrast the psychological ego agency is an abstraction par excellence. It is the hypostatic reification of certain phenomena of the unobjectifiable *Da-sein*."[47] To approach life from the point of view of an ego is a restricted approach, the ego is clung to as a refusal of the task, which is to face up to what addresses man, a response to the call of the openness of Being. An adequate response is a resoluteness which faces anxiety and death. Anxiety is the "disclosure accompanying a *Dasein's* preontological sense that it is not the source of the meanings it uses to understand itself."[48]

Similarities between Existentialism and such Eastern philosophies as Buddhism and Taoism were pointed out in the first major work of existential psychology published in the United States.

> "The likenesses between these Eastern philosophies and existentialism go much deeper than the chance similarity of words. Both are concerned with ontology, the study of being. Both seek a relation to reality which cuts below the cleavage between subject and object. Both would insist that the Western absorption in conquering and gaining power over nature has resulted not only in the estrangement of man from nature but also in the estrangement of man from himself. The basic reason for these similarities is that Eastern thought never suffered the radical split between subject and object that has characterised Western thought, and this dichotomy is exactly what existentialism seeks to overcome."[49]

So according to this view, human being is no thing but a perceptive, responsive openness, and any illness or mental disturbance encroaches on this openness and becomes a restriction of it. Treatment is treatment of constriction of Dasein and its ontological structures of existence. Modes of illness are classified according to the particular impairments that affect manifestation of these existential characteristics.[50] Authentic living requires facing up to and accepting one's position. The prime objects of repression for Existential Psychology are anxiety and death.

This existential foundation for medicine and psychiatry was also reflected in a different way of being with the patient. The discovery that man's existence is his essence, that "man is essentially one in whose meaning-disclosing relationships the phenomena of our world make their appearance, develops in the *Daseinsanalytic* therapist a basic respect for the intrinsic value and essential content of everything that shines forth and comes into its being in the light of a *Dasein.*"[51] Everything that appears is to be taken seriously as the truth and reality of that patient's existence, rather than as a symbolic account of a drama of underlying forces as in a psychodynamic interpretation. The *Daseinsanalyst* rather than being tied to a theoretical interpretation of the patient's life and symptoms, is free to look for the limitations imposed by the patient's outlook on her own life, and expose and questions these limitations, opening up the possibility of a wider, richer existence.

In turn the transference relationship in Existential psychology is seen as a genuine interpersonal relationship between analyst and analysand, and the fact that the analysand may behave in an infantile manner, and thus misjudge the actual situation, is not allowed to detract from acknowledgement of the genuineness of their present feelings. This also has the effect of bringing the focus of work into the present rather than excavating the past.

All forms of existential psychotherapy, and indeed of Humanistic Psychology in general, display this movement away from the earlier theoretical efforts to achieve purely scientific respectability towards an understanding of man according to his existential reality. As Ludwig Binswanger wrote " Psychology and psychotherapy as sciences are admittedly concerned with 'man' but not at all primarily with mentally *ill* man, but with *man as such.* The new understanding of man which we owe to Heidegger's analysis of existence, has its basis in the new conception that man is no longer understood in terms of some theory, be it a mechanistic, a biologic or a psychological one."[52] The shift was towards the specifically human; man as existential centre in his dealings with society or environment with an emphasis on awareness, self-consciousness and presence. It was, as Binswanger's statement shows, a shift towards the exploration of freedom, authenticity and integration for all, in which neurosis is seen as a failure of personal growth. The influence of Existential Psychology in America was profound, its most well-known protagonists being Rollo May, Irving Yalom, and James Bugental.

However perhaps the most influential figure connected both with Humanistic Psychology and, as we shall see, with the foundation of Transpersonal Psychology was Abraham Maslow. Maslow was instrumental in turning Humanistic Psychology away from the medical model towards a field of growth and human potential. Starting from a position of admiration and gratitude towards individuals whom he saw as supremely well-functioning, Maslow set out to see if these models could lead him towards any conclusions about the healthy human. This led to his theory of the hierarchies of human needs and the process of self actualisation and his conclusion that growth itself is a motivating experience, and one which will occur naturally and healthily whenever the attractions of growth outweigh the perceived dangers. He believed Freud's greatest discovery to be that the cause of much psychological illness is the fear of knowledge of oneself.

The first hierarchy of needs are those he called the deficiency needs, concerned with basic homeostasis, physical needs and security, followed by those for love and esteem. When these are met he felt a further hierarchy of needs came into play that he called Being needs, which are concerned with value and meaning. He described these needs as instinctoid in nature, claiming them to be necessary for avoidance of illness and achievement of full humanness and growth. Indeed Maslow finally postulated that spiritual needs are a biological necessity, and with this belief he was instrumental in founding a fourth psychology, the Transpersonal school.

Another figure of central importance to the development of Humanistic Psychology was Carl Rogers, who, with his Person-Centered approach to therapy continued the trend away from theory and towards a real meeting with the client. Rogers believed that all clients have within themselves the ability to guide their lives in a healthy and constructive manner, and it is the job of the therapist to help free the troubled individual from the blocks and restrictions which separate them from their own inner wisdom. As with the Existentialist foundation, this led to an altered view of the therapeutic relationship, and was Roger's most profound contribution to psychotherapy. According to him there are three conditions that constitute the "person-centered" approach that are growth-promoting. All these conditions relate to the presence of the therapist. The first is congruence or genuineness. It is incumbent upon the therapist to be real and open in the encounter. The second element is what he termed "unconditional positive regard", within which the therapist expresses a positive, non-judgmental and accepting attitude towards whatever the client presents. The third facilitative aspect of the relationship is empathic understanding. This means that the therapist should enter the client's world, sensing accurately the feelings and meanings that the client is experiencing, and communicating her acceptant understanding back to the client in a clarifying reflection. This is listening of a particularly skilful and active kind, and can be of immense value for change. I should like to return to these principles later in terms of the manner in which Buddhist meditative practices may facilitate them.

The other major component of Humanistic Psychology, and of many therapies generally considered under this umbrella is the emphasis on the body, and on psychosomatic unity.[53] Here, possibly more than in other therapies so far mentioned, come changes in techniques and praxis to match those in foundational theory and approach. Human health and potential are seen as concerns not only of a disembodied mind or psyche, but also of the body and its energies. Techniques using bodily exercise, posture, breathing etc. are used to expose, release and heal energetic blocks which cause neurosis and hindrance to expression, growth and freedom. In the Analytic therapies although psychic disturbances are seen to cause somatic trouble, there was yet no appreciation of the possibility of the converse situation, that somatic work could release psychic and emotional tensions.

The change of emphasis goes along with the fundamental belief of Humanistic Psychology that in order for a therapeutic result, thoughts and insights must be accompanied by concomitant affect. Although this had been noticed by Freud, subsequent psychoanalytic work had concentrated on the verbal and cognitive. Indeed Freud had also mentioned the body, writing: "The ego is ultimately derived from bodily sensations, chiefly from those springing from the surface of the body. It may thus be regarded as a mental projection of the surface of the body."[54] This has profound therapeutic implications which, however, he did not follow up. It implied that lack of ego-forming bodily sensations will hinder the development of ego, and that bodily experiences which are ego-developing will be needed to bring about change and restitution. Freud's student Ferenczi continued work in this area, developing "activity techniques" which paid attention to muscular activity and bodily expressions. It was Ferenczi's student, Wilhelm Reich, however, who brought the body into central focus in psychotherapy. Reich's major theoretical contribution was the concept of "muscular amouring"; a bodily response to the continual conflict between instinctual demands and those of society and culture. Character is seen as a structural formation developed as defence against unacceptable instinctual expression. Reich's theory dealt with the economy of the libido, which he saw as a measurable physical energy, which he termed orgone energy. Muscular armouring, corresponding to psychological character structure, binds this energy and interferes with its homeostasis. Various practices of breath and movements are utilised to release energy blocks. Somatic therapies such as Reichian, Bioenergetics, Biodynamics and Biosynthesis and concepts such as muscular armouring and character structures have provided an important new area of development for the field of psychotherapy.

In some senses forming a bridge between Heidegger's thought and somatic therapies, Eugene Gendlin has interpreted Heidegger's concept of "*befindlichkeit*," translated as "mood" or "attunement", the way we sense ourselves within a situation[55], in the context of the therapeutic encounter, and has produced the very important concept of "felt sense." Gendlin's research into the results of psychotherapy suggested that some clients benefited far more than others from therapy, and that it was possible to predict the successful ones. He found that the difference lay not in the therapists' techniques, nor in *what* clients talk about, but in *how* they talk; giving outward sign of what is going on inside, gaining access to the subtle shifts of internal body movement, those preconscious unverbalised infinitely subtle feelings or moods. Gendlin calls this skill "focusing," and has written about it and taught it. Focusing is now a most useful tool or technique which can be used in conjunction with many different approaches to therapy. Basically it is a method for gaining access to the "felt sense". "A felt sense is not an emotion. We recognize emotions. We know when we are angry, or sad, or glad. A felt sense is something you do not at first recognize – it is vague and murky. It feels meaningful, but not known. It is a body-sense of meaning. When you learn how to focus, you will discover that the body finding its own way provides its own answers to many of your problems."[56] Gendlin set out a six step method for accessing and listening to this felt sense, for he says that in the movement from being implicit to becoming explicit the feeling itself changes, and it is in this change that the effectiveness of psychotherapy lies. This is the experiential shift that must accompany, or replace, purely rational talk if there is to be long-term and deep change, and is a skill which may be learned and practised. I will discuss this further in consideration of methods of meditation[57].

These are perhaps some of the most important themes which occur through the heterogeneous school of Humanistic Psychology under whose umbrella shelter a numerous array of different therapies, techniques and trainings quite impossible to do justice to. However one which has escaped previous mention, should be noticed here. This is Gestalt therapy, many of whose techniques and approaches are used by all kinds of therapists professing different allegiances. In fact, ironically, one of its founders, Fritz Perls was wary of techniques. He considered Gestalt to be one of the existential therapies with an emphasis on integration rather than analysis. Perls was influenced by Freud, by Reich, by the findings of German Gestalt psychology that human beings do not perceive things as isolated and unrelated, but within the perceptual process organise them into meaningful wholes, and by the Eastern philosophies of Taoism and Buddhism. He believed "that awareness per se – by and of itself – can be curative."[58] Thus the emphasis in Gestalt therapy is not on asking "why" questions, but consistently on sensing and feeling '*HOW*' – how you experience, how things happen. It exemplifies the experiential holistic outlook important to Humanistic Psychology.

Transpersonal Psychology

As we saw earlier it was in the work of Abraham Maslow that the movement from Humanistic to Transpersonal Psychology began. Maslow came to believe that spiritual needs are a biological necessity, and in 1968 he wrote: "I consider Humanistic Third Force Psychology to be transitional, a preparation to a still 'higher' Fourth Psychology, transpersonal, transhuman, centred in the cosmos rather than in human needs and interest, going beyond humanness, identity, self-actualisation and the like."[59] This was to be Transpersonal Psychology. In the words of Frances Vaughan, one of the school's leading writers and practitioners, it is "an open-ended endeavour to facilitate human growth and expand awareness beyond limits implied by most traditional Western models of mental health ... in this the therapist may employ traditional therapeutic techniques as well as meditation and other awareness exercises derived from Eastern consciousness disciplines."[60] A chief objective of transpersonal theory is to integrate spiritual experience within the understanding of the human psyche. It attempts to achieve a synthesis of spiritual and psychological approaches to the psyche. Only through the belief that human development ultimately points towards spiritual ends and that it is only from this perspective that human nature can be fully understood, can the final integration between man and the cosmos, man and meaning take place.

If Maslow was the actual Founding Father of Transpersonal Psychology, it has important godfathers who lived long before the school as such was founded in the late 1960s, but whose work in retrospect opened the way towards it. One is Carl Jung, who as we have already seen was one of the first psychologists to be deeply interested in Eastern religions, alongside the even less-travelled paths of Western mysticism and alchemy. He broke away from Freud in opposition to Freud's insistence upon the primacy of the instinctual drives, his biological orientation and his emphasis purely on the personal. Jung's psychology describes both the importance of the unconscious and a very different conception of it. In his clinical work Jung came face to face time and again with recurring images and themes which led to his belief in an "authentic religious function in the unconscious", and to his formulation of the theory of the collective unconscious. I will give his own definitions of his key terms.

> "The collective unconscious is a part of the psyche which can be negatively distinguished from a personal unconscious by the fact that it does not, like the latter, owe its existence to personal experience and consequently is not a personal acquisition. While the personal unconscious is made up essentially of contents which have at one time been conscious but which have disappeared from consciousness through having been forgotten or repressed, the contents of the collective unconscious have never been in consciousness, and therefore have never been individually acquired, but owe their existence exclusively to heredity. Whereas the personal unconscious consists for the most part of *complexes,* the contents of the collective unconscious is made up essentially of archetypes."
>
> "The concept of the archetype, which is an indispensable correlate of the idea of the collective unconscious, indicates the existence of definite forms in the psyche which seem to be present always and everywhere. Mythological research called them 'motifs'."[61]

With this theory Jung opened up exploration of the symbolic world, particularly through the practice of dream interpretation and active imagination. His approach to symbols however, differs from that of Freud. Whereas for the latter the symbol represents another known but repressed object, for Jung the true symbol points beyond itself to a something that is truly unknown and unknowable, the archetype that cannot be represented more specifically. Thus the psychological endeavour is immeasurably extended into that of the inexpressible, the mysterious.

As noted earlier, Jung came to believe that "psychoneurosis must be understood, ultimately, as the suffering of a soul, which has not discovered its meaning."[62] Such meaning is the realisation of the self and its destiny in what he termed the "individuation process." This, his analysand, personal secretary and biographer, Aniela Jaffé has written: "has to be understood as the realisation of the 'divine' in man,"[63] a realisation of "how vast is the nexus of life and the goal towards which it is striving, no matter whether this be interpreted as sense or nonsense, and no matter whether any such interpretation is sought or not."[64] The process of individuation requires first a ruthless confrontation with the contents of the unconscious, an integration of the previously rejected "shadow" side of the personality with the accepted "persona," and of all the divergent and dualistic tendencies into wholeness. It is a finally unattainable task. As Jung himself wrote; "The goal is important only as an idea. The essential thing is the *opus* which leads to the goal; *that* is the goal of a lifetime."[65] It is a progressive realisation of wholeness taking the form of confrontation between conscious and unconscious, ego and self. It is to Jung that we owe both the typology according to introverted or extraverted orientations of personality, further distinguished by the predominance of one or more of the functions of sensation, thought, feeling or intuition, and also the concept of the acausal principle of synchronicity.[66]

Further exploration in the symbolic realms of the imagination have followed with Archetypal Psychology, an offshoot of Jung's Analytical Psychology. Unlike Jung, who radically distinguished between the noumenal archetype and the phenomenal archetypal image, the concern of Archetypal Psychology is with the archetypal image rather than the archetype per se. The realm of Archetypal Psychology is the realm of the imagination. Its strategies involve attention to phenomena and to the way in which one sees. It undertakes a deconstruction of the world by "seeing through" accustomed structures of thought, and a reconstruction through attention to the self display of an ensouled cosmos. Although Archetypal Psychology is a prime explorer in the transpersonal symbolic world of images, it is necessary to point out that holding to the central aspiration of its work as "soul-making", it is resistant to spiritual disciplines, eastern or western, and techniques of cultivation whether of meditation or operant conditioning, all of which it sees as belonging to the "spirit position", "with its rhetoric of order, number, knowledge, permanency, and self-defensive logic ... its rhetoric of clarity and detached observation ... of unity, ultimacy, identity..."[67] rather than to the soul position. In his most recent book and talks, Hillman has strongly criticised psychotherapy for its lack of involvement with the world and narcissistic obsession with the individual, referring to a wish to turn from therapy as narcissistic mirror to therapy as window.[68]

Both Jungian and Archetypal Psychology are still based on the word, with their origins in the Freudian talking cure. Another of Freud's students Roberto Assagioli and his Psychosynthesis unites a transpersonal or spiritual dimension with some of the outlook and the diverse techniques of Humanistic Psychology. The aim of Psychosynthesis, as its name suggests, is synthesis rather than analysis. The synthesis is firstly personal synthesis of parts of the self, the subpersonalities, and later, transpersonal synthesis of the self with the Higher Self, however that may be conceived by the individual. Assagioli presents a cartography of the personality containing seven dynamic constituents. The lower unconscious contains the elementary psychological activities which direct the life of the body, the middle unconscious corresponds roughly to the Freudian preconscious containing those elements similar to waking consciousness and easily accessible to it, and the superconscious is the house of higher feeling and capacities such as intuitions and inspirations. The field of consciousness designates the part of the personality of which we are directly aware – the changing experience we can observe, analyse and judge. The conscious Self or I is the point of pure awareness. It differs from the field of consciousness as the difference between a lighted screen and pictures projected upon it. The Higher Self is a noumenal, permanent or true self, situated above and unaffected by, the consciousness of the mind stream and bodily conditions. All the above are enclosed within the collective unconscious. The therapeutic process of Psychosynthesis involves four stages; first recognition of the elements of the personality, second, disidentification from them and acquisition of control over them. This is based on the psychological principle stating: "We are dominated by everything with which our self is identified. We can dominate and control everything from which we disidentify ourselves."[69] The third stage is the realisation of one's true self, and the creation or discovery of a unifying centre. In terms of the earlier cartographic model, this involves uniting the conscious Self with the Higher Self. The final stage is Psychosynthesis itself, the formation or reconstruction of the personality around the new centre.

Contemporary Transpersonal Psychotherapy believes in the transpersonal perspective and experiences in which the sense of identity or self extends beyond the individual and personal to encompass wider aspects of life, psyche and cosmos. To this end it holds assumptions of the potential of human development beyond common definitions of normality in the context of ancient wisdom traditions.[70] Not only opening up the realm of spiritual search as a legitimate area of concern for psychotherapy, it may also actively encourage the experience of expanded states of consciousness. In a recent article in *The Journal of Transpersonal Psychology*, the home of much contemporary discourse in this field, two of the more central Transpersonal therapists and writers discuss the elements of transpersonal practices that they consider constitute the art of transcendence.[71] They enumerate six elements ; a foundation in Ethics (1), is the basis for Attentional Training (2), which assists in Emotional Transformation (3), comprising the reduction of destructive emotions, the cultivation of positive emotions, and the cultivation of equanimity. These practices redirect Motivation (4) and Refine Awareness (5), leading to the realisation of Wisdom (6). Such a list betrays a strong Buddhist influence with reminders of the Eightfold Path and the six Paramitā of the Mahāyāna. The philosophical foundations of such teachings are of equal import as their practices, for as Stanislav Grof, another leading contemporary Transpersonal Psychologist has written;

> "Modern psychotherapy ... faces an interesting paradoxical situation. Whereas in the earlier stages it tried to bypass intellect and eliminate it from the process, at present a new intellectual understanding of reality is an important catalyst for therapeutic progress. While the resistances in more superficial forms of psychotherapy are of an emotional and psychosomatic nature, the ultimate obstacle for radical therapies is a cognitive and philosophical barrier. Many of the transpersonal experiences that are potentially of great therapeutic value involve such a basic challenge to the individual's world view that he or she will have serious difficulty in letting them happen unless properly intellectually prepared."[72]

Grof himself is one of the most active explorers of altered states of consciousness, from prenatal to transpersonal experiences. To accommodate his findings in these fields, he has had to reappraise the relationship between scientific theories and reality, and seek new theoretical frameworks from within the findings of the new physics beyond the Newtonian-Cartesian paradigm, and from ancient non-Western systems of thought.

One towering figure has been absent from mention within any of the four schools or approaches. This is William James, who was present at the very birth of Western psychology, and whose breadth, wisdom and prescience are still breathtaking when read today. Indeed it is the figure of James to whom I look in this enterprise. Alone in Western terms he provides the holistic unity of philosophy, psychology and religious meaning which has been lacking in Western psychology and therapy for so long. Indeed James' psychology as, perhaps also his philosophy, has been eclipsed for much of the past century but is now reappearing in many places to surprise, and perhaps still to shock by its freshness and genuiness. Perhaps James sits most comfortably within the transpersonal approach because of its very lack of boundaries, having written in 1901:

> "The whole drift of my education goes to persuade me that the world of our present consciousness is only one out of many worlds of consciousness that exist, and that those other worlds must contain experiences which have a meaning for our life also; and that although in the main their experiences and those of this world keep discrete, yet the two become continuous at certain points, and higher energies filter in."[73]

Indeed William James is mentioned twice in the article by Vaughan and Walsh mentioned above. The authors cite James in support of their contention that one of the two most important "breakthroughs" in Western psychology of the twentieth century is the rediscovery that, as James put it; "most people live, whether physically, intellectually or morally, in a very restricted circle of their potential being. They make use of a very small portion of their possible consciousness ... We all have reservoirs of life to draw upon, of which we do not dream."[74] James is quoted once again with respect to his comments on attention, having written in 1899: "The faculty of voluntarily bringing back a wandering attention over and over again is the very root of judgement, character and will. No one is *compos sui* if he have it not. An education which would improve this faculty would be the education par excellence."[75] Even more pertinent is his continuation on the same page that "each of us literally *chooses,* by his ways of attending to things, what sort of a universe he shall appear to himself to inhabit."[76] James' views on consciousness which he believed "connotes a kind of external relation, and does not denote a special stuff or way of being,"[77] are so non-substantialist, so rooted in interrelationship that they often appear strangely compatible both with a Buddhist view and with much of contemporary cognitive science.

So too do his views on the self; distributing it between the material Self, including the body, the family and possessions, the social Self, the recognition we receive from others, the spiritual Self, the inner or psychic dispositions and the pure Ego; concluding that "*the 'self of selves' when carefully examined, is found to consist mainly of the collection of these peculiar motions in the head or between the head and the throat*"[78] Perhaps this compatibility comes with an almost ruthless concern with experience itself, not with conceptualisation; a determination to take experience as James describes "just as we feel it, and not to confuse ourselves with abstract talk *about* it, involving words that drive us to invent secondary conceptions in order to neutralize their suggestions and to make our actual experience again seem rationally possible."[79] James' psychology demonstrates many of the postulates of Transpersonal Psychology; emphasis on awareness, the awakening to a greater identity beyond the bounds of the conventional self, and the training of attention and intuition.

The Integrative Perspective

It is important, however, not to overlook the predominance of the integrative approach. In practice, many if not most, therapeutic approaches today partake of a variety of different techniques and concepts. In the 1991 edition of *Theory and Practice of Counselling and Psychotherapy*, Gerald Corey stated that: "There are clear indications that since the early 1980s psychotherapy has been characterized by a rapidly developing movement towards integration and eclecticism".[80] His prediction, reiterated in the 1996 edition is that this trend will continue, accompanied by increased emphasis on both multicultural and spiritual perspectives. Most of the trainings which would consider themselves under the umbrellas of the Humanistic or Transpersonal schools take an eclectic approach to psychotherapy. Basic principles of psychoanalysis, the theories of Freud, Jung and Object Relations will be known and taught today for aspiring therapists in all trainings. The Rogerian principles of therapist presence are now generally upheld by many other branches of psychotherapy, and techniques and approaches originally founded in one or another major school are now frequently used in very different settings. In his latest book Gendlin writes of the understanding of the felt sense and the use of his focusing technique within different avenues of therapy.[81] As psychotherapy becomes more available in the mainstream of health care, short term and goal oriented therapy taking from Cognitive-Behaviourist principles, is currently receiving much attention, supported in UK by the National Health Service and in USA by insurance companies. Buddhist influence itself is to be found in the work of practitioners and writers following all the major schools.[82] Such eclecticism does, however, require, careful consideration of the underlying philosophical foundations of different therapies and techniques, with discriminative awareness of their compatibility in terms of outlook, goal and therapist function.

Ken Wilber's model of the Spectrum of Consciousness (Fig. 1)[83] presents a simple and comparative model around which to organise the aims and developments of the four major schools of western psychology. From a unified ground emerges the first of a series of dualities or splits. Each division is accompanied by repression, projection and identification; repression of the former unity, projection of this into two distinct parts, accompanied by rejection of one and identification with the other. From the base of unity or mind arises the Primary Dualism of self versus other, organism versus environment, subject versus object. Immediately above the level of Mind are the Transpersonal Bands where man is no longer conscious of his identity with Mind, but neither is his identity confined to the boundaries of the individual organism. Here is the place of the transpersonal, the Jungian Archetypes

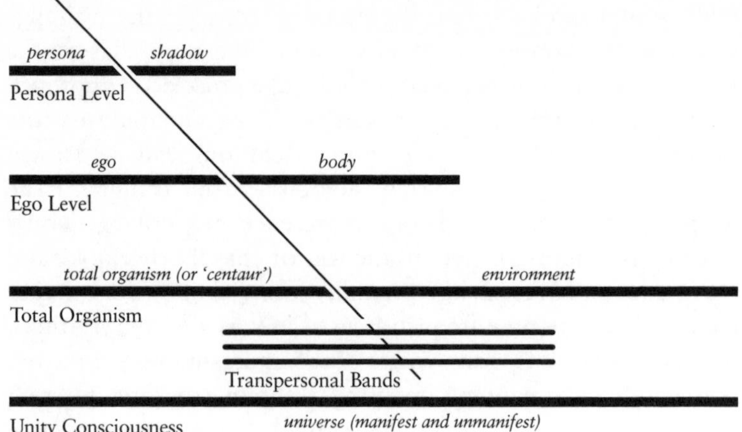

Figure 1: The Spectrum of Consciousness
From *No Boundary* by Ken Wilber. © 1979 by Ken Wilber. Reprinted by arrangement with Shambhala Publications, Inc., 300 Massachusetts Avenue, Boston, MA 02115.

and much mystical experience, where there is a way of looking *at* emotional and ideational complexes without being totally identified *with,* and thus looking *through* them. The Primary Dualism is accompanied by the Secondary Dualism of existence and non-existence, life and death which brings us onto the existential level of the Total Organism. Here man is identified with his total psycho-physical organism as it exists in space and time, and boundaries between self and other, organism and environment are firmly drawn. The upper limits of this level contain the BioSocial Bands "the internalised matrix of cultural premises, familial relationships, and social glosses, as well as the all-pervading social institutions of language, logic, ethics and law."[84] Driven by the anxiety that flees from death, the life of the organism itself is then divided into *psyche* and *soma*, the Tertiary Dualism of the Ego Level where the unity of the total organism is repressed and projected into the ego or self image, a mental representation of his organism with which man identifies in neglect of his actual body. Finally, within the mind or self image, on the Persona Level, the Quaternary Dualism is imposed, the division of the many faceted self into those aspects with which we identify (the *persona*), and those we repress or reject (the shadow). Each level, thus is constituted by a central dualism, with ensuing repression of unity, and projection of the divided parts with accompanying identification and rejection. The schools of psychology and their therapies address and attempt to integrate different dualities.

Broadly speaking, each new historical development has expanded the territory, from the intra-personal, to interpersonal to transpersonal dimensions. Analytic Psychology is concerned primarily with the intra-personal, divisions between *id* and *ego*, conscious and unconscious, the identified *persona* and the rejected shadow. Later developments of this school confront the interpersonal and the Biosocial Bands more strongly. Humanistic Psychology with its emphasis on actualising the full human being is concerned with the total psycho-physical organism in its existentiality, in the interface of self and other, self and environment. Here the aim is to reveal the true self rather than the false self, the individuated self rather than the persona, the integrated I rather than sub-personalities, to use the terminologies of different schools. This real self is the integrated body/mind of fulfilled personal authenticity, at ease within relationship in a world truly experienced. In terms of Existentialism, the prime object of repression is no longer sexual impulse as with Psychoanalysis, but death, giving rise to existential *"angst"*, the anxiety provoked by the duality of being versus nullity.

Finally Transpersonal Psychology enlarging the territory still further to include the Transpersonal Bands, addresses all levels of the spectrum, egoic, existential and transpersonal, including levels of consciousness that are supra individual. It is concerned with the primary dualism of self and other, organism and environment. Recently David Loy has attempted to re-interpret the Freudian Oedipal process yet again, in Buddhist terms, suggesting that the prime object of repression is neither sexual drive nor death, but "lack of being", in Buddhist terms "*annatta*". Interpreted thus, the Oedipal project is the attempt of the developing self to become one's own father.

> "To become one's own father is to become what Nāgārjuna described (and refuted) as *self-existing* ... In Buddhist terms, the Oedipal project is the attempt to attain closure on itself, foreclosing its dependence on others by becoming autonomous. *To be one's own father is to be one's own origin.* Rather than just a way to conquer death, this makes even more sense as the quest to deny one's own groundlessness by becoming one's own ground: the ground (socially sanctioned but nonetheless illusory) of being an independent person."[85]

It is an attempt to heal the division between self and other, self and world, the repression of non-duality.[86] From the Buddhist point of view this sense of self is seen in fact as a mental construct rather than as something self-existing. This constructed and constricted sense of self wants to make itself real, to ground itself, thus "the ego self is this *attempt* of awareness to objectify itself, by grasping itself – which it can no more do than a hand can grasp itself ... The consequence of this is that the sense-of-*self* always has, as its inescapable shadow, a sense-of-*lack*."[87] This sense of lack we have met earlier in descriptions of various psychotherapies, for as Madan Sarup has written with reference to Lacan whose theories, as we have seen, are permeated with this sense of lack: "If one allows that philosophy's concern is with being, one must also recognise that the concern of psychoanalysis is with lack of being."[88] Indeed it is perhaps an attempt to evade this sense of lack that is the basis of all our identifications, and of the sense of ontological anxiety or guilt that accompanies our lack of success in these enterprises. Loy argues that, from the Buddhist perspective, the answer to this lack is not another foundation for the self but rather its deconstruction, revealing that *both* the feeling of self, and the feeling of lack are unnecessary and illusory, since there neither is nor has ever been a self-existing self apart from the world. In short the way of existing of both desire *and* lack is emptiness. This discussion logically leads us to consider these and other Buddhist concepts.

CHAPTER THREE

The Buddhist View

> *"Mind itself is buddha.*
> *Practice is difficult. Explanation is not difficult.*
> *Not-mind. Not-buddha.*
> *Explanation is difficult. Practice is not difficult."*[1]

> *" – a man looking at reality brings his own limitations to the world. If he has strength and energy of mind the tide pool stretches both ways, digs back to electrons and leaps space into the universe and fights out of the moment into non-conceptual time. Then ecology has a synonym which is ALL.*[2]

Just as there are many differences of theory within the broad field of psychotherapy, so within Buddhism also there are many schools and differences of belief and practice. It is my intention here, as far as possible to present the core teachings which remain, with difference of emphasis, at the heart of all Buddhist discourse. Where there is substantial divergence I shall name the specific schools or approaches concerned. I will concentrate especially on the teachings which I consider to be both at the very heart of Buddhism, and also of most importance for a psychotherapy able to meet today's needs. Although Pickering has noted that Buddhism cannot be treated as if it were a Western science, and that: "there is no such thing as Buddhist psychology apart from Buddhism *in toto*"[3], many commentators have done just that, discussing 'Buddhist psychology' in isolation from the philosophy that supports it, and Buddhist meditation practices in isolation from either. As Pickering continues to point out, the whole nature of Buddhism is therapeutic, based on the understanding that "the psycho-physical processes underlying the flow of human experience are not psychological absolutes, but skills that may be improved."[4] Buddhist philosophy promotes the understanding of the development and function of psycho-physical processes and a definition of desirable goals, and its practices promote the improvement of skills. For its therapeutic purpose these are inseparable. Thus within a discussion of the Four Noble Truths I shall emphasise the importance of dependent origination (*pratītyasamutpāda*), and its relationship to the concept of emptiness or transparency (*śūnyatā*). To help explicate this difficult subject I will consider the history and development of Western interpretations of *śūnyatā*.[5] Most importantly, I will then consider the idea of *śūnyatā* as a "way" rather than as a purely intellectual or cognitive concept. Arising from the fact that for Buddhist thought ontology and epistemology coincide, I will present a very brief excursion into the simpler regions of Buddhist epistemology. Finally I will introduce the concept of Buddha Nature (*tathāgatagarbha*) which is an idea of some central importance for a Buddhist approach to psychotherapy.

The Four Noble Truths and Dependent Origination (Pratītyasamutpāda)

The root teachings of Buddhism are encapsulated within the four noble truths; the existence of suffering in all life, the cause of suffering, the cessation of suffering, and the path.[6] Buddha Śākyamuni presented a soteriology based on the individual human life; an analysis of ordinary human life, diagnosis of its problem, prognosis, and prescription. However, rather than seeing these truths as imperatives, in terms of the actions they invoke, there has been a tendency to present them as propositions, statements of fact. Yet the emphasis in the Buddha's first sermon, the Turning of the Wheel of Dharma is on what is to be *done*. The first truth, of the existence of suffering, is "to be known absolutely." The second, the cause of suffering, is "to be abandoned." The third, the possibility of cessation, is "to be realised", and the fourth, the path to such cessation, is "to be cultivated." These actions may also be said to provide a model for psychotherapy – to become aware, to abandon harmful patterns, to realise the possibility of greater freedom and to cultivate the means to achieve it.[7] The first truth asks us to clearly know that life itself, from our normal standpoint, is never entirely satisfactory. We are drawn to what we like, which causes suffering when it is unattainable, or disappears due to inevitable change and decay, and we attempt to avoid what we dislike, which causes suffering when our attempts at avoidance are unsuccessful. Perhaps the ultimate and inescapable unsatisfactoriness or suffering from the point of view of the egocentric individual is death. It is also important to note that the first truth presents suffering as impersonal. There is suffering – suffering exists. Thus we may negotiate a relationship with it. In actuality, what normally happens is that we grasp it or identify with it; it becomes *my* suffering.

The second truth fundamentally relates to causation. Gombrich has pointed out that Buddhism's great innovation was the ethicisation of the pan-Indian doctrine of *karma*, the law of cause and effect, by re-interpreting it in terms of intention.[8] This at a stroke ethicised and, I would add, psychologised Buddhist teachings which become centrally concerned with the analysis of the functioning of mind, how willing comes about. Underlying this is the doctrine of dependent origination (*pratītyasamutpāda*). The Buddha said: "One who sees dependent origination sees the Dhamma; one who sees the Dhamma sees dependent origination."[9] Later, at the beginning of Mahāyāna Buddhism, Nāgārjuna wrote: "One who sees all things as arising in dependence, sees unregenerate existence and its origin, its cessation and the path to its cessation as they truly are."[10] In 1984 in a lecture the Dalai Lama spoke of it as "the general philosophy of all Buddhist systems."[11] It is this teaching, at the heart of the Buddhist view that I contend is of great importance in relation to contemporary discourse and to good psychotherapeutic practice. Due to this foundation in dependent origination, the outlook of Buddhism is one of dynamic interrelationship rather than linearity of cause and effect. It is this that allows it to escape dualism and the logic or either/or and take the "middle way" between eternalism and nihilism, self and world, inner and outer.[12] Dependent origination is at the heart of the Buddhist explanation of causality, and in the twelvefold form relating to human existence describes the mechanism underlying the existence of suffering, its arising and its cessation. It both describes the arising of *saṃsāra*, or unregenerate existence, and provides for a way of liberation. For if *saṃsāra* signifies conditioned existence, then *nirvāṇa* or liberation means unconditioned existence, the extinguishing of the very conditions which determine our limited and restricted existence.

In its simplest form, dependent origination describes the dependence of all phenomena upon causes and conditions, thus:

> "When this exists, that comes to be;
> with the arising of this, that arises.
> When this does not exist, that does not come to be;
> with the cessation of this, that ceases."[13]

In the longer form dependent origination in terms of the individual human life is presented in the twelve links which are often illustrated as the Wheel of Becoming or cyclic existence.

> "When this exists, that comes to be; with the arising of this, that arises. That is, with ignorance as condition, formations (come to be); with formations as condition, consciousness; with consciousness as condition, mentality-materiality; with mentality-materiality as condition, the sixfold base; with the sixfold base as condition, contact; with contact as condition, feeling; with feeling as condition, craving; with craving as condition, clinging; with clinging as condition, being; with being as condition, birth; with birth as condition, ageing and death, sorrow, lamentation, pain, grief and despair come to be. Such is the origin of this whole mass of suffering."[14]

These links may be presented either in forward or in reverse order, emphasising either arising, or dependence, because each link is both conditioned and conditioning, providing a theory of causality that, in contradistinction to most Western ways of thought up to present time, is not linear and substantial, but circular, and reciprocal. In this model everything is interdependent and interconnected, nothing is absolute and independent and the emphasis is shifted from individual things to process and relationship. Mind and body, belief and action, object and environment are seen in reciprocal relationship, all constituent parts of a dynamic and mutually causative whole. In the Theravāda commentarial tradition the cycle was interpreted over three successive lifetimes; ignorance and determinations of previous life give rise to consciousness etc. in this life which gives rise in time to the next life, but it may also be seen as simultaneous within every moment. A Tibetan oral description of *saṃsāra* is "taking birth again and again without autonomy or free will."[15] Psychologically interpreted this explains how the dispositions of ignorance in every moment infect every subsequent perception and understanding of self and world, giving birth to an endless and inescapable cycle of misperception. Seen from the point of view of cessation, this same cycle points to a way of liberation, starting with the cessation of ignorance or nescience, the formations or mental dispositions will cease; on their cessation, consciousness will cease; on the cessation of consciousness, the psychophysical person, i.e. mentality-materiality will not arise, with no psychophysical person, there will be no six senses, giving rise to no contact, no feelings, no craving and holding, and thus no being or becoming, no birth and concomitant ageing, death and suffering. Since the model presents a distinction between the different stages of the process, it also presents the possibility that through training of the mind the stages may be delinked and their progression need not become inevitable. Psychologically the pivotal links are, from the cognitive standpoint, that of ignorance giving rise to the dispositions, and from the emotional perspective, that between feelings and craving. Ignorance may be abandoned through the application of wisdom, and feelings may be uncoupled from craving through cultivation of a different way of life. Obviously the more subtle and early the awareness and identification of feeling, the more opportunity there will be to introduce choice before the reaction of craving. This, I would suggest, is a significant part of the work of psychotherapy.[16]

The first node of this cycle is ignorance or nescience; ignorance specifically, that is, of the three marks of existence; that all things are impermanent, unsatisfactory and without self or fixed essence. In Early Buddhism non-self referred specifically to the non-self of persons. I would like to look at the teachings about self in detail in the following chapter, merely noting here that in Buddhism there is not considered to be an essential self. Self is ascertained primarily in terms of five aggregates, which we have already met in different form within the twelvefold chain of dependent origination. These are form or matter, feelings, perceptions, determinations and consciousness. What we name and identify with as our self is actually the interaction of these causal factors which form a system. From a Buddhist point of view ignorance arises when this sense of self is grasped and identified with as an individual entity rather than as a changing process; when words or concepts relating to this process are apprehended as if they referred to something ultimately real rather than to a useful concept. The Buddhist explanation of self provides a model of process; a non reifying model of human being in its dimensions of body, speech and mind; a description of how the self works rather than a description of parts.

As well as the provision of an explanation of causality, there may be said to be a second level of dependent origination applying to all phenomena, which is an explanation of the dependence of wholes upon their parts. A third linguistic level of dependent origination, more discussed by Mahāyāna Buddhism, refers to the dependence of phenomena upon their imputation by name and concept.[17]

Emptiness (Śūnyatā)

In the Mahāyāna the concept of selflessness of the person was extended to distinguish both the selflessness of persons and that of phenomena In fact the root of such teaching exists in the early

Buddhist work, the *Dhammapada*; "All *dhammas* are without self."[18] However, in the Mahāyāna, and in particular, in what became known as the Madhyamaka school, this lack of self in all things, persons and phenomena, was expanded into the central doctrine of emptiness or *śūnyatā*, and it is this doctrine that is at the heart of Mahāyāna Buddhism, and of the subsequent Vājrayāna or Tantric Buddhism, and schools of East Asian Buddhism such as Zen and Hua Yen. Emptiness is grounded in, and indeed *is*, the very interdependence expressed by dependent origination in its simplest form; the emptiness of inherent existence or self-sufficient essence of mutually dependent processes. As Nāgārjuna wrote in the dedicatory verses of the *Mūlamadyamakakārikā*, the primary text of Madhyamaka Buddhism:

> "I pay homage to the Fully Awakened One,
> the supreme Teacher who has taught
> the doctrine of relational origination,
> the blissful cessation of all phenomenal thought
> constructions."[19]

He then continues to explain that due to dependent origination (relational origination in Inada's translation) every event is marked by eight negations:

> "Non-origination, non-extinction,
> non-destruction, non-permanence,
> non-identity, non-differentiation,
> non-coming (into being), non-going (out of being)."[20]

Due to these qualities, Nāgārjuna sets out to prove the emptiness of all phenomena by a series of arguments that deconstruct every possible opponent's position by reducing it to absurdity. Towards the conclusion of the work he declares that dependent origination (here translated as contingency) and emptiness are one and the same, and constitute the middle way of Buddhism.

> "Contingency is emptiness
> which, contingently configured
> is the central path."[21]

It may be helpful here to introduce the concept of Two Truths, conventional truth (*saṃvṛti satya*) and absolute truth (*paramārtha satya*). The term for conventional or confined truth in Sanskrit, *saṃvṛti*, comes from a term implying veiled or covered and is the ordinary everyday truth of language in which we may acceptably say "I", "you", "individual" and "self". The absolute or liberated truth is that there is no indivisible and essential self. From this fundamental ignorance of the absolute truth of selflessness, as we have seen, arises the emotional grasping, identification and self-cherishing that puts the ego at the centre of the world. All else is then related to it.[22]

In terms of the two truths, a thing's conventional truth is its appearance and apparent existence, its absolute truth is its emptiness of essential existence. Ultimately it is necessary to see the two as non-dually indivisible, in order to rest in the middle way between the two extreme views of eternalism and nihilism. As Tsong Kha pa states:

> "So long as the two understandings,
> The unfailing (nature) of appearances – the dependent arising,
> And the emptiness – lacking assertion of (independent existence),
> Appear as separate, still,
> He has not realized the thought of the Muni.
>
> When the (two realizations) exist simultaneously without alteration,
> Merely from seeing the dependent arising as unfailing,
> And, if the ascertained understanding of (non-inherent existence)
> Destroys all modes of misapprehension of objects,
> At that time the analysis of the view of (emptiness) is complete.
>
> Further, the extreme of existence is avoided by the appearances,
> And the extreme of non-existence is avoided by the emptiness."[23]

Emptiness is a subtle concept, difficult to grasp. As Nāgārjuna himself described;

> "Misconstruing emptiness
> injures you,
> like mishandling a snake
> or miscasting a spell"[24]

The supreme fault is the fault of turning emptiness itself into a something, rather than a provisional name or thought construction. Ultimately Buddhism teaches the emptiness of emptiness itself.

Perhaps the most poetic, positive and easily-accessible contemporary presentation of dependent origination and emptiness comes from Vietnamese Buddhist monk and writer Thich Nhat Hanh. He presents the concept in terms of the piece of paper you are reading:

> "If you are a poet, you will see clearly that there is a cloud floating in this sheet of paper. Without a cloud, there will be no rain; without rain, the trees cannot grow; and without trees, we cannot make paper. The cloud is essential for the paper to exist. ...
>
> If we look into this sheet of paper even more deeply, we can see the sunshine in it. If the sunshine is not there, the forest cannot grow. In fact nothing can grow ... And if we continue to look, we can see the logger who cut the tree and brought it to the mill to be transformed into paper. And we see the wheat. We know that the logger cannot exist without his daily bread, and therefore the wheat that became his bread is also in this sheet of paper..."[25]

And so, within the sheet of paper he includes the clouds, the rain, the sunshine, the trees, the logger, his food, his parents, and finally you, the reader, for your mind and perception are found there too. All these things, in his term "inter-are" through their dependent origination, their relative and dependent existence within a web of interconnection. Emptiness is merely the description of this from another angle; from that of the phenomena themselves, which are empty of being autonomous entities, possessors of some essential nature, independent of causes, conditions or a designating mind. Such a presentation as Thich Nhat Hanh's leads surely to a participative and enriched rather than an impoverished sense of world. It leads to a positive appreciation of emptiness, as source of possibility. Perhaps the translations, occasionally found, of openness or transparency for *śūnyatā* convey this connotation more fully.[26]

However within Buddhist philosophy there are many different arguments and interpretations of *śūnyatā*, which very broadly hinge on leaning towards a positivistic interpretation leading in the eyes of opponents to the dangers of a substantialist understanding, or a more negative interpretation, leading in opponents' eyes to the fault of nihilism. Nāgārjuna represents what later became known as the Prāsaṅgika Madhyamaka position, the most extreme anti-substantial position which refuses to accept that it represents a logically-defined position or view itself, and argues by deconstruction of the propositions of their opponents.

Another main area of disputation has to do with interpretations of *śūnyatā* itself in Tibetan Buddhism, arguments between adherents of the *rang stong* or self-empty position, and those of the *gzhan stong* or other-empty position who maintain a more positive view of emptiness.[27] Yet the message behind the concept of emptiness is by no means nihilistic. Later on in the East Asian school of Hua Yen (Japanese, Kegon) the eight negations of Nāgārjuna are re-interpreted cataphatically in the doctrine of the non-obstruction and interpenetration of the six characteristics delineated by Fa Tsang. These observe the interdependence of three pairs of antitheses; universality and particularity, identity and difference, integration and disintegration.[28] It is to the Hua Yen school that we are indebted for the image of the net of Indra, the image we suggested as a contemporary symbol.

In this view emptiness is seen as possibility, indeed as that without which nothing is possible. Nāgārjuna himself spoke of this:

> "Nothing fails to happen in this way,
> nothing is not empty."[29]

I would suggest that it is this quality of emptiness which allows for growth and change, and is so important in psychotherapeutic attempts to free ourselves from the frames and conditions which we impose on awareness, and with which we subsequently identify ourselves.

When emptiness is realised what is seen is suchness, *Tathatā,* the suchness of things as they are, freshly presented rather than represented through the individualistic veils of conceptuality and emotion. Nāgārjuna describes this as:

> "Not known through others, peaceful, not fixed by fixations, without conceptual thought, without differentiation: these are the characteristics of suchness."[30]

This is the liberation pointed to by the third truth which is to be realised. As noted earlier and to be further discussed later, psychotherapy is less concerned with the transcendental and religious aspects of Buddhism, but it is concerned with the ideas and practices which lead to liberation, since they may equally well lead to a more mundane liberation from the fixed concepts and frames of reference which cause us daily and continuing suffering.

When behind the conventional truth of appearance is seen the absolute truth of emptiness, then

> "Life's no different from nirvana,
> nirvana's no different from life.
> Life's horizon is nirvana's horizon.
> The two are exactly the same."[31]

Nirvāṇa is thus not another world, it is perhaps a different understanding of the one we inhabit, which, if we believe it to be essentially as it appears, is *saṃsāra.* In effect neither term *paramārtha* nor *saṃvṛtti* can be utterly separated since what is called *saṃvṛtti* is not pure *saṃvṛtti* in so far as its true nature is *paramārtha* or *śūnyatā*, *paramārtha* is not pure *paramārtha* since it is *śūnyatā* which always appears, to the perception of all but Buddhas, as *saṃvṛtti.* Ultimately *paramārtha* is not to be known by any reifying or dichotomising conceptuality inherent in language. It is to be realised by non-dual wisdom, and while discussion and discourse may, at least according to Tsong Kha pa, point to this, and lead to understanding, it does not subsume and contain that understanding. In fact as Nāgārjuna states, both absolute and conventional or confining truth is necessary:

> "The dharma of the awakened
> hinges on two truths:
> ambiguous truths of the world
> and truths which are sublime.
> Not distinguishing between them,
> you cannot plumb the depths.
> Without conventions,
> you cannot reveal the sublime,
> you cannot nirvana"[32]

As Andrew Tuck perceptively writes in his study of the Western interpretation of Nāgārjuna: "... *śūnyatā* is a provisional heuristic term for the nature of the universe as seen without such absolutistic mental constructions. It is reality without an 'illusory veil' of conceptional formations that impose a conventional view of reality. *Paramārtha-satya* is thus, in this description, a psychological state."[33]

Although, as we have noted, psychotherapy is predominantly concerned with the mundane, from the perspective of a Buddhist inspired psychotherapy this relationship of the two truths, *nirvāṇa* and *saṃsāra,* the unconditioned and the conditioned is important. It widens the field and scope of psychotherapy, opening, if only in intention, the domain of the possibility of the unconfined and unconditioned around, within and among the confined, conditioned and conventional. It listens attentively for the silence behind and between speech and breath and thought. There is another factor arising from this linkage of the worldly and the transcendent, expressed most succinctly in the well-known opening of the Heart Sutra: "Form is emptiness, Emptiness is form." From the perspective of the unconditioned, and from that of the conditioned as delineated in dependent origination, all phenomena and their qualities partake of what they are not as well as what they are. Spaciousness speaks also of confinement, clarity of ignorance, compassion of separation. This may be helpful to the therapeutic approach bringing awareness both to what manifests overtly and to its shadow or unspoken aspect. In daily living what occurs is an ever-increasing confinement of the open transparent potential of the unconfined. One Buddhist psychotherapist describes ordinary psychological development as "a gradual thickening of the psyche's arteries as layers of patterned responses deposit themselves on the open potential of being."[34] This perhaps explains one definition of emptiness (Tibetan, *Stong nyid*) in the Tibetan dictionary as *spros med*, free of conceptual proliferation.[35]

Other echoes of the value of this idea of seeing things as they are, are found in unexpected places. Novelist Italo Calvino quoting from another Italian writer that "to know is to insert something into what is real, and hence to distort reality", notes of any writer that "from this arises his invariably distorting way of representing things, and the tension he always establishes between himself and the thing represented, so that the more the world becomes distorted before his eyes, the more the author's self becomes involved in this process and is itself distorted and confused."[36] Surely this is exactly what the doctrine of emptiness is seen as a remedy for? Indeed in a statement close to Buddhist thought, Calvino continues "Think what it would be to have a work conceived from outside the *self*, a work that would let us escape the limited perspective of the individual ego, not only to enter into selves like our own but to give speech to that which has no language, to the bird perching on the edge of the gutter, to the tree in spring and the tree in fall, to stone, to cement, to plastic. . . ."[37]

Scientists, Varela, Thompson and Rosch also describe a similar state: "As mind/world keeps happening in its interdependent continuity, there is nothing extra on the side of mind or on the side of world to know or be known further. Whatever experience happens is open, perfectly revealed as it is."[38] There is no additional reality apart from itself, the interdependent whole needs no foundation outside itself. It is perhaps similar to the non-dual reality which Heidegger described: "Nothing is never nothing; it is just as little a something in the sense of an object – it is Being itself, whose truth will be given over to man when he has overcome himself as subject, and that means when he no longer represents that which is as object."[39]

The lack of distinction between subject and object is much emphasised in the Yōgacāra school. According to the teaching of the *Saṃdinirmocana Sutra* the Buddha's teachings are to be divided into three turnings of the wheel of Dharma. The first turning refers to teachings based on the Four Truths and the second to teachings on emptiness. Teachings of the third turning are broadly those of the Yōgacāra school which chronologically succeeded the Madhyamaka or middle way school, whose most outstanding representative was Nāgārjuna. The Yōgacāra presentation differs from that of the Madhyamaka. Firmly based in meditative practice and reacting to a perceived overnegation tending toward the nihilistic in Madhyamaka teachings, Yōgacāra doctrines are concerned with the non duality of subject and object, which for them are impositions upon the non-dual flow of perceptions, sometimes termed Mind.[40] The Yōgacāra is generally considered to be a school of idealism, yet recent studies have questioned this view, and designated at least two variant strands of Yōgacāra thought; the earlier and original strand expounded in the works of Maitreya, Asaṅga, Vasubandhu and Sthiramati which is not in conventional terms "idealist", and a later strand following Dharmapāla and the Chinese translations of Hsuan Tsang, which may be so designated.[41] Asaṅga explains emptiness through exposing the false dualities of subject and object and designation and base of designation, and bases his argument on the theory of three natures and what may be called a nominalist approach. Confusion of the two strands of Yōgacāra teaching arises from interpretation of the term "*cittamātra*" or "mind only" which is often given as another name for the school. Willis argues that for Asaṅga, "mind only" or "only mind" describes the nominalist position; the discovery that the object in meditation is mind-made is simultaneously the realisation of emptiness. Moreover, through meditation, the subject too is found to be also illusory, a creation of the mind, thus "merely mind", which is by definition, impermanent and empty. Later more idealist interpreters upheld a more positive belief in "mind only" as "mind alone" as the true non-dual reality.

For the Yōgacāra the Madhyamaka presentation of the two truths is expanded into a model of three natures or ways of being. This is intended to present a better understanding of the conventional existence of phenomena and of absolute emptiness, and to act as an antidote to misconceptions of Madhyamaka doctrine leading to a misplaced belief that things do not exist at all, even conventionally, and are entirely illusory. According to this model *parikalpitasvabhāva* is the imagined nature, *paratantrasvabhāva*, the other-dependent or relative nature and *parinispannasvabhāva,* perfected nature. *Parikalpita* denotes conventional reality when apprehended as real, *Parinispanna* denotes absolute reality, or to avoid substantiality, the consummated understanding of a practitioner. Mediating between these two, *Paratantra* denotes the understanding of reality in its dependent origination, which is the basis of the other two natures. On this base the imagined nature presents itself as false imagination which the worldly person takes to be real and becomes attached to. Similarly the consummated nature is to be understood on the same basis by the enlightened. This transformation of the basis *(āśrayaparāvṛtti)* describes the achievement of enlightenment for the Yōgacārin. The positive interpretation of emptiness, the *gzhan stong* interpretation, rests on an understanding of emptiness as *parinispanna,* empty of both *paratantra* and *parikalpita*. Empty thus, of all "other", it is yet not empty of the inseparable Buddha qualities.[42] Certainly the Yōgacāra view of non-dual mind, whether ultimately empty or not, was and is of great influence both to Vajrayāna, and to the development of Far Eastern Buddhism.

Western Interpretation of Emptiness

Both the difficulties and the contemporary relevance of presenting emptiness may be seen in considering its changing interpretation in the West.[43] The initial Western reaction to Mādhyamika thought, as also that of earlier Indian opponents, was one of repudiation on the grounds of its nihilism. Nineteenth century interpreters, principally E. Burnouf called it "*nihilisme scholastique*". Following on this, what we may call the second phase of scholars favoured an absolutist interpretation under the influence of German idealism and Vedanta. Here we find the works of Scherbatsky and Murti. However, it is more recently both that Nāgārjuna has seemed to be speaking directly to the contemporary Western condition, and that Western discourse has itself led to fresh interpretations of Madhyamaka, and a dialogue has ensued.[44] This is the third phase of Madhyamaka scholarship in the West, which may be termed the "linguistic interpretation" after the work of Wittgenstein. Both Nāgārjuna and the contemporary philosophers mentioned are reacting against the prevailing beliefs that meaningful language propositions faithfully reflect existing objects. According to the linguistic interpretation the Madhyamaka analysis is to be read as a critique of this referential theory of meaning and correspondence theory of truth. As philosophical discourse in the West has swept away the grounds of legitimation for earlier systems of philosophy or belief, the Madhyamaka analysis of just such a condition becomes of greater interest and of greater value. Following Nietzsche's announcement of the death of God, Heidegger's argument of the death of metaphysics, and Derrida's of the death of logocentrism, it becomes urgent for the West to seek for some view which will both accept basic groundlessness and perhaps allow for some value; some future more meaningful than either nihilism, or providing more guidance than the "conversation" put forward by Rorty.[45]

Derrida, writing of "*différance*", a key term in his discourse, standing for the impossibility and continual deferring of self-identity states: "It is because of *différance* that the movement of signification is possible only if each so-called 'present' element, each element appearing on the scene of presence, is related to something other than itself, thereby keeping within itself the mark of the past element, and already letting itself be vitiated by the mark of its relation to the future element, this trace being related no less to what is called the future than to what is called the past, and constituting what is called the present by means of this very relation to what it is not: what it absolutely is not, not even as past or a future as a modified present."[46] That, surely sounds like dependent origination, and like *śūnyatā*, *différance* itself has no absolute existence; "différance is not. It is not a present being, however excellent, unique, principal or transcendent. It governs nothing, reigns over nothing and nowhere exercises any authority . . . not only is there no kingdom of différance, but différance instigates the subversion of every kingdom, which makes it obviously threatening and infallibly dreaded by everything within us that desires a kingdom, the past or future presence of a kingdom."[47] The deconstruction of the Mādhyamika is no less rigorous than that of Derrida, but at the end of the deconstruction we are, I suggest, left with something more than mere ruins. Ann Klein has suggested that: ". . . from a Buddhist perspective, postmodern emphasis on the constructed, endlessly diffuse nature of things, combined with its unwillingness to admit to any category outside the process of diffusion, is like talking about dependent arising without emptiness."[48] The ontological status of any thing may be discussed only in terms of its association with other things, and the meaning of any proposition may be defined only by being viewed in the full context of its usage, so that both existence and meaning are grounded in a contextual matrix. Yet this kind of contingent significance does not detract from its value and usefulness, but as we saw in the description of Thich Nhat Hanh may even enrich it, opening it upon the unconditioned, the ultimate truth of emptiness. Moreover, as Klein carefully describes in connected with feminist discourse, it is emptiness that may be taken as a connection between essentialist and constructivist postmodern stances. For emptiness is both dependently originated and unconditioned.

Emptiness as a Way

For above all things, it must not be forgotten that Buddhist philosophy, and Madhyamaka is considered the highest pinnacle of Buddhist philosophy, is not merely polemic but soteriology. The fourth noble truth which is to be cultivated is the truth of the path, whose eight stages are divided into the three divisions of wisdom, morality and meditation. In subsequent chapters I will consider these more fully; what is of prime importance is to realise that for Buddhism, wisdom is inseparable from practice and skilful means. Thus Buddhist philosophy is, in Wittgenstein's terms, "therapeutic", and in Rorty's, "edifying" rather than "systematic". It is not a theory but, for Edward Conze, "a ladder that reaches out into the infinite." and for Mervyn Sprung, the termination of philosophy as "the transmutation of knowing into something else."[49]

The Buddhist Mahāyāna path rests on the twin foundations of wisdom, that wisdom of the understanding of dependent origination and emptiness, and of compassion. Compassion relates not only to the benevolence which wishes well to all beings but also to the way in which one practises such wisdom. It is often referred to as "skill in means." Within the circular logic we have noted before, it is compassion which gives rise to the Bodhisattva's initial wish to achieve wisdom and enlightenment for the sake of all beings, and it is also this compassion which as a result of achieving such wisdom, sees the equality and sameness of all beings in their dependence and emptiness, and acting under the influence of that understanding, ceases to operate from an egocentric perspective.

The contemporary problem has been described as that of nihilism, as the great systems of belief and philosophy have lost their sources of legitimation, and we have moved into a postmodern universe of signs. When the paradigms of knowledge, truth and reality that have dominated modern history have lost their ground, we are left groundless, and such loss of meaning is found in the psychopathologies of the age.[50] Hubert Dreyfus distinguishes between philosophers like Sartre and Derrida for whom the lack of an ultimate ground is an abyss, and those such as Heidegger and Wittgenstein for whom the nonground is no abyss, since what remains are shared practices. "Giving grounds (must) come to an end sometime. But the end is not in ungrounded presupposition: it is an ungrounded way of acting."[51] Like Wittgenstein who stated the aim of philosophy was to show the fly the way out of the fly bottle,[52] and Heidegger,[53] the Madhyamaka philosopher certainly sees the end of philosophy in action, not only in the shared practices of conventional reality, though these are important, but also in the transmutation of the conventional into the absolute truth of emptiness and suchness. Buddhist critiques of Derrida's philosophy argue that Derrida's own critique of Western philosophy fails to go far enough, remaining in the realm of pure textuality, while Nāgārjuna puts forward a transformed mode of experiencing the world; that the middle way goes beyond Derrida in that "it frequents the 'unheard-of-thought', and also, 'with one and the same stroke' allows the reinstatement of the logocentric too."[54]

For the Mādhyamika emptiness is taught with a specific purpose, as a medicine prescribed as a remedy for the disease of conceptual proliferation and clinging which arises from ignorance about the real nature of existence, its emptiness. Realisation of emptiness is the base for an entire way of life grounded in compassion, and understanding is achieved through a deconstruction of all present conventional beliefs, views, signs and frames through entering into specific mind training. A recent Western study discusses how our experience is shaped by our conceptual framework, and how that framework and its expression in language develops through a process of metaphorically structuring one concept in terms of another, layer upon layer.[55] For example, we structure our concepts of argument through metaphors of war, using such terms as attacking, defending, winning and losing. Perhaps if explicated within a different conceptual framework, e.g. that of dance, both experience and resultant behaviour would be different, perhaps less antagonistic. A Buddhist scholar responded to this work with the comment that from a Buddhist point of view the authors have omitted the "most deeply rooted and pernicious of all metaphors, 'reality as substance.'"[56] It is the replacement of the metaphor "reality as substance" with that of "reality as emptiness" that Buddhism attempts, or indeed the conscious retention of the idea of metaphor itself, thus cutting through and deliteralizing all the conceptual layers and proliferation, returning us to the suchness of phenomena. As the same scholar beautifully described it:

> "The Madhyamika is radically deconstructive, pragmatic philosophy designed to be *used* for exposing, defusing and dismantling the reifying tendencies inherent in language and conceptual thought. ... All it does is dissolve the old questions which are seen to have been misguided from the start, leaving behind nothing other than a dramatic awareness of the living present – an epiphany of one's entire form of life. No form of conceptual diffusion remains, and no questions begging for answers that reinforce a deep-seated resistance to acceptance that this life, as it is now lived, is the only arbiter of truth and reality."[57]

Buddhist Epistemology and Psychology

From the above it will appear that in Madhyamaka thought ontology and epistemology become indivisible. As we noted earlier this is clearly stated at the beginning of the *Dhammapada*:

"We are what we think.
All that we are arises with our thoughts.
With our thoughts we make the world."

The difference between conventional and absolute truth is a different way of knowing or understanding. Thus it would be helpful here to take a very brief look at Buddhist epistemology and psychology of perception. To do justice to this subject is beyond the scope of this work, but I would like to point out that here again we find models of interdependence, wherein all mind states are seen to arise from the interaction of interdependent causes and conditions.

The aim in Buddhist practice is to train the mind in a progression from false views to valid perception. From an epistemological perspective, relying largely on the teachings of Dharmakīrti,[58] perception is analysed into the six sense organs; eye, ear, nose, tongue, body and mind, with their respective objective sense fields of form, sounds, smells, tastes, tangibles and concepts, and the six consciousnesses; visual etc.[59] In a dynamic process in which both self and world, knower and known are reciprocally dependent, a visual perception comes into being through the contact between a form, an eye, and a visual consciousness. Again this presentation reveals the interaction and interdependence of inner and outer, subjective and objective, world and person. In its first arising it may be considered ideal if it has the characteristics of freshness, infallibility and cognition. However, this first perception lasts for only a fraction of a second, and serves as the condition for the arising of a moment of mental consciousness. Due to the power of secondary mental factors derived from emotions, memories etc., (i.e. *samskaras,* formations or dispositions), a memory or mental image will arise at the same moment as the arising of the mental consciousness, and the subsequent moments of that visual consciousness, will be overlaid by memories, images and emotional responses. It is described thus in the Honeyball sutra:

> "Dependent on the eye and forms, eye-consciousness arrises. The meeting of the three is contact. With contact as condition there is feeling. What one feels, one perceives. What one perceives, that one thinks about. What one thinks about, that one mentally proliferates. With what one has mentally proliferated as the source, perceptions and notions tinged by mental proliferation beset with respect to past, future, and present form cognizable through the eye."[60]

Thus the problem of conceptual cognition according to Buddhism is the inevitable mixing of subsequent mental images with initial perceptions. The only ideal cognitions are these ideal perceptions, which are defined as fresh, infallible cognitions that are free from conceptuality, and ideal conceptions or inferences which are initial states of inferential understanding based upon perfect reasoning.[61] It is interesting here to note briefly the different methods of direct sensory perception and inference. Though both are considered valid cognitions, their methods of perception are contrasted. Sense perception is said to enter its object in a positive way, and all the qualities of an apprehended object appear to a sense consciousness simultaneously and without differentiation. In contrast conceptual thought engages with its object in a negative manner. It is selective and works through exclusion of all but the specific object or quality ascertained.

The psychological aim of Buddhism is to convert mistaken conceptions first into correct beliefs, and eventually into valid cognitions. Cognition of an unrealistic nature is the source of samsaric states, and conception of a realistic type is the source of liberation. This model has much resonance for psychotherapy, both in its emphasis on the importance of cognitions and in the manner of delineating how a first fresh moment of valid perception is eroded by instantaneous cognitive predispositions, accretions of emotion, memory etc. Also from a Western perspective, philosopher Suzanne Langer has noted the same process: "A concept is all that a symbol really conveys. But just as quickly as the concept is symbolized to us, our own imagination dresses it up in a private personal *conception* which we can distinguish from the communicable concept only by a process of abstraction."[62]

From a more psychological perspective, mind or primary consciousness is distinguished in the teachings of the Abhidharma from the secondary mental factors. According to the later Mahayāna Abhidharma system of Asanga, there are fifty one secondary mental factors arranged into six categories in accordance with their manner of function.[63] Thirty seven of these fall into three categories, wholesome, unwholesome or indifferent from the point of view of liberation. The remaining fourteen fall into three categories: the five omnipresent factors of intention, attention, perception, feeling and contact; the five object-ascertaining factors of interest, intensified interest, recollection, concentration and insight which come into play whenever the mind is actively engaged in a task; and the four variable mental factors of sleep, regret, general examination and precise analysis which may be either wholesome, unwholesome or unspecified according to motivation or situation. Thus ethical considerations are fundamental to Buddhist psychology. The aim is to eliminate those factors which are unwholesome, while cultivating those that are wholesome. For, as we have seen, the nature of objects as we construct them in perception is determined by the characteristics of the concepts employed in discerning them. It is by cultivating one's powers of wisdom, concentration and altruism that conceptual cognition can be transformed.

The Yōgacāra school also presented a model of the structure of mind. As they expanded the model of Two Truths to Three Natures, so the Yōgācarins expanded the model of six consciousnesses, the five physical sense consciousnesses plus mental consciousness, into an eightfold model. They added a foundation or store consciousness, the *ālayavijñāna* which contains all the dispositions or determinations accumulated from all time, lying dormant in the form of seeds which create agitation. However these have not solidified and the *ālaya* also contains within it the possibility of liberation. Between the *ālayavijñāna* and the mental consciousness lies *manas* mind, (or *kliṣṭamanas*, afflicted mind, as it is often termed) which is responsible for belief in the ego, and from which originates an ego-centred approach to the world. The achievement of liberation must be accomplished by a turning around (parāvṛtti) of consciousness from its entrapment in *manas,* which brings about the conversion from the perception of the imagined nature to that of the perfected nature, as discussed earlier.

Buddha Nature

Associated primarily with the Yōgacāra school, indeed in some texts conflated with the *ālayavijñāna* is another theory of particular import to the psychotherapeutic outlook.[64] This is the idea of *Tathāgatagarbha* or Buddha Nature; that all beings possess a core nature which is basically pure and luminous with qualities of openness, clarity and sensitivity, though veiled by the obstruction of thought and desires.[65] The attainment of *nirvāna* is the re-attainment of this pure state, clarified from its obscurations. This idea that the mind's fundamental nature is that of luminosity and clarity[66] is to be found in the canonical works in the *Aṅguttara Nikāya*; "Luminous is this mind, but sometimes it is defiled by chance passions, sometimes it is free of chance passions."[67] The Mādhyamikas as one might expect refuse to hypostatize this luminous mind, seeing it as ultimately empty, and as non-thought: "... the Perfection of Wisdom is exempt from thought, and the natural luminosity of thought, the natural purity of thought does not consist in any thought production."[68] Other traditions, primarily the Tibetan rDzogs chen speak of the specific qualities of Buddha Nature as those of pure Mind; emptiness or spaciousness, clarity or awareness and compassion or unimpededness.[69]

However, in any form this has important implications for therapy. This basic model of an original core and progressive obscuration is found underlying many therapies. In the Psychodynamic model the natural drives are distorted by defences and repression in support of social requirements; in Existential terms Being-in-itself becomes Being-for-itself; for Jungians the Self is split into Persona and Shadow. Each model shows proliferating dualities and densification. However the Tathāgatagarbha model has a specific implication for psychotherapy since it contains the notion that the core is fundamentally good.[70] Buddhist psychotherapy thus starts from a belief in what Chogyam Trungpa called "brilliant sanity." The implications in terms of therapy are explained in an interview with psychotherapist and writer John Welwood:

> "The idea would be that the mind or our basic nature is intrinsically pure from the very beginning, and wholesome from the beginning, because it's not solid, because its open, because its nature is undefinable, ungraspable, unpackageable. In it's very nature, therefore it has an intrinsic purity and wholesomeness. There is no sort of sinful quality of the mind, broken or unhealthy or confused. Intrinsically this is not the nature of the mind, what is intrinsic is the basic healthiness. The basic healthiness emerges when you actually can relax a little with whatever is going on. So instead of trying to change what's going on, then, in that state of relaxation, one can start to just let go a little bit, and then one can try and taste some kind of basic goodness, basic healthiness, some kind of basic wholesomeness."[71]

Such an underlying attitude may be of immense assistance in therapy, where, as research noted above has shown, the attitude and personality of the therapist is seen to be the most important factor in the success of therapy. It is a far cry from the medical models of sickness which informed the early history of psychotherapy. Further therapeutic resonance springs from the presentation of Buddha nature as clear light mind, in its separation of pure awareness and the structures of mind. On the religious path to nirvāṇa all structures are to be loosened and ultimately disidentified with; on the therapeutic path more frequently one seeks merely to replace unhealthy identifications with more wholesome ones. But the idea is the same; mental structures are not engraved upon stone and permanent, but are to be seen through, worked with, and are capable of transformation. All the existent trainings based on Buddhist principles take their inspiration from the more positive approach to *Tathāgatagarbha* of the Tibetan rNying ma and bKa' rgyud pa schools.

The Buddhist view, then, is one of an interdependent universe, empty of isolated things, a continual process of interconnected events in which world and self mutually unfold. It is perhaps fitting that we have considered Buddhist epistemology and psychology in the absence of detailed consideration of the view of the self. However, I would now like to consider this topic, the "consciousness that views", and consider some ideas of the self, both from the Buddhist perspective and from contemporary Western discourse, comparing these, and contrasting them with the traditional, historical, 'modern' view.

CHAPTER FOUR

The Consciousness that Views

Some Ideas of the Self

If body and mind were me,
I'd come and go like them.
If I were other than body and mind,
They'd say nothing about me at all."[1]

"...
calling farewell
to the ears that forget to listen,
to the nerve-ends fraying with use,
to the breathing that retrenches into itself,
to the beautiful skin grown tired of dividing the earth
into ours, not ours,
as we tire too, of holding separate,
and love of self that was once so clear
grows suddenly simple, widens,
as a mother's hand smoothing a sheet,
as water that broadens and flattens,
taking the shape of the darkened, still-reflecting world."[2]

Turning from the view to "the consciousness that views", I would like to look at concepts of self and human identity. For it is with selves that psychotherapy is concerned and it is here that a central contradiction between Buddhist and Western psychotherapy is often assumed to occur. Surely Buddhism denies the existence of a self (or an ego), and the work of psychotherapy is just to strengthen that self (or ego)? This may be a good place at which to start considering ideas of self, as it will force us, firstly to consider what we mean by self in western terms, and secondly, to define what it is in Buddhism that is to be negated under the heading of self.

First, terminology. Not only are we confronted with different conceptions of self, but also similar ideas expressed in different terms. One man's ego is another man's self.[3] The immediate response to the conception of self, I would suggest, is usually, or perhaps until very recently has been, that which philosopher Charles Taylor has called the "punctual self", the point of self awareness in abstraction, in isolation from its constitutive concerns. It is that self which John Locke described when he wrote: "We must consider what Person stands for; which, I think, is a thinking intelligent Being, that has reason and reflection, and can consider it self as it self, the same thinking thing in different times and places."[4] However, if we look more closely and follow recent studies we find a sense of self that is above all, a construct, and one that appears to be considered as ever more widely distributed. As Taylor has pointed out: "much of the most insightful philosophy of the twentieth century has gone to refute this picture of the disengaged subject."[5]

William James was one of the first to consider thus. In the early days of the century and of academic psychology, he suggested: "In its widest possible sense, however, a man's Self is the sum total of all that he can call his."[6] Working from experience James divided the self into the I as knower and doer, and the me, the empirical self, the known or experienced; a division which we will find continually, perhaps best labelled self and self concept. He distributed the empirical self over a wide ground, designating it as "material self" which encompasses body, family and possessions; "social self", the recognition that one gets from others; "spiritual self", one's inner being and psychic dispositions; and the "pure Ego", that core sense of continuity which, he says, when carefully examined, is found to consist mainly of the collection of peculiar motions in the head or between the head and the throat ...

> "... the part of the innermost Self which is most vividly felt turns out to consist for the most part of a collection of

> cephalic movements of 'adjustments' which, for want of attention and reflection, usually fail to be perceived and classed as what they are; that over and above these there is an obscurer feeling of something more; but whether it be of fainter physiological processes, or of nothing objective at all, but rather of subjectivity as such, of thought become 'its own object,' must at present remain an open question, – like the question whether it be an indivisible active soul-substance, or the question whether it be a personification of the pronoun I, or any other of the guesses as to what its nature may be."[7]

Psychologist Jerome Bruner has criticised the conventional 'punctual' view of self on four counts; as being too concerned, firstly with egocentric perspective and secondly, with privacy. Thirdly he criticises the idea of immediate conceptualism; that a child's knowledge of the world is achieved through her own direct encounter with the world, rather than being mediated through various encounters in interaction and negotiation with others. Fourthly, Bruner believes that cognition, affect and action are far more closely interconnected than allowed for in the standard view.[8] Changes in contemporary views of the self not only move away from the punctual self to a more distributed one, but also display a shift away from the separation of epistemology and ontology, in so far as they believe the stance we take towards knowledge and reality becomes in time a feature of that very reality.[9] Expressing both these views Bruner writes:

> "I have tried to show how the lives and Selves we construct are the outcomes of this process of meaning construction. But I have also tried to make it clear that Selves are not isolated nuclei of consciousness locked in the head, but are 'distributed' interpersonally. Nor do Selves arise rootlessly in response only to the present; they take meaning as well from the historical circumstances that gave shape to the culture of which they are an expression."[10]

In the light of that can Buddhism, coming from such a different and culturally varied background, have anything useful to say to us today? I would first like to consider Buddhist views on the self, before considering some contemporary ideas relating to the ontogenetic and phylogentic development of self, following which I would like to discuss some concepts of self arising in postmodern discourse. Then I will turn to views of the self in psychotherapy, before attempting to compare and contrast the Buddhist and the contemporary views, suggesting that intellectually they are now similar, but Buddhism has much to offer to aid us to come to terms emotionally with a realisation of such views.

The Buddhist View of the Self

The third of the three marks of existence relating to all dharmas is *anattā*, (Pāli) non-self, and the concept of selflessness is one of the distinguishing marks of Buddhism. Yet when we look at the life of the Buddha Śākyamuni, we see a man who possessed personal continuity, identity and personality, and who clearly referred to himself as "I". What then is the self which is to be rejected, and what is the self that Buddhism denies? The Tibetan dGe lugs pa tradition makes a distinction between the "mere self", the transactional self which functions conventionally in the world, and a fictitious self, an absolute or essential self which is to be denied. The general definition of self rests on the term "I", imputed in dependence upon any or all five of the psychosomatic aggregates; material form or appearance (*rūpa*), and feelings (*vedanā*), perceptions (*saṃjnā*), determinations (*saṃskāras*) and consciousness (*vijñāna*). The sense of self which we experience is comprised of these five *skandhas* or aggregates, and it is the interplay of these rather than any permanent partless ontological entity. From the Buddhist point of view, ignorance or delusion arises when this process of selfing is grasped at as an entity and identified with, rather than experienced as an ever-changing expression of dynamic interaction. In mindful awareness we can become aware of the arising and falling, coming and going of the discontinuous thoughts, perceptions, feelings and sensations which make up what we like to imagine as a single coherent and continuous self.

> "This arising and subsiding, emerging and decay, is just that emptiness of self in the aggregate of experience. In other words, the very fact that the aggregates are full of experience is the same as the fact that they are empty of self. If there were a solid, really existing self hidden in or behind the aggregates, its unchangeableness would prevent any experience from occurring; its static nature would make the constant arising and subsiding of experience come to a screeching halt."[11]

In the twelvefold description of dependent origination (*pratītyasamutpāda*) these same factors, as we saw earlier, appear in different order. From basic ignorance of the three marks of existence; impermanence, unsatisfactoriness and lack of essential self, arise the mental tendencies or determinations (*saṃskāras*) which give rise to consciousness (*vijñāna*) which in turn gives rise to *nāma/rūpa*. As we have seen *nāma/rūpa* comprises the five aggregates, since the last four are attributed to *nāma* which is often translated as mind, with *rūpa* as body or form. A more helpful translation of the pair however as name and physical form uses them as the basis for a Buddhist theory of identity which would incorporate both the conventional self which is acceptable and that which is to be denied.[12] It is name and form which individualises, identifying us to ourselves and to others, and which creates the divisions between inner and outer identity. "Name" also introduces the function of language. It is important to point out that these five factors are mutually dependent and implicated in each other.

An exposition of the five *skandhas* by Susan Hamilton is, I find, most compatible with a psychotherapeutic point of view, as she suggests that the model of the *skandhas* is not presented as a description of what a human being is, but as a description of the faculties pertaining to the cognitive process, underlining again Buddhism's concern with *how* rather than *what*.[13] The result is a picture of the physical and conceptual identity of the person. According to this, *rūpa* refers to the physical attributes of the living body. *Vedanā*, usually translated as feeling, are, I feel most helpfully described by Hamilton as experiences, as she considers them as part of the cognitive process rather than as merely sensory processes. Moreover experience is, in English, a more value-free term than feelings. The locus of valuing is rather in the *saṁskara skandha*. *Samjñā* is the process of apperception and conception, the process of recognising what one experiences, the process by which one conceives and imagines. *Saṃskāra* is perhaps the most difficult term of translation and ascription, sometimes translated as volition, intention, or karmic formations. It is that faculty which influences choice and attention, covering all intention from life force to sensual desire. *Saṃskāra* conveys those dispositions or conditions which we impose on our experience. *Vijñāna* is the faculty of being conscious of things, and with it resides the sense of continuity.

One may single out the *saṃskāra skandha* as the link in the cognitive process which gives rise to unhealthiness, suggesting that what has to be guarded is in fact one's reaction to what one has experienced through the senses. I would consider this to be the very core of psychotherapeutic work; to uncover original reactions to experience, seeing how they have become incorporated as unchanging parts of the self image, thus influencing all subsequent perception and feeling. Seeing this, one may then loosen the hold of such predispositions and reactions so that choice, change and transformation may occur.[14]

Freud in a paper entitled *Note on the Mystic Writing Pad* used a child's toy as an image for the workings of the psyche similar to that described in this Buddhist model. The Mystic Writing Pad was a device upon which writing was displayed according to its impression upon a wax pad. When the paper was lifted from the pad the impression was destroyed. However, a permanent trace of what was written was retained by the wax slab. Similarly perception, feelings and consciousness receive stimuli, but do not retain the traces which are held in a different process, that of the dispositions.[15] Dispositions such as passions form permanent traces in the psychic apparatus which preclude the subsequent possibility of immediate, unclouded perception.

Interpreters differ as to the extent they see the individuating factor of the dispositional aggregate (*saṃskāra skandha*) as harmful in itself, but all point to the dispositions as the source of individuation, which either in itself, or through subsequent solidification and identification of initial interest, leads to *saṃsāra.* Dr. Hamilton suggests in a recent paper that this *skandha* need not, indeed *should* not be activated in the functioning of the human being.[16] Kalupahana points to its inevitable presence with consciousness in the initial form of interest or selectivity, describing it as "that which processes material form, feeling, perception, disposition (itself) and consciousness into their particular forms."[17] Certainly it is the dispositions which at some stage generate the influxes of desire, becoming, views and ignorance which are the causes of suffering and saṃsāra. Without these influxes perhaps one can aspire to the purity of perception suggested in the *Bāhiyasutta* of the *Udāna:*

> In the seen there will just be the seen; in the heard, just the heard; in the reflected, just the reflected; in the cognized, just the cognized. This is how, Bāhiya, you must train yourself. Now Bāhiya, when in the seen there will be to you just the seen; ... just the heard; ... just the reflected; ... just the cognized, then, Bāhiya, you will not identify with it. When you will not identify yourself with it, you will not locate yourself therein. When you do not locate yourself therein, it follows that you will have no 'here' or 'beyond' or 'midway-between' and this would be the end of suffering."[18]

In the *Majjhima Nikāya* the Buddha said that name was comprised of the five factors of intention (*cetanā*), attention (*manasikāra*), perception (*saṃjñā*), stimulation or contact (*sparśa*) and feeling (*vedanā*). These same five factors were given as the five constant factors of consciousness in the Theravāda Abhidhamma and in the Mahāyāna by Asaṅga. Thus they may form the foundation for a working sense of self. The illusory self with its concomitant egoic grasping is a superimposition, resultant primarily of the naming process of language. Ignorance of the three marks of existence conceives of this fluid transactional self as permanent, partless and autonomous.

The process of selfing works in three main ways, both instinctually and intellectually: craving occurring in the linguistic form "This is mine", conceit manifesting in the linguistic form "This I am", and false views manifesting in the linguistic form "This is myself."[19] Once one identifies with a permanent, partless self concept, pride and craving adhering to this, become the pivot from which an egocentric world arises.

Again William James has something somewhat similar to say:

> "This me is an empirical aggregate of things objectively known. The *I* which knows them cannot itself be an aggregate; neither for psychological purposes need it be considered to be an unchanging metaphysical entity like the Soul, or a principle like the pure Ego, viewed as 'out of time.' It is a *Thought*, at each moment different from that of the last moment, but *appropriative* of the latter, together with all that the latter called its own."[20]

In a recent meeting between the Dalai Lama and Western scientists at the end of a presentation of self in Western philosophy, His Holiness asked Charles Taylor, if, when one thinks 'I am', this necessarily implies that the self must be independent and autonomous? Taylor relied "If you ask people they say no. But in the way they actually live it, the answer is yes, very powerfully, and much more so than our ancestors who thought of themselves more as part of a larger cosmos."[21] One may think here of the seemingly inbuilt commitment to hypostatisation and substance ontology that Feyerabend has called "the natural interpretation".

The self then, which in Buddhism is to be negated, is an illusion; it is the imposition of a self with attributes of independence and permanence upon the foundation of the conventional or transactional self, when all that exists is the interaction of various factors forming a system. This imposition arises not from the lack of an essential self itself, but from the emotional reaction to that lack; from the grasping which is the nature of the conditioned mind, which itself arises from the dispositions or mental tendencies (*saṃskāra*) Thus Stephen Batchelor suggests that; "The Buddha's sense of self would thus not be different from an ordinary person's in terms of structure, but only in the apprehension of that structure."[22] However I would agreed with Hamilton in seeing this in terms of process rather than of structure.

Central to this process of expansion and solidification is *prapañca*. We have noted *prapañca* earlier in its Tibetan translation *spros pa* in relation to a definition of emptiness as *spros med*, free from *prapañca*.[23] It is another difficult term to translate, and Bhikkhu Ñāṇananda has devoted an entire book length essay to the subject, such is its importance. As a translation he suggests that "*prapañca* may refer to the consequent prolificity in ideation" which follows upon initial application of thought.[24] Ñāṇananda considers the following passage central to his interpretation of what occurs in perception, an interpretation somewhat differing from the traditional understanding based upon the commentaries of Buddhaghosa with whom he disagrees.

> "Because of eye and material object, O brethren, arises visual consciousness; the meeting of the three is sensory impingement, because of sensory impingement arises feeling; what one feels, one perceives; what one perceives, one reasons about; what one reasons about, one proliferates conceptually; what one proliferates conceptually, due to that, concepts characterised by the prolific tendency assail him in regard to material shapes cognisable by the eye, belonging to the past, the future and the present."[25]

Most interestingly Ñāṇananada points out that there are three stages. The formula is impersonal up to the point at which feeling enters, where it takes up a personal verb ending suggestive of deliberate activity and ego grasping. This personalisation ceases after the entrance of conceptual proliferation, at which stage "the concepts are, as it were, invested with an objective character."[26] He suggests this is brought about due to characteristics inherent in language. This is certainly interesting when related to such contemporary ideas as that of Heidegger that language is the house of Being, and the works of Derrida and the deconstructionists indicating that finally it is language that speaks us.

Here again Hamilton makes perceptive comment concerning *prapañca*, noting that Ñāṇananda and other commentators fail to observe the idea of separateness which adheres to the term *prapañca*. She translates the verb *papañceti* (Pali), which Ñāṇananda gives as "one proliferates conceptually", as "one causes to become manifold." Thus after perception comes reasoning, which gives rise to making manifold. Hamilton suggests that *prapañca* is associated with perception in this *sutta* in a way that suggest both that manifoldness is a concomitant of identification, and that this manifoldness implies the attribution of separate independent existence to the phenomena perceived; implies, in fact, an erroneous imposition of separateness upon things which are really dependently originated.[27]

It is this same term *prapañca* which Nāgārjuna used in the dedicatory verses at the opening of MMK:

> I pay homage to the Fully Awakened One
> the supreme teacher who has taught
> the doctrine of relational origination,
> the blissful cessation of all phenomenal thought
> constructions."[28]

This does make more sense when *prapañca* is understood with its connotations of manifoldness and separateness. This connotation was also noted earlier by Mervyn Sprung who translated the final line of this verse as: "the serene coming to rest of the manifold of named things."[29]

The most important attribution of separate independent existence is that to the self. The pivotal separation is the statement "I am" from which all further attributions of separateness spring. It is this that is spoken of in *Sutta Nipāta* 916: "The wise man should put a stop to the thought 'I am', which is the root of all naming in terms of manifoldness."

In Mahāyāna Yōgacāra philosophy Asaṇga unites discussion of self, discursive reasoning (*vikalpa*) and consequent conceptual proliferation (*prapañca*).[30] Asaṇga describes how eight kinds of discursive reasoning, being the foundation of proliferation, create three bases upon which all the realms of *saṁsāra* are founded. Discursive thought about essential nature, about particularity and about "whole shapes" is responsible for producing things or referents, which then become named, and the foundation for conceptual proliferation. Discursive thoughts about "I" and "mine" produce the basis for the view of self and egocentricity. Lastly discursive thought about what is agreeable, disagreeable or neither, gives rise to the three primary obstructions of desire, hatred and delusion. Asaṇga states that these three bases are closely interrelated, such that the view of self has support only when there is a view of an object in contradistinction to which it is defined in self/other, subject/object dualism. Similarly the obstructions of desire, hatred and delusion can only arise when there are ideas of self and its possessions. The antidote is to understand that discursive thought and the given thing which becomes the support for discursive thought are mutually dependent and without beginning. If one considers discursive thought in terms of "name" or "designation", then thorough investigation of the name, the given thing, the designations for essential nature and for particularity, reveals the emptiness or transparency of all designations and of given thing. Investigation of name gives rise to understanding that it is just a designation. Likewise with regard to the object, investigation will only reveal its emptiness of inherent nature. Through such investigation both names, things, essential nature and particularity in isolation are found to be groundless, without referent, and transparent or empty. Realising the nature of name as it really is, as merely a linguistic symbol which facilitates discursive thought and with which discursive thought operates and conceptually proliferates, one understands that in its ultimate or liberating nature the given thing is inexpressible and separated from discursive thought. Such realisation allows a middle-way understanding of reality without exaggeration leading to clinging, or underestimation leading to nihilism. For the given thing is neither completely present, nor completely absent. "It is not present, since it is not 'perfected' (*pariniṣpannatva*), owing to its having an expressible 'self'. And it is not altogether absent, since in fact is it determined to have an inexpressible essence. Thus from the stance of absolute truth (*paramārthasatya*) it is not formed (*rūpī*), yet from the stance of relative truth (*saṃvṛtisatya*) it is not formless, since form is attributed to it."[31] Through such investigations, one may learn the interdependence and ultimate emptiness of both selves and given things, and how they arise together through discursive thought and conceptual proliferation.

Thus we see that for Buddhism it is not so much that there is no self as often stated, but rather that the imposition of a permanent, separate self onto the interaction of self processes is an error. The experiencing of life from the perspective of identification with this unchanging centre, this independent separate identity is the ignorant premise that underlies life in *saṁsāra*. If, as we are told in the second noble truth, desire is the cause of continual suffering, it is fuelled by the erroneous perception which sees and separates one who desires, the object of desire, and desires themselves. When one no longer sees in this way and things are seen as they really are, such desires and the traces they leave on mental processes will cease since they are the result of thinking in terms of the separateness or selfhood of oneself and all things. Concomitant with the relinquishment of this grasping of separateness arises compassion, a concern for that from which one is not separate. In the Mahāyāna specific attention is drawn to compassion as the necessary adjunct to the wisdom which sees the truth of emptiness; sees things and selves as dependently originated and devoid of separateness.

Some Western Views on the Development of Consciousness

Before considering views of self in psychotherapy, I believe it would be helpful to look at some Western ideas concerning the ontogenetic and phylogenetic development of consciousness and self consciousness. In recent years the field of consciousness studies, after some earlier neglect during the hegemony of strict behaviourism, has become a rich and exciting one. New theories are arriving constantly aided both by advances in neuroscience increasing knowledge of the working of the brain, and by enlargements in the parameters and paradigms within which such science is undertaken.

As far as the evolution of consciousness is concerned, a generally accepted view would seem to trace development from an intuitive and non-analytic body awareness to awareness of self as agent, then through a developed apprehension of self in relation to others, to more complex social interaction leading in turn to an increase in comprehension and introspection of the interactive self. From the imputation of self onto system, and especially with that imputation in language we enter the sphere of cultural evolution. A Systems Theory description of this development sees the process as deeply embedded in its environment. From this viewpoint, self is a construction, and as conventionally understood, an illusory one. In the words of Gregory Bateson: "the 'self' as ordinarily understood is only a small part of a much larger trial-and-error system which does the thinking, acting and deciding. This system includes all the informational pathways which are relevant at any given moment to any given decision. The 'self' is a "false reification of an improperly delineated part of this much larger field of interlocking processes."[32] The apparently stable structure of organisms are, in actuality, only maintained through a constant process of exchanging matter, energy and information with their environment. An evolutionary view of the development of consciousness and self awareness starts with the response of simple organisms of irritability, the ability to react to fluctuations of energy in the internal and external environment. Progress occurs with the development both of biological capability to attune to variations in the environment, and more developed and skilful methods of tuning, such as attending and experimenting, and above all anticipating. A significant stage occurs with the development of social learning animals. As the tasks become too complex for the mind as a whole to deal with them, sub-systems evolve to handle different tasks, bringing with them the problem of communication between these sub-systems. The needs of dealing with ever greater complexity necessitates representation of self as well as world. Accurate perception must involve some level of self representation, however this self representation does not exist as a separate understanding in most animals up to chimpanzees. Beyond this we enter the zone of community, allowing the ability to learn not only from observation but also from communication, and with the advent of sophisticated language, cultural evolution occurs with the agent of replication being no longer the gene, but rather the idea, or in Dawkins term the *meme,* a unit of cultural transmission.

Interestingly, from a different perspective, David Abram writes of the linking of self and language. He argues that with the advent of alphabetical (rather than iconic) writing, a new and reflexive sense of self was engendered. He notes that this seemingly autonomous reflexive awareness was called by Socrates, *psyche*, a term which had previously held the meaning, as found in Homer, of the "invisible breath that animates the living body."[33] Such a change in the reference of the term mirrors a stage in the strengthening of the individual sense of self and its separation both from participation in the world and its own sensory being.

Psychologist Margaret Donaldson has written of the development of the individual in psychological terms somewhat similar to the phylogenetic development described: "some sense of one's self as an agent is probably present very early indeed, ... But the construction of a self-concept, or self-image, is another matter. The development of the ability to think about, or conceptualize one's self seems to have its origin around the age of eighteen months."[34] She delineates four core stages of development. The first she calls Point Mode, that of present awareness. This is followed by Line Mode which incorporates narrative ability. This leads speedily on to what she calls Core Construct Mode, in which can occur representation, abstraction and modelling. This Core Construct Mode occurs in two forms, relating to intellectual constructs, and to value-sensing constructs. This latter is concerned with emotional rather than rational response, but refers to a responsiveness to what she terms "sources of importance". This Core Construct mode may be followed by a fourth stage, again divided into two parts, Intellectual Transcendent and Value-Sensing Transcendent. From the point of view of the self/nonself dilemma which we have spoken of, she notes that:

> "Development beyond the core modes requires, by definition, cultivation of the ability to hold concern for the self-image in check, so that it can at least be laid aside for certain lengths of time. If these lengths of time are to be more than momentary, then some level of personal (not material) security may first have to be achieved. For when you are deeply and persistently worried about the 'sort of person' you are, concern about this will soon intrude; and instead of wanting to solve a problem you will be wanting to prove that you are the sort of person who can solve the problem."[35]

As a Western scientist who is not a Buddhist, Donaldson shows a great interest in Buddhism as a source of a different kind of education in value-sensing modes which she considers as important and insufficiently addressed in Western culture.[36]

Having looked at its development, what can be said about this evolved consciousness and self? In the field of cognitive science, there are many positions. All hold that the self is compounded and divided, and see some distinction between transactional self system, and self concept. According to a recent work by Baars: "All unified threories of cognition today involve theater metaphors. In this version, conscious contents are limited to a brightly lit spot of attention on stage, while the rest of the stage corresponds to immediate working memory. Behind the scenes are executive process, including a director, and a great variety of contextual operators that shape conscious experience without themselves becoming conscious. In the audience are a vast array of intelligent unconscious mechanisms."[37] However, their theories as to the manner of cognition of world and self vary. Strict cognitivists upholding the idea that cognition is mental representation, posit mental processes of which we are not, and cannot be, aware, seeing self as not only non-unified but basically as unnecessary for cognition. Connectivists see mental processes not as sequential and localised and speak of neural networks, emergent properties and self organisation in which a great number of elementary agents equipped with simple properties may be united to give rise to that which appears from outside to be an integrated whole, yet is without any necessity for central supervision. Most radically, those upholding an enactive view, move right away from any idea of representation, seeing a lack of distinction in principle between logical and material, or between symbols and non-symbols. According to this view knowledge is the result of ongoing interpretation emerging from our capacities for understanding, and a world is "enacted" through structural coupling between properties of our psychophysical organism and the environment.

We can return once again to William James for one of the earliest and still exceedingly relevant distinctions between self as agent and self as object. "The total self (is) partly known and partly knower, partly object and partly subject ... we may call the one the Me and the other the I."[38] James' work is much quoted by Baars who sees the acting self as the deep context of experience. Speaking of the relationship of self to consciousness, he says: "They're not the same thing, but stand in the relation of context to content."[39] The self is that which has access to consciousness, in the words of Dennett: "That of which I am conscious is that to which I have *access* or (to put the emphasis where it belongs), that to which *I* have access."[40] Baars himself suggests that access to a self system may be a necessary condition for conscious experience.[41] More recently Dennett has said that: "A self, according to my theory, is not any old mathematical point, but an abstraction defined by the myriads of attributions and interpretations (including self-attributions and self-interpretations) that have composed the biography of the living body whose Centre of Narrative Gravity it is."[42] The creation of such a centre of narrative gravity, the spinning of a self out of a narrative web of words and actions, he says, is a fundamental human act of self-protection, self-control and self definition. It plays an important role since of all the things in the environment which a body needs to make models of, the most vital is the model of itself. Baars distinguishes clearly between self as self system which is the I, and self concepts, being a set of beliefs which one has *about* oneself, which he sees as corresponding to James' "Me". This consists of aspects of self decontextualised and experienced as objects of consciousness, used to create a model of self, which is not the self itself, but is rather a content within the self system.

Gerald Edelman who is at the forefront of current research into brains, minds and selves writes that in order to acquire the capacity to become "conscious of being conscious", "systems of memory must be related to a conceptual representation of a true self (or social self) acting on an environment and vice versa. A conceptual model of selfhood must be built, as well as a model of the past."[43] Edelman speaks of the development of primary consciousness which is achieved by the reconnection of a value-category memory to current ongoing perceptual processes, and of higher consciousness which arises with the evolution of semantic capabilities, and the accession of language and symbolic reference. As he says: " A conceptual explosion and ontological revolution – a world, not just an environment – are made possible by the interaction between conceptual and language centers. By these means, concepts of self and of a past and a future emerge. Higher-order consciousness depends on building a self through affective intersubjective exchanges."[44]

More controversially, science writer Danah Zohar attempts to describe the self and the relationship between man and world in terms of quantum mechanics and the complementarity of wave and particle: "Viewed quantum mechanically I am my relationships – my relationships to the sub-selves within my own self and my relationships to others, my living relationship to my own past through quantum memory and to my future through my possibilities. Without relationship I am nothing."[45]

From all perspectives we are presented with models with two levels; first self image as process, representing a simple and implicit notion of self with inner coherence and position in the world, on top of which develops the self concept, bolstered by language and culture, which becomes increasingly reified and considered autonomous, and to which emotional components adhere, in turn affecting the concept. The former is "a kind of rough summary of who I am, always open to question, retaining the sense of absolute connectedness with the environment as an organism/environment field, whereas the other is a self representation which is bounded, causative and persistent through space and time."[46]

Perhaps one of the simplest ways to underline the difference between the two "selves" as Polly Young-Eisendrath and James Hall show in their essay, "Ways of Speaking of the Self", is by the common phrase; "I am not myself today."[47] The first "I" is the immediate changing sense of self as centre of personal subjectivity responding to environmental conditions, the second is the more unchanging self concept or self image. I would now like to consider some views of the self in current nonscientific discourse.

Views of the Self in Contemporary Discourse

Scientific views of self appear to have taken us quite a way from any unitary, essential and "punctual" view. This is reflected in the worlds of theory and art. One of the characteristics of the postmodern stance is the idea of the vanishing subject. This may take different forms, but in all cases a substantial representation of the self at the centre of its world is replaced with a more relational and distributed concept of subjectivity. According to a recent study of psychology and postmodernism: "What has died is . . . the unified, reified and essentialized subject" which is replaced "by a provisional, contingent and constructed subject, a subject whose self-identity is constituted and reconstituted relationally."[48] Constantly in postmodern discourse the emphasis is on the 'other', on alterity. Whether what is privileged are certain types of alterity such as women or minorities, or otherness in general, the emphasis has shifted from unity and identity to difference. Geoffrey Bennington writing of Derrida speaks of one of the most constant themes: "in order to be itself, a subject must already relate to itself as to an other. Identity comes only from alterity, called by the other."[49] It is only from the point of view of the other that I can be perceived as a whole, from outside my own happening. This returns us to the difference between self as centre of action and self as representation in which language is deeply implicated. Beautifully put by Bahktin: "Much as Peter Pan's shadow is sewn to his body, 'I' is the needle that stitches the abstraction of language to the particularity of lived experience."[50] In this stitching there is loss as a result of the addition. Holquist writing of Bakhtin comparing the difference between the time of the self which is always open and unfinished to the time we assume for others or for a representation of ourselves, time which is closed, finalisable, describes that process:

> "in order to be known, to be perceived as a figure that can be 'seen', a person or thing *must* be put into the categories of the other, categories that reduce, finish, consummate. We see not only ourselves, but the world, in the finalizing categories of the other. In other words, we see the world by authoring it, by making sense of it through the activity of turning it into a text, by translating it into finalizing schemes that can order its potential chaos – but only by paying the price of reducing the world's variety and endlessness."[51]

In both agreement and contrast to this the philosopher Emanuel Levinas exhorts us to acknowledge, and be open to, the infinite alterity of the other in the face-to-face situation, which alone can precede and escape representation, in a project which I find strangely complementary to the Buddhist one. Thus, this necessity of the other may also be viewed from two sides, from what we might call following Dogen, the side of enlightenment or from the egocentric perspective.[52]

> "To practice and confirm all things by conveying one's self to them is illusion, for all things to advance forward and practise and confirm the self is enlightenment ... To learn the Buddha Way is to learn one's own self. To learn one's own self is to forget one's self. To forget one's self is to be confirmed by all dharmas."[53]

As Gans writes of Levinas: "From within the perspective of egology, others seem to have no other status than that of stimulus to my own pleasure.... The ego's self-identification and reduction of difference (the not me) to the same (the for me) is the totalization process *par excellence* which Levinas undertakes to critique in *Totality and Infinity*."[54] Gans convincingly argues that the aim of Levinas' phenomenological ethics is the same as that of psychotherapeutic practice since "both show the way toward the transformation of egoic *need* into interpersonal *desire*."[55] Levinas describes the position of egoic interiority of Western man; as Gans describes it: "Western man *looks* out for his enjoyment. From the invisible centre of his hidden presence, he represents and constitutes a world which he in turn penetrates, manipulates and controls, so that he can accumulate power and might in order to deploy resources to satisfy his needs and defend against loss."[56] Levinas' answer to this is to found his philosophy on the priority of the ethical over the ontological, on the Platonic Good beyond being, and on the prior claim of the face to face encounter with the Other, which calls us to break with "the narcissism of the imaginary in order to live in the promised land of the real and the good."[57] According to Levinas' approach narcissism represents a refusal of the extension of self into the world, a failure of nerve, a failure to respond to the call of "otherness," a constriction of defensive posture. Perhaps it is not so far from Heidegger's call of Being, although Levinas considered Heidegger's prioritisation of Being to be still in the realm of theory rather than of the "face-to-face." To answer the call of the other is "to move toward an ethics of love, toward the celebration of our interrelatedness."[58]

Such language seems familiar to that of Buddhist discourse. According to Gans, also following Lacan, need is deficient desire, "a void in the heart of interiority", and it is this which initiates the objectification process as defence against loss, limitation and death. Philosopher Richard Rorty addressing the topic of the contingency of selfhood writes of "the unconscious need everyone has: the need to come to terms with the blind impress which chance has given him, to make a self for himself by redescribing that impress in terms which are, if only marginally, his own."[59] There are three factors here: first description or representation of the "blind impress", second redescription in terms of grasping, and third an emotional concomitant in terms of identification and value judgement.

In Buddhist terms this loss is illusory, the result of the ill-conceived sense of self as ultimately separate from other. In discussion of Wilber's Spectrum model in chapter two, I considered David Loy's views on the lack of being of the self. Loy speaks of "the nondualist claim that the ontological self is a delusion and that this delusive sense of self is the fundamental *duḥkha* (frustration) which distorts our experience and disturbs our lives. Contrary to all schools of ego psychology, such a self can never become secure because its very nature is to be insecure ... the sense of self is not a thing but a *lack*, which can conceal its own emptiness only by keeping ahead of itself – that is, by projecting itself into the next thought, action, and so on – which process is craving..."[60] Loy suggests that the prime object of repression is awareness of lack of "being", a lack of inherent existence, or groundlessness. In terms of Buddhism it is such fears themselves, or rather the preceding unsatisfied desire to be an independent entity, which is groundless and misguided since the sense of self itself is not an existent reality, but merely a mental construction which falsely experiences its own perceived groundlessness as a lack. Investigation of the mental constructions which give rise to this constructed sense of self, as we saw in Asaṇga's analysis nearly two thousand years ago, reveals its emptiness, loosening at one stroke both the conceptual proliferation which supports the sense of self, that self itself and the anxiety unconsciously defending its fragility. What is left is not nothing, but a greater non-egocentric grounding, as Loy describes: "If each link of *pratitya-samutpada* is conditioned by all the others, then to become completely groundless is also to become completely grounded, not in some particular, but in the whole network of interdependent relations that constitute the world. The supreme irony of my struggle to ground myself is that it cannot succeed because I am already grounded *in the totality*."[61] Such an understanding may also help to heal the antagonism which Lacan finds between being and meaning, whereby to be a subject incurs an 'aphanasis' of meaning, while choosing being, the subject disappears. Against the background of interdepence there is a non-dual alternative to either/or.

Bakhtin takes particular note of relationship in the composition of self In his exposition of existence, language and self as dialogue, he notes that dialogue is composed of an utterance, a reply and the relation between; the self is a centre, a not-centre and the relationship between them.[62] He writes that "the psyche enjoys extraterritorial status within the organism. It is a social entity that penetrates inside the organism of the individual person." He was influenced by the views of psychologist Lev Vygotsky who believed that maturation of the infant and the dissemination of culture occurs first in intersubjective space, in what he termed the "zone of proximal development." According to this view the direction of the development of thinking is from the social to the individual and not, as usually perceived, vice versa. Research by Jerome Bruner has explored what he calls this "loan of consciousness" from parent or tutor to infant, with, as we saw above Bruner's similar conclusion that conceptualism is not unmediated, but acquired in interaction and negotiation with others.[63] Sociologist Kenneth Gergen has also written widely on the distribution of the self and has pointed towards change from an understanding based on an individualistic and dualistic concept of persons to an understanding as "relational activity" or intersubjectivity. He suggest also that in abandoning the assumption that knowledge lies within the minds of single individuals, we may be able to move away from the high value which we now place on individualism which is problematic for contemporary Western culture. [64]

In the Madhyamaka view, as we have seen, deconstruction of the solidity of self is linked to that of world and of the relation between the two, until only changing process remains. However what seems most difficult to dislodge are the last traces of reification of the relationship itself, for even process can be hypostatized. We need to remember what Bruner calls the "ability to subjunctivize". Ideas of metaphor and narrative belong to the project of subjunctification. As we have seen, a concern with narrative, by which self creates coherence and consistency, and a focus on the meanings, private and cultural by which self is defined, and on the practices in which these meanings are achieved, has accompanied the deconstruction of the punctual self. As George Lakoff & Mark Johnson explain:

> "A large part of self-understanding is the search for appropriate personal metaphors that make sense of our lives. Self-understanding requires unending negotiation and renegotiation of the meaning of your experience to yourself. In therapy, for example, much of self-understanding involves consciously recognizing previously unconscious metaphors and how we live by them. It involves the constant construction of new coherences in your life, coherences that give new meaning to old experiences. The process of self-understanding is the continual development of new life stories for yourself."[65]

Indeed it has been suggested that psychotherapy may be seen as "a process of challenging and rebuilding models, and metaphor can be a conscious tool toward exploring ways for expanding models."[66] However only Buddhism suggests that all constructs can or should be held lightly and seen through as metaphors, rather than being hypostatized and identified with. This ability and the practices used to facilitate it has been noticed. Margaret Donaldson advocates switching our modes of mental functioning and speaks of Buddhism as "a particularly resolute attempt to develop skill in leaving undesirable modes at will."[67] I should now like to look at some of the ways different psychotherapeutic approaches consider the self.

The Self in Psychotherapy

Psychoanalysis provided perhaps the first coherent model of the divided self, a model which has almost insidiously invaded contemporary discourse. Examples from the fields of art and literature abound, perhaps Cubist painting is the most obvious example of portraiture equally valuing different perspectives. Freud, as we have discussed above, put forward different models over time; divisions into conscious, unconscious and preconscious and into ego, id and superego, but the emphasis is always on conflict and division. Mark Epstein both a psychoanalyst and a Buddhist practitioner has frequently pointed out that the seeming contradiction between ego and the Buddhist self which is to be negated are easily dissolved if the concepts are analysed clearly. "It is not ego, in the Freudian sense, that is the actual target of the Buddhist insight. It is, rather, the self concept, the *representational* component of the ego, the actual internal experience of one's self that is targeted."[68] As the result of Buddhist practice: "It is not that the ego disappears, but that the belief in the ego's solidity, the identification with ego's representation, is abandoned in the realization of egolessness."[69] In Freudian terms he suggests that realisation of the construction of self concept is not to be confused with loss of self or dissolution of ego boundaries. It is the "ideal ego" rather than the "ego ideal" that is the target of Buddhist meditation, and which is responsible for feelings of solidarity, permanence and inherent existence.[70] In psychotherapy we work constantly with representations, analysing and experiencing their causation, their experience and our identification with them, attempting thereby to encourage disidentification or reframing, a widening of possibilities or of models that are holding back our clients, helping them to open out to new possibilities, new selves, stories and representations. And this is where most therapy ends. Perhaps the task of a Buddhist therapy is to be open-ended, to *see through* all models. I would like to return to this idea later.

Kohut's Self Psychology also, developing from the demands of different pathologies from those addressed by Freud; pathologies of fragmentation, draws attention to the pragmatic needs of developing a coherent and consistent self as centre of action. Although it does not advocate a unitary and independent self, it may be in danger of reifying the self, by its very emphasis upon it.[71] Philip Cushman has recently written perceptively about psychotherapy's participation in the creation of the essentially empty self of Western culture which is to be filled with the goods of a consumer society. Cushman while valuing both Kohut's Self Psychology and Object Relations in many ways, also sees them both as having inadvertently conspired in the development of the isolated interiority of the empty self by presenting a model of an inherently empty self constructed from its "consumption" or introjection of selfobjects and significant others. This is strengthened by their disregard of wider historical, political and cultural horizons. If, as Ann Klein suggests, postmodern discourse is like talking about dependent origination without emptiness, perhaps the emptiness of the empty self may be likened in Buddhist terms to emptiness without dependent origination, an emptiness, which far from being beyond duality, is merely privation.

Paradoxically, both Kohut and Winnicott may be seen both as contributing to the interiority of the self in this way *and* as simultaneously broadening the scope of the self by emphasising the interpersonal as well as the intrapsychic. As Winnicott wrote: "A description of the emotional development of the individual cannot be made entirely in terms of the individual, but that in certain areas ... the behaviour of the environment is part of the individual's own personal development and must therefore be included."[72] Yet, as we said before, perhaps it is only Lacan who sees that both the structure of language and the structure of self are articulations of difference, and who, with his exposition of the mirror stage and the construction of self as imago and identification, emphasises the "*méconnaissance*", and sees the very constructed self as not only constructed, but false, an identification in resistance to a perceived lack of being.

Behavioural and Cognitive psychotherapies are closest to the findings of academic psychology for which the idea of a central self or unified centre of organisation in the consciousness has long been dismissed. RET, for instance strives for an egoless state of being, in an manner which, according to Ellis, is only matched by Zen Buddhism.[73] In RET, actions and performance may be judged, but not the self, for the essence of a human being is found as process in a state of flux; any judgements will fail, as they are artificial attempts to stop an ongoing development. Even if a representative sample of such process is taken at random of all the aspects of the self, such judgement would be, according to Kwee "a 'pars in toto' and an identification of the concept with the self."[74]

Humanistic and Existential Psychotherapy is centrally concerned with the individual in the world, with *Dasein*, "being-in-the-world," and *Mitsein*, "being-with." The humanistic conception of the self is concerned with the influence of environment, experience, responsibility and choice, and with issues of congruence between self and self image. "The self is made up of all the truly objective aspects of our being ... It includes images of our bodies, our ideas of what sorts of persons we are, our generalizations about how others see us, and our personal histories. The self, so conceived, is an abstraction, a perceptual and conceptual object."[75] Yet it is an abstraction to which we cling instinctively, as Heidegger appeared to note: "Dasein ... also interprets itself as having a fixed and self-sufficient nature like the occurrent in order to hide 'the inessentiality of the self.'"[76]

Carl Rogers contended that the human infant has an inherent tendency toward actualising his organism, part of which is a tendency towards differentiation, due to which a portion of experience becomes differentiated and symbolised in an awareness of functioning which he describes as self experience. Such representation is elaborated through interaction with the environment, particularly through interaction with significant others, into a concept of self which is a perceptual object in the experiential field. If all experience is available to awareness and nothing is shut off due to defensive reactions, then all symbolisation will be as accurate as possible, leading to a self concept which is congruent with experience.[77] Ideally the self concept will be a fluid *gestalt* flexibly changing as it interacts with its experience of world. However, in actuality, various aspects of experience become repressed or defended against perceived pain, and the horizon of potential experience becomes limited and the self concept rigid. Psychotherapeutic work attempts to expose and loosen the defensive structures which prevent experience being available to awareness, thus allowing for more flexible self concepts which can be congruent with ever-changing experience.

Transpersonal psychotherapies travel beyond Humanistic and Existential therapies in their definition of the needs of actualisation, leading them into the territory of religion. They, therefore, have perhaps most clearly addressed the self/non-self, ego-strengthening/ego-loosening issues. If we take a definition of religion as relating to the Latin *religere* to tie back, reconnect, it connotes the connection to that which is greater; to relations between the Many and the One in both directions, and is thus at the very heart of the self/no-self debate.

C.G. Jung attempted to counterbalance the emphasis on fragmentation by putting forward wholeness as the ultimate, if unreachable, goal of the individuation process. In fact there is more than a little confusion within Jung's writings due to his use of self both as in common usage in terms of the *individual* as him or herself, and as self standing for wholeness, as a transcendental archetype explained in terms of its function in uniting opposites. This latter self, often written Self, does come close to that kind of hypostatized self which is to be negated in Buddhism, in such statements as; "The self: as the essence of individuality it is unitemporal and unique; as an archetypal symbol it is a God-image and therefore universal and eternal."[78]

On the other hand, Jung definitely believed that in the second half of life it was necessary to go beyond the frame of the ego, and his Self is certainly not an individual self. Several comparisons have been made between Jungian Analytical Psychology and Buddhism.[79] One of those writers notes that "Neither of the two sides advocates complete egolessness, and neither the Buddhists nor Jung have an understanding of the negation of the ego that implies the utter eradication or non-existence of the ego. Each in their own way, shows that it is the exaggeration of the importance of the ego, a wrong view and a misapprehension of its relative and dependent nature that is the cause of pain and suffering."[80]

Jack Engler, an American psychologist and *vipaśyana* meditation teacher has written most clearly and convincingly on this subject, in a way which links back to many of the arguments and topics we have been considering above. I shall, therefore, quote at length:

> "Though they value ego-development differently, both Buddhist psychology and psycho-analytic object relations theory *define the essence of the ego in a similar way*: as a process of synthesis and adaptation between the inner life and outer reality which produces a sense of personal continuity and sameness in the felt experience of being a 'self,' a feeling of being and ongoingness in existence. Object relations theory explains this experience of personal continuity and selfhood as the outcome of a gradual differentiation of internalized images of a 'self' as distinct from internalized images of object and the eventual consolidation of these images into a composite schema or self-representation. Theravada Abhidhamma explains the emergence of the sense of 'I' in a similar way

as the end product of a process of identification in which we learn to take one or more of the various components (*khandhas*) which make up our experience of objects as 'me' or 'myself'. ...

In both psychologies then, the sense of 'I', of personal unity and continuity, ... is conceived as something which is not innate in personality, not inherent in our psychological or spiritual makeup, but as *evolving developmentally out of our experience of objects and the kinds of interactions we have with them.* In other words, the 'self' is literally *constructed* out of our experience with the object world. ... In fact, the self is viewed in both psychologies as a representation which is *actually being constructed anew from moment to moment.*"[81]

In this view the issue is a developmental one, first to acquire a coherent and cohesive functioning sense of self, then to recognize or acknowledge it as a construct.[82] In fact in Engler's terms: "you have to be somebody before you can be nobody"[83] and the issue is not self or no-self, but self *and* no-self.[84] Wilber himself follows a developmental model, and has described in detail what he calls the pre/trans fallacy, the danger of mistaking early states of undifferentiated ego with later states of transcended or "seen-through" ego. It has been suggested that the essential difference between the prepersonal and the transpersonal states is a question of awareness.[85] It is a view utterly in contradiction to Freud's description of all mystical experience as the regression to the former. However confusion between these states is a very real danger both in meditation and in therapeutic work. There have been many cases of those with borderline personality or problems of ego-stability being drawn to meditative experience, which is unhelpful to their prior need to strengthen ego boundaries. John Welwood has called this the problem of "spiritual bypassing."[86]

A somewhat different view of this topic is presented by Washburn who presents what he calls a "dynamic-dialectical" paradigm in contrast to Wilber's "structural-hierarchical" model. Whereas Wilber presents a structural conception wherein development proceeds through ascending levels, Washburn presents a bipolar conception of the psyche and shows development as a triphasic dialectical interplay between the two poles, ego and dynamic ground. In the first stage, the pre-egoic, ego emerges out of the ground and is still under the dominating influence of the ground. In the second stage, the Egoic stage, ego differentiates and disassociates itself from ground, while in the final stage, the Transegoic, the ego undergoes a return to the ground followed by a higher synthesis with ground which is an integration of the two poles of the psyche.[87] Though this view is less hierarchical, both models show that relationship requires distinction if not separation; that there is a necessary movement from union through distinction to relation. All these tripartite schema may be mapped onto the Bakhtin/Mumford model presented in Introduction above.

Thus we see that each school of psychotherapy is attempting according to its own model, to heal the divisions in the fragmented self, to describe and clarify the relationships between parts whether intra, inter or transpersonally, and to encourage a sense of functional coherence and wholeness. The primary division, according to Wilber's Spectrum model, is that of subject from object, self from other, and our views of the self, and the goals for the achievement of a suitable self concept will be constituted from the ways we view this split, both in terms of the divided parts and the relationship between them. In some sense our lives may be seen as an attempt to regain some idea of impossible wholeness, whether this is seen as lost unity with the mother, or with implacable Desire or with God. The therapeutic endeavour is dependent upon the way in which the coming into being of egoic consciousness is envisaged, and the particular explanation of the fact that the self always already finds itself with the world. Reviewing the different definitions of selves and the description of the development of desirable selves according to the different therapeutic models, we have seen contradictory trends. On the one hand, the increasing dispersal of self over a wide area, from intrapersonal to interpersonal to transpersonal dimensions. At the same time there has been an increased emphasis on the importance of that self, on actualisation of its potential, accompanied by the danger of reconsolidation and reification of the construct. The generation of Humanistic psychology has been termed narcissistic in the most pejorative sense, the "me" generation. Although the sense of self is no longer unitary, yet the operational view of it as an egocentric centre of operations has been strengthened. Paradoxically theoretical models of the widely-distributed self seem to be accompanied by an ever stronger focus on the interiority and individuality of that self. Psychotherapies addressing the problems of the contemporary self in practice remain largely fixated on the individual experience, narrative and feelings, ignoring the wider social horizons.

Working against this trend EcoPsychology, Systems Theory and some Structuralists attempt to place the ego firmly in the context of some greater whole. This, like Buddhism, may point to a middle way between subjectivity and objectivity, one that escapes the extremism of either side, a non-dual view like that of Koestler's Janus-faced "holon" showing both autonomy towards its parts and integration within larger systems.[88] For in terms of recent prevalent dualities the obverse of objectivism is renewed subjectivism, which in its turn initiates objectivism again. Heidegger pointed out the unsatisfactory nature of this in "The Age of the World Picture" describing this age as that in which there has never been greater subjectivism and individualism, and at the same time a comparable objectivism, an impoverishment of world as representation. According to his vision, as man has become the "primary and only real subiectum ... Man becomes that being upon which all that is, is grounded as regards the manner of its Being and its truth."[89] "To represent (*vor-stellen*) means to bring what is present at hand (*das Vorhandene*) before oneself as something standing over against, to relate it to oneself, to the one representing it, and to force it back into this relationship to oneself as the normative realm."[90] But in that man puts himself into the picture in this way, thereby he becomes himself the "representative (*der Repräsentant*) of that which is, in the sense of that which has the character of object."[91] Such a state of being might be contrasted with that described by Dogen and quoted earlier.[92]

Conclusion

In 1987 in the introduction to *The Book of the Self,* subtitled *Person, Pretext and Process* the editors see "person" as subjective coherence or agency, while "pretext" "expresses the possibility that presuppositions of a continuous and unified self are illusory. The self may be a project of deception, a masking of discontinuity and disintegration ... a construction based on language, a cultural point of view on human life, expressing a desire for unity in the face of dissolution and death."[93] This differentiates, as so many of the examples cited have also done, between self as agency and self as concept built up of processes, reified and identified with, as a search for security and unity in the face of the primary and secondary dualities of Wilber's Spectrum model as described earlier. It presents a view not incompatible with that of Buddhism.

However paradoxically, along with the weakening of the certainty of world and of the punctual self the West has seen a both rise in nihilistic thought and a reactionary emotional clinging to the concept of self and self actualisation, rather than attempts to discover ways of keeping our balance *within* and *upon* metaphor, movement, fluidity and interconnection. If the sense of self is upheld according to the Buddhist view by craving, conceit and false views, perhaps Western approaches may be said to have come to terms intellectually with views of self rather better than they have emotionally with craving and conceit. Contemporary views of self are, as we have seen, most definitely no longer those of a single, unitary and permanent self, and everywhere we find a distinction between transactional self, and self image or self concept. Yet our conceit, "this is me", and our craving, "this is mine," would not appear to have yet caught up with our intellectual knowledge.[94] This was emphasised in the interchange between the Dalai Lama and Charles Taylor quoted earlier.

However, there is also an important difference between the historical and cultural preconceptions between traditional Buddhism and contemporary Western discourse which must not be overlooked. This concerns the importance given in the West to the individual as a locus of experience with the consequent importance of personal narrative in the construction of a coherent and self sufficient self. No direct tracing of Buddhist concepts of nonself onto Western psychotherapy will be helpful if this difference is ignored. Nor, perhaps, will Buddhist teachings be easily and helpfully accepted widely in the West without acknowledgement of such cultural differences. Yet an understanding of ultimate emptiness, impermanence and dependent origination may certainly be helpful in enabling us to hold our personal stories more lightly, and to retain awareness of their metaphoricity, and their embeddedness in a wider framework. As a contemporary Western writer has suggested: "It may be that to understand ourselves as fictions, is to understand ourselves as fully as we can."[95]

Psychotherapy hardly seems to have followed through with the implications of these views of the plurality of the self. In terms of resultant therapy such discourse is only just appearing in the work of individuals. James Hillman has recently addressed them, as has Philip Cushman with his hermeneutic approach, and ecopsychologists are attempting to widen the scope of psychology to embrace environment.[96] Psychotherapist Petruska Clarkson in a very recent book points out that recent conceptual changes in our psychosocial and cultural environment are conspicuous by their absence in the practice of psychotherapy; that despite the views which we have explored above, which distribute the self ever more widely, the paradigm for psychotherapy is still pre-eminently that of psychotherapist and client in a one-to-one individual relationship. At the very least she believes "that counselling, psychology and all their associated disciplines need to take on the challenges of the new contexts – not to be learnt by rote, but to be held at the mind as a constant resource, otherwise they may become a symptom of those conditions which called them into being."[97]

Buddhism has in its long history not only effected the intellectual deconstruction of substantial views of world, self and their relationship but has also instituted methods of practice for vitiating the emotional attachment to such views as self and the grasping for reified security as illusory defence. It engages both with the philosophical and psychological sense of lack and its concurrent desire, for the philosophical and the psychological are inextricably interwoven. Buddhism sees how belief in self is upheld by desire to be and to have a self, and how from the central pivot of identification with a self, the notion of mine and the entire egocentric world arises.

For the Western view the perceived loss of self may well lead either to nihilism or to a reactive narcissistic grasping of self.[98] For Buddhism the realisation that self and world are interdependent and ultimately empty allows one not merely to ride on the processual wave, but to be it. When world is not viewed from an egocentric position, self may be seen not as a solitary unit but as immanent and embedded within a larger network of relationship with world, and both self and even death take on a different aspect. For, as Gregory Bateson pointed out: "the individual nexus of pathways which I call 'me' is no longer so precious because that nexus is only part of a larger mind."[99] The bridge between self and emptiness, which carries one over the abyss of nihilism is interconnection and interdependence. Such an understanding is instantiated through the ways of the Path, through morality and meditation, which encourage disidentification with the ways of egocentricity, with the cries of "this is me" and "this is mine".

Part Two

Path

PREAMBLE

Path

"Water birds
going and coming
their traces disappear
but they never
forget their path."[1]

Buddhist texts traditionally divide the Path into Morality, Meditation and Wisdom. Within the framework of the eightfold path, two factors, right thought and right understanding belong to Wisdom (*prajñā*), three factors, right effort, right mindfulness and right concentration belong to Meditation (*samādhi*) and three factors, right speech, right action and right livelihood belong to Morality (*śīla*). Right thought and right understanding rest on the ground or views which we have considered in the previous section. Here I would like to discuss Morality and Meditation with relation to a contemporary psychotherapy. First, however it may be appropriate to say a few words about the stages of the path itself. Descriptions of the stages of the path form an important topic in Buddhist thought, and a complicated one, since different schools and vehicles delineate the stages in different manner. It is outside the intention of this work to go into details of the stages of the path in general, yet it is of interest and importance to note both that the simple and nearly ubiquitous fivefold map of the path may be interpreted in psychological terms, and that this description itself fits well with the experience of psychotherapy. The fivefold model presents the path in terms of the Path of Accumulation, the Path of

Practice, the Path of Vision, the Path of Meditation or Cultivation, and the Path of the Arhat who is beyond training. In the context of the psychotherapeutic experience this relates happily to the experience of accumulating information, practising the therapeutic relationship and interaction, achieving insight into behavioural or mental patterns, cultivating the implications of such insights and finally integrating them into new and healthier patterns.[2]

CHAPTER FIVE

Ethics

"Two things fill the mind with ever new and increasing wonder and awe, the more often and the more seriously reflection concentrates upon them: the starry heaven above me and the moral law within me."[1]

Śīla is usually translated Morality or Discipline and I am aware of how unfashionable and unfavoured such a concept currently is.[2] Walpola Rahula gives a translation, perhaps more suited to the contemporary scene, that of Ethical Conduct.[3] Yet under whatever name, this is an area which also receives only limited consideration in contemporary discussion of psychotherapy.[4] Thus in this section I wish to look at the Buddhist sense of ethical conduct, and what this entails, and how it changed from early Buddhism, through the Mahāyāna, and Vājrayāna. I will then consider the subject of ethics in relation to psychotherapy. Here, although we find much written about the contract between therapist and client, and the ethical behaviour required of the therapist, there is little consideration of the wider field of ethics and value. Indeed this reflects the modern scientific world view with its distinct attempt to separate facts from values. An attempt which psychology in its pursuit of scientific status wholeheartedly embraced. Yet psychotherapists are constantly called on to answer moral questions, implicitly if not explicitly. Some definition of the good; good health, good life or good intention is surely implicit in every facet of therapy. At the same time an acceptable moral framework within which to position such questions or to legitimate their answers is difficult to find.

Most recently both science and philosophy tell us that these very attempts to be value-free are themselves "value-laden", it is merely that the implicit values are unacknowledged. Here Buddhist epistemology concurs with the results of research in Cognitive Science in rejecting the separation of fact from value, and asserting that perception is from its inception value-laden.[5] I would, therefore, like to consider both the modern separation of fact and value, and some postmodern attempts to ground a sense of values in something other than ideology. Finally I will consider whether we can usefully find any links between the Buddhist view of ethics and the contemporary ones, and thus present an interpretation of ethical conduct in a way that is meaningful and valuable for contemporary psychotherapy. I will suggest that such an interpretation will be through the idea of responsibility.

Buddhist Ethics

As seen earlier ethics is fundamental to Buddhism. Concluding his study of the nature of Buddhist ethics Keown states that it is objective and naturalist, based on a conception of the good that is "governed by the facts of human nature and the inalienable characteristics of the world we inhabit, such as impermanence and change."[6] The interpretation of *karma* as intention shifted the emphasis from the natural law of the *Vedas* to one concerned with more individual morality. Following on from this, the human being moves to the centre of Buddhist teachings, and an understanding of the working of the mind becomes of the highest importance, resulting in an overlap of psychology and ethics. Walpola Rahula says that Early Buddhism based the framework of Buddhist ethics on two factors; the spiritual experience of the Buddha and analysis of the human mind.[7] The analysis of mind has also been considered earlier, and we have seen the importance placed upon the generation of healthy mind states. For unethical or unhealthy mind states are per se seen as harmful to the mind and inevitably conducive to suffering and entrapment, just as physical trauma results in damage to the body. A morally good intention will give rise to healthy action and mind states, and likewise for a morally unhealthy intention. This may be seen traditionally as occurring across many lifetimes, or interpreted more psychologically to describe the tendencies and dispositions which arise during the current life. How dispositions in turn colour perceptions and the interconnectedness of the five *skandhas* or personality factors has been described. Thus an ethics may be discovered by close enquiry into our mind states, and the consequences of intentions and actions.

If the path consists of wisdom, ethics and meditation, that wisdom is concerned with experience and conduct, rather than with metaphysical speculation. Since the central aim of Buddhism is the attainment of liberation from *saṃsāra*, emphasis is upon the behaviour most likely to achieve this and upon the understanding and the training leading to that understanding which will support such ethical conduct. Outside this focus lie the metaphysical questions upon which the Buddha refused to pronounce. The *sūtra* regarding Malunkyaputta is probably the most repeated example of this. Describing the event of a man struck by an arrow, the Buddha suggests that it is more helpful to call the doctor to attend to the wound, than to pay attention to who shot the arrow, to what family he belonged, how he looked, and what the weapon was; such delay undoubtedly leading to the death of the wounded man. Similarly Buddha explained that he had not explained matters the knowledge of which would not lead to peace.[8] Wisdom and ethics are inextricably linked. In the words of the Buddha; "For wisdom is purified by morality and morality is purified by wisdom; where one is, the other is."[9]

Śīla is divided into right speech, right action and right livelihood.[10] Right speech includes abstention from telling lies, from slander and speech bringing about disunity and disharmony, from rude and abusive language and from idle gossip. Rules of right action prevent us from taking life or property, from illegitimate sexual conduct and from indulging in intoxicating substances. Right Livelihood prohibits making one's living from any profession which would bring harm to others such as trading in lethal weapons or alcohol or killing animals or cheating. Such rules obviously aim at promoting a harmonious life for both the individual and society. Observation of morality is considered more valuable when it is accompanied by commitments or vows.[11] The layman may commit to the Five Central Precepts of not taking life, stealing, telling lies, indulging in unlawful sexual conduct or taking stimulants, or to any one or more of those. The novice will accept ten precepts, up to the full commitment of up to two hundred and fifty for a monk and more for a nun. Ethical conduct in Early Buddhism is pre-eminently that of monastic discipline and training the senses to eliminate sense desire and grasping. In general it tends towards the ascetic and prescriptive and in spirit it may be said to be world-shunning.

Ethical conduct is considered an indispensable foundation for all higher spiritual attainments which are achieved through the path of meditation or mental discipline. Research studies show that meditation students without such disciplinary preparation for meditation progress far slower, and tend to fill their meditation with "therapy." Since they have not prepared themselves to carry out a meditative training, they become "stuck" on the contents of mind and personal issues.[12] The ethical man is he who achieves guardianship of the sense doors – who is in control of unskilful mental states and has developed restraint of the mind faculty.[13] Unhealthy mind states are to be restrained or let go of, healthy mind states to be encouraged, through the methods of meditation and mindfulness. This outlook does have important implications for psychotherapy in relation to the expression of negative mind states such as anger. Western therapy is skilful in its understanding of unconscious mind states and their repression, and in its creation of techniques for facilitating awareness and expression of these. However charges of over-expression, excessive catharsis and reactivation of negative mind states may sometimes rightfully be placed against it. From a Buddhist point of view continual expression and re-enactment of negative mind states may increase the strength and the karmic traces of such harmful emotions, if there is no transformation and integration.[14] Interestingly, current research by neuroscientist Gerald Edelman would seem to support this idea. Edelman's researches show that the neural pathways and connections which are activated during actions which bring about a desired result are strengthened, and will subsequently be activated more easily, while those resulting in undesired ends are weakened.[15]

Ethics, however, is not just a means to the end of enlightenment, but is also an essential component of that enlightenment. It involves, as Keown points out, "a gradual emotional realignment and must be cultivated slowly."[16] If wisdom cultivates cognitive realignment in accordance with the way things are according to Buddhist philosophy, so ethics form the ground for emotional transformation.

In the Mahāyāna the association between the view, a critical insight into emptiness, and authentic moral activity is further emphasised.[17] As the focus of the Mahāyāna becomes less monastic and more concerned with the lay sangha, the emphasis is placed more on intention and relationship, less on retreat from the world, and this influences its ethical stance. The essence of Mahāyāna ethics is altruism and compassion. According to the *Māhāyānasaṃgraha* of Asanga, the higher ethics of the Māhāyāna is superior in classification, in rules, in breadth and in depth.[18] In its classification it has three aspects; morality of abstention, morality of cultivation of virtue and morality in the service of others. The first of these which is seen as the support of the other two is shared with Early Buddhism, morality as the cultivation of virtue, which is the support for the acquisition of the attributes of Buddha, and altruistic morality which is the support for the maturation of sentient beings belong to the Māhāyāna alone.

The path of the Bodhisattva, central to Mahāyāna thought, precludes the search for liberation for oneself alone; it is to be undertaken for all beings. Skilful means which is identified with compassion becomes the equal of wisdom, and the wisdom of early Buddhism becomes the perfection of wisdom, *Prajñāpāramitā,* the wisdom of emptiness. Such wisdom is expressed in compassion, wherein ethical conduct is no longer a matter of comporting to external discipline but becomes the spontaneous expression of perfected awareness. In the Mahāyāna, morality is seen not only in terms of the more external discipline of speech, action and livelihood, but concerned primarily with mind. Thus there is a re-emphasis on the importance of intention which was clearly set out earlier, for instance in the *Dhammapada*.[19] In Mahāyāna literature we find expression of the perfected virtues as set out in the six perfections, the *Pāramitās* of Generosity, Morality, Patience, Energy, Concentration and Wisdom, rather than of the more negative restrictions of Early Buddhism. In the *Bodhicaryāvatāra,* one of the most important treatises of the Mahāyāna and central to the Tibetan tradition, Śāntideva makes mind the central figure of his chapter addressing the *Pāramitā* or virtue of *Śīla*. Stephen Batchelor translates the heading of this chapter as "Guarding Alertness." All fear and miseries arise from mind, thus taming the "elephant of mind" will achieve the cessation of all fear and misery.

> "Unruly beings are as (unlimited) as space:
> They cannot possibly all be overcome,
> But if I overcome thoughts of anger alone
> This will be the equivalent to vanishing all foes."[20]

It is impossible to find sufficient leather to cover all the world, but wearing just the amount to cover our own feet achieves the same end. Thus morality is interpreted at base as a question of mental training, of mindfulness; a question of guarding "the wound of my mind."

> "The defining characteristic of guarding alertness
> In brief is only this:
> To examine again and again
> The condition of my body and mind."[21]

In the Mahāyāna the identity of *saṃsāra* and *nirvāṇa* as demonstrated by Nāgārjuna emphasises the belief that it is the mind or understanding that is to change.[22] In Yōgacāra terms this is the *paravṛtti*, the turning around of understanding from its entrapment by *manas* or egological conceptual thought. According to this view egocentrism becomes transcended in understanding of relationship, friendliness leads to selflessness in the perfection of non-dual understanding. From the point of view of this higher plane of awareness there is a more relative view of ethical conduct, more spontaneous, more situational, less rule-bound. The central virtue is compassion, and in the light of compassion, there are occasions in which a Bodhisattva may justifiably transgress moral precepts.[23] Ethical conduct is no longer a matter of external discipline but is instead the spontaneous expression of perfected awareness. Identified with suchness one's acts are the expression of dharma.

> "Not only is the reality of identity and interdependence the basis for Bodhisattva activities, but it also acts as a moral imperative, leaving the truly moral being with no option but to act in accordance with this reality. For if my own existence is unthinkable apart from the existence of this infinite other, and if my own actions touch these being in some manner, then I must have an obligation to act in such a way that all benefit from the acts. I may, of course, choose otherwise, but then I am not acting in a fundamentally ethical manner, nor, of course, am I making any progress in my own development."[24]

The Vājrayāna propounds the most relative approach towards the rules of external morality; they are viewed as a raft, no longer applicable on reaching the farther shore, where non-dual understanding transcends such differentiation as absolute good and evil. In the words of one of the *mahāsiddhas* or great attainers, Tilopada: "I am the void, the world is void, all the three worlds are void; as such in pure Sahāja, there is neither sin nor virtue."[25] Speaking of the Māhāyāna rather than Vājrayāna, Keown refutes what he terms the "transcendency thesis" of the raft metaphor, but does distinguish between two types of skilful means.[26] The first skilful means is concerned with normative ethics during the process of self cultivation through the *pāramitās*, and the second refers to skilful means as symbolic statement of altruism, for those who have achieved the perfection of insight and attained to an advanced stage in the career of the bodhisattva. The second meaning of skilful means, he suggests, arises from the Madhyamaka interpretation of wisdom as emptiness, which leaves nothing to impede the activity of compassion, as is revealed in the quotation above.

The evolution of Buddhist ethics may be seen in terms of the three major periods outlined in the Bakhtinian model, although from another perspective aspects of each of the three phases may be found within each one of them. Change occurs concurrently with change in the conception of the relationship between individual and world, mind and world. First in the Vedic period moral law is natural law. Later Buddhist ideas of karma with its concepts of intention and choice regarding whether or not to follow the eightfold path, introduced ideas of individual moral retribution, and raised the status of the individual as, at least partially, mistress of her own destiny. Although the present may be caused by the past, yet liberation may be worked for, and even achieved through present deeds. This supports a belief in the importance of individual mind training, and the classification of mind states as healthy or unhealthy. Thirdly the individual is again, to an extent subsumed or recontextualised in the doctrine of *śūnyatā* expressed in terms of *prajñā* and *karuṇā*. The relativity, polyphony and non-finality of conventional truth are seen as aspects of non-dual absolute truth of emptiness. Morality is seen not only in terms of discipline of action, but primarily concerned with mind, which is no longer seen as separate from world. Here the perfected expression of suchness as an expression of dharma carries an echo of the first phase, though it is now seen to be the final outcome of individual efforts.

Ethics and Psychotherapy

Turning to Western views of morality, we find again how the view of the world will influence concepts of ethical conduct.

Historically religion has been the support and foundation for Western morality. With the rise of secular scientific culture with a view of man as an isolated individual 'thing' pursuing his destiny in a world organised according to impersonal scientific laws of causality, time and space, the 'modern' tendency has been to segregate fact from value. In a recent work philosopher and novelist Iris Murdoch suggests that the purpose of such segregation, certainly as used by Kant and Wittgenstein, was to keep moral value pure, untainted by, and underived from empirical facts. Such a well-intentioned move, however, has resulted in a diminished account of morality and "a marginalisation of the ethical."[27] More recently, the era of value-free science and the embrace of the objective point of view has been strongly criticised both by contemporary science itself and by philosophy, concurring that such an approach is not only impoverished but also impossible.[28] Entirely objective, value-free cognition is now seen through the eyes of the Cognitive Sciences to be impossible. The theory of relativity has also shown the impossibility of separating the experimenter from the experiment. What was value-free, has come to be seen as merely value-unacknowledged. Similarly, Buddhist epistemology clearly shows the arising of values and dispositions within the cycle of dependent arising, and in the five aggregates. Yet at the same time as this realisation that fact and value cannot be separated, the sources of legitimation for morality, the systems of thoughts and religion upon which they were traditionally founded have been laid open to criticism and deconstruction as never before.

Psychology, as pre-eminently a child of the modern, has been deeply imbued with this spirit of separation of fact and value. Similarly psychotherapy, though concerned with the ethics of therapist responsibility, is rarely concerned with an explicit moral stance in relation to the client's ethical behaviour, which is considered a private matter; the criteria for acceptability being rather whether or not it is conducive to the client's health, rather than being seen in a wider social involvement. Behaviourist psychology was committed to the segregation of fact from value. In Psychoanalytic theory Freud portrayed a sense of morality as developing from the external constraints of civilisation, which became in time internalised into the super-ego, a kind of internal detective, monitor or judge. Within his writing morality wears a negative and repressive aura. In the *Three Essays on the Theory of Sexuality* references to morality are always conjoined within a triad of disgust, shame and morality.

Humanistic and Existential theory with its foundation in Existential philosophy, and such concepts as Heideggerian authenticity and care has a much greater potential for exploring the place of moral reflection in self-understanding. However, I believe that it is ironic that the situated attributes of *Dasein* have often led via the path of Sartrean freedom to a far more self-centred actualisation of the decontextualised and isolated individual in many forms of humanistic and existential therapies; have, in fact, led to the terms and goals of the "me generation" pursuing ever greater individual satisfaction. The potential for egocentric interpretation of Fritz Perls' *Gestalt* prayer is obvious:

> "I do my thing, and you do your thing.
> I am not in this world to live up to your expectation
> And you are not in this world to live up to mine.
> You are you and I am I,
> And if by chance we find each other, it is beautiful
> If not, it can't be helped."[29]

For the view of the world underlying much psychotherapeutic theory is that of the "self as an essentially isolated individual in a morally neutral, objectified universe."[30] This view itself may be seen as itself a source of the emotional and behavioural problems which bring clients to seek therapy. Thus psychotherapy based on such views, risks perpetrating rather than ameliorating such problems.[31] Different theory, emphasising embeddedness and connection rather than isolation – indeed dependent origination – may provide a foundation for a more helpful practice. Gregory Bateson again was one of the first to point this out: "But when you separate mind from the structure in which it is immanent, such as human relationship, the human society or the ecosystem, you thereby embark, I believe on fundamental error, which in the end will surely hurt you."[32] Contemporary transpersonal therapies, ecopsychology and the general drift of the postmodern would seem to be attempts at recontextualisation of the individual, and a re-recognition of ethical and social embeddedness.[33] We may find in both Buddhist and postmodern discourse various different arguments as to the construction of world and self, and the relationship between; arguments which run counter to the separation of fact and value and offer different pictures which call upon a new ethics.

Some Contemporary Western Views of Ethics

The very failure of philosophy to totalize the world, to enclose it within a system is its success for Emmanuel Levinas. We have considered above his views of the appeal of the other in the construction of the self, and the primacy of the ethical relationship, the "call of the face." In his own words: "I am trying to show that man's ethical relationship to the other is ultimately prior to his ontological relation to himself (egology) or to the totality of things that we call the world. (cosmology)."[34] Moreover it is through the appeal of the other that the way is open to transcendence and escape from totality. "Man's relationship with the other is *better* as difference than as unity, sociality is better than fusion."[35] Once again we hear the postmodern theme of difference, with once again, I would suggest, its echo of *śūnyatā,* the non-totalizable, non-simultaneity of presence, and the move away from egology to the acknowledgement of relationship. "My duty to respond to the other suspends my natural right to self-survival, *le droit vitale*. My ethical relation of love for the other stems from the fact that the self cannot survive by itself alone, cannot find meaning within its own being-in-the world, within the ontology of sameness."[36] Alterity opens us up to transcendence, to desire, and leads us away from the need of the same, for "the possibility of possessing, that is, of suspending the very alterity of what is only at first other, and other relative to me, is the *way* of the same.[37] Indeed "the identification of the same IS ... the concreteness of egoism."[38]

In some ways this appears against nature; against the Darwinian survival of the fittest, and it requires the backing of discipline, emphasised by Buddhism with its path of training in morality and mind training to correct or 'see through' the primal ignorance. In the words of Levinas: "Ethics is not derived from an ontology of nature; it is its opposite, a meontology, which affirms a meaning beyond being, a primary mode of non-being (me-on).[39] Indeed one commentator has described Levinas' analysis of God as "an impossibility of being or being-present."[40] which sounds much like an attempt at a description of *śūnyatā*. For Levinas too, metaphysics is enacted in ethical relations,[41] a similar linkage to that of emptiness and compassion. That ethical altruism is 'against nature' is also linked with the perceived advantages of the single unified and separate self considered in the previous chapter. The view of the distributed self and that of the necessity for altruism are interconnected. At first both seem contrary to experience and there is an emotional pull against accepting them. Perhaps at this stage, one can only note how these two ideas are interlinked, and hypothesise that as cultural evolution comes into play alongside somatic evolution with the arrival of human beings and language, the advantages of participation and communality will become apparent in the future.

In a somewhat comparable manner, for Bakhtin too, the foundation of ethics lies in the relationship of the individual to the world, most especially the relation to the other, in all the concrete actuality of the experienced act. Against the background of his belief in the dialogic network of relationship which surrounds and constitutes each event, Bakhtin posits the necessity for the individual to authenticate and fulfil each act. We have, he believed, "no-alibi in being," but a requirement, the "ought" to actualize our own place in "the once occurent event of Being."[42] Such an obligation is grounded in everyday experience, in concrete events rather than in any abstract rules belonging to the "world of cognition", and thus is not selfish, since it must be seen against the background of dialogic relations, in which every moment of Being is organized around the polyphonic value centres of self and others. Thus this "ought to actualize one's unique place in once-occurent Being-as-event ... is determined first and foremost as a contraposition of I and the *other.*"[43] For Bakhtin the monologic view is deaf to the response of the other, just as for Levinas the reduction of difference and the reduction of the other to the same, is the violence of totalization. Monologue attempts both to achieve closure, to say the final word, and to objectivise reality. The dialogic position allows the other to remain another consciousness, another centre beyond integration or reduction. Speaking in relation to Dostoevsky, Bakhtin suggests: "The most important moment of this surplus is love (one cannot love oneself, it is a coordinated relation); then, confession, forgiveness ... finally, simply an active understanding (that does not reduplicate), watchful listening."[44]

Both Systems Theory and the enactive approach from Cognitive Science uphold an interconnected view of the relationship of the individual and the world, which emphasises the moral nature of knowing itself and a naturalistic and normative ethics defining the good as a state of maximum adaptation of natural and cognitive systems. In asking where error or sin enters, Ervin Laszlo argues that it is on the level of reflective consciousness; conscious representation of basically sound attempts at achieving goals become distorted by misrepresentation. He contends that one principal way in which this occurs is in misunderstanding of system status, resulting in misidentification of goals, interpreted solely in individualistic mode rather than in part status in relation to the larger system; i.e. putting the egocentric desires of the individual to the fore at the expense of the needs of the higher level system.[45] From this way of thinking which gives rise to a relational ethics, comes not only the re-unification of fact and value that we have discussed above, but also that of means and ends. Ends are no longer considered to be something separated, ahead or "out there", but are a function of thoughts and actions, interdependent with means. Similarly theory is not seen as an isolated supratemporal foundation for praxis, but is emergent, and changing in a mutual process or feedback loop, within an open-ended rather than a closed system. Means and ends are part of process, similar to that of insight and act as we saw in the Dīgha Nikāya in discussing Buddhist ethics: "From morality comes wisdom and from wisdom comes morality."[46]

The ethical norms for such views do not rely on outside legitimation but are grounded in the interdependence that conditions all existence. They can perhaps be compared to those revealed by Carol Gilligan's research into womens' conception of morality.[47] Gilligan distinguishes between what she terms "ethics of principal" and "ethics of relatedness", suggesting that women have a different approach to ethical problems than men; a morality based on responsibilities rather than on rights, grounded in connection rather than separation, within which relationship rather than the individual is primary. Within a view that upholds the participation of the individual in the world, and that is concerned both with differentiation and integration, it is seen that the health of the individual and society are interlinked.

From within the Cognitive Sciences comes another new view of the grounds of morality, propounded by Mark Johnson following on his work with George Lakoff on the metaphoric and imaginative foundations of language and his own work grounding this within embodiment which I will discuss in later chapters.[48] Johnson believes that the scope of moral understanding is far broader than 'institutions of morality' allow for, and pervades all aspects of life. Such a belief "confronts us with the task of always trying to see as broadly as possible the implications of our attitudes, judgements, and way of life. It simply tries to make us more finely attuned to our interconnectedness with other people, animals, and organic processes as a whole."[49] Johnson finds the grounding of our conceptual systems in the structures of bodily experience. Since such concepts are often implicated in and extended by conceptual metaphors, he contends that no account of morality that fails to examine the use of metaphor and imagination in moral understanding can be adequate. His central thesis is that moral understanding is situated in narrative understanding, and is fundamentally imaginative in character.[50] It is derived from the experience of prototypical situations, imaginatively extended to wider contexts, rather than from abstract concepts.

His particular researches lead him to the belief, frequently encountered in contemporary discourse, that there is no absolute, final or objective, context-free truth, and that in freeing ourselves from such a notion, rather than losing something valuable and necessary, we are, in fact, merely releasing ourselves from the influence of an illusory ideal that is counterproductive to human well-being and community. In place of this illusion he believes we need a number of competing methods, views and practices, a multiplicity of meanings in continuing dialogue, tested by experience. In response to charges of relativism he believes that the fact of human embodiment, with its shared set of needs and instincts guarantees a certain level of commensurability between competing moral themes, based on the constraints of human experience, its biological purposes, cognitive structures, social relations and ecological concerns. Once again central to this theory is the idea of the interrelationship of the individual and the world, as Johnson believes: "We are beings whose identities emerge and develop in an ongoing process of interactions within our physical, interpersonal and cultural environments."[51]

More recently, similarly yet from very different perspectives, two other writers have put forward suggestions and hopes for a new approach to ethics founded on the understanding of interconnection. Francisco Varela, whose work in neuro-biology has been mentioned throughout, has brought together phenomenology, cognitive science and Buddhism in an attempt to ground contemporary ethics.[52] He argues that truly ethical behaviour comes from personal transformation rather than from moral judgement. He believes that ethics is a situationally-based *know-how* rather than *knowledge of*, involving an ethical way of acting rather than adherence to a fixed set of rules. He shows from a cognitive science perspective, how consciousness is contextualised and incarnated. For him the link point between Buddhism and cognitive science is their common understanding of non-self. Buddhism provides methods of transformation and a model of ethical comportment which arise from, and also evoke, deep realisation of the emptiness of self, which gives rise to compassion. A true realisation, rather than a mere intellectual argumentation of the non-self found by cognitive science could bring to an end not only views of self, but also the emotional clinging and selfishness, as discussed in the previous chapter.

From a more Western and ecological perspective, David Abram also argues that a new 'environmental ethic' "that would lead us to respect and heed not only the lives of our fellow humans but also the life and well-being of the rest of nature – will come into existence not primarily through the logical elucidation of new philosophical principles and legislative strictures, but through a renewed attentiveness to this perceptual dimension that underlies all our logics, through a rejuvenation of our carnal, sensorial empathy with the living land that sustains us."[53] He believes that such embodied perception can appreciate and understand the interconnection of perceiver and perceived.

Conclusions

Within these different approaches to morality, we find definite themes which recur, and contrast to the earlier 'modern' views which saw man as a thing within a world of things, pursuing his individual destiny according either to externally given moral authority, or to natural laws. With the deconstruction of the legitimation of external authority, and the understanding of both the impoverishment and impossibility of a value-free stance, a more pluralistic, relative and perspectival view now prevails, with a different concept of the individual and their relationship to the world. Recontextualised within society, culture and history, the individual is perhaps seen in a middle way between total participation and total isolation and egocentricity; as a 'holon', both whole facing in one direction, and part of a larger system facing in the other.[54] Gilligan's research on womens' responses to abortion illustrates this pattern. She found a specifically female three-stage sequence of development towards moral problems which she termed the development of the "ethic of care." According to this sequence an initial emphasis on caring for the survival of the self is followed by a phase in which this stance is critically judged as selfish, at which point the good is seen as caring for others. The third perspective, focusing on the dynamics of relationship, forges a middle way between selfishness and responsibility, through a new understanding of the interconnection between self and other. This ethic of care, as she acknowledges, "evolves around a central insight that self and other are interdependent."[55] In place of a privileging of either subjectivity or objectivity (which as we have seen earlier are not so different), these new views favour transperspectivity rather than mutual contradiction, pluralism and dialogue rather than monologue. The guiding image again might well be the net of Indra.

Thus I would contend that the morality implied by these views, and indeed also by Mahāyāna Buddhism is an ethics of responsibility and responsible behaviour. A responsibility engendered by a view of interdependence, our answerability to the other, to the planet, in an openness to the claims of interrelationship that decentre the ego and encourage us to live in the world with compassion.

Just as Varela has written of ethical behaviour as know-how rather than adherence to moral rule, so this responsibility also includes the aspect of response-ability, an aspect of particular relevance to psychotherapy, particularly spoken of in Gestalt therapy. For the healthier the human being, the more they are wholly available for free response. In terms of Buddhist epistemology, as we saw earlier, a *pramāṇa* or ideal cognition means ideal and fresh cognition, free from subsequent conceptuality. In a somewhat similar way, the more areas of the personality are bound by rigid defensive and cognitive structures, the less is available for spontaneous and open response. The very work of psychotherapy is to bring awareness to these structures and in exploring them, loosening them, freeing the energy bound up therein, allowing moment to moment free response to events, in contrast to being confined within a pre-determined script written with fear or resentment or whatever, often relevant to a time now past. Likewise selfishness is a constriction of response and responsibility in ignorance of our embeddedness in a greater whole; it is a terrified grasping of a limited part. Understanding of this leads to compassion, the foundation of Mahāyāna and Vajrayāna ethics, based on the non-duality of self and other.

This link between responsibility and response-ability is also noted by Levinas; "I think that the beginning of language is in the face. In a certain way, in its silence, it calls you. Your reaction to the face is a response. Not just a response, but a responsibility. These two words (réponse, responsabilité) are closely related."[56] Thus, as we have seen, Levinas places the ethical prior to the ontological, the Good prior to, and transcendent to, Being. For Levinas this responsibility is unique to man, and through it the human breaks with pure being. "The aim of Being is being itself. However, with the appearance of the human – and this is my entire philosophy – there is something more important than my life, and that is the life of the other."[57]

Perhaps today we can find ground for an inescapable morality in responsibility; understanding of the contingency or self and interrelationship of life giving rise to action founded upon responsibility and compassion. And such contingency need not be utterly relativistic, if we join such understanding with a return to close attention of the things of this world for their own sakes, not as means to further ends. For we share embodiment with all humans, we share a planet with nature, these are the natural constraints if we view them without egocentricity. Such a view must be part of a conception of health. Perhaps this has been most perfectly expressed in the lines which we have quoted before by Dogen:

> "Studying the Buddha way is studying oneself,
> Studying oneself is forgetting oneself.
> Forgetting oneself is being enlightened by all things."

and in the same essay:

> "To practice and confirm all things by conveying oneself to them is illusion: for all things to advance toward and practise and confirm the self, is enlightenment."[58]

This attention must be cultivated: both attention to things as ends in themselves rather than as means to our egocentric ends, and the attention that through close mindfulness of the consequences, outwardly of our actions and inwardly of our intentions and mind states, experiences the inevitability of suffering arising from harmful thoughts and deeds. It is to Buddhism that we may turn to find a long tradition of methods of mind training in mindfulness and meditation. These methods, as also ethical conduct, are grounded in the view of a changing, impermanent and interconnected world of which we are a part, and in which it behoves us to participate with responsibility, both to ourselves, to other parts, and to the whole, not to manipulate merely from the nescient position of a grasping separative egocentrism.

CHAPTER SIX

Meditation

> "*. . . a man becomes his attentions. His observations and curiosity, they make and remake him.*
>
> *Etymology:* curious, *related to* cure, once meant 'carefully observant.' *Maybe a tonic of curiosity would counter my numbing sense that life inevitably creeps toward the absurd.* Absurd, *by the way, derives from a L*atin word meaning 'deaf, dulled.' *Maybe the road could provide a therapy through observation of the ordinary and obvious, a means whereby the outer eye opens an inner one. STOP, LOOK, LISTEN, the old rail*road crossing signs warned. Whitman calls it '*th*e profound lesson of reception."[1]

It is with the practices of awareness and mind training that Buddhism provides the greatest specific tools for psychotherapy. Just as Śāntideva over a thousand years ago, encouraged his students to guard their minds, so today we are similarly assured that happiness "does not depend on outside events, but, rather, on how we interpret them."[2] Indeed many people expect discussion about Buddhism and psychotherapy to concentrate primarily on meditation. It is the intention of this work, however, to try and contextualise such practices within the theoretical framework both of Buddhist philosophy and of Western therapy. In this chapter, therefore, I would like first to look at Buddhist meditation itself, considering the two main approaches and defining their differences. Then I would like to turn to considerations of meditation and mindfulness within the field of psychotherapy; firstly from the perspective of the therapist, then from that of the client, and thirdly in the context of the therapeutic relationship itself. Thus, I shall consider meditative practices first as an aid in the training of therapists, then I shall discuss mindfulness practices, both Buddhist and Western, for the client, and finally I shall look at meditation as a model for the therapeutic encounter itself.

Buddhist Meditation

In the 1890s, as we have already noted, William James wrote: "The faculty of voluntarily bringing back a wandering attention over and over again is the very root of judgement, character and will. No one is *compos sui* if he have it not. An education which should improve this faculty would be the education par excellence."[3] In 1990s as noted earlier, Margaret Donaldson turns to Buddhism for methods of education in developmental modes underdeveloped and undervalued in current Western society; modes she terms "value sensing", concerned with affect as opposed to intellect.[4] It would seem that there is within meditative cultivation a resource which has been largely ignored in the West. Buddhist meditation is seen as a training in the cultivation of tranquillity and insight, which are the names of two distinct types of meditation which ideally and finally are to be yoked together to give rise to wisdom. Sometimes they are described as concentrative and analytic meditations.

Tranquillity meditation or meditative stabilisation *(śamatha;* Tibetan: *shi gnas)* is that in which the mind is focused upon an object, whether external like a pot, or internal like the breath, to the exclusion of all else, devoid of reflection. In the Theravadin commentary the *Visudhimagga,* detailed instructions are given as to objects of meditation, situation, and methods of meditation for different types of person.[5] Detailed descriptions are also provided for the path, events and achievements of trance-like states. However, such achievements in Buddhist meditation are generally considered to be a by-product of attainment of concentration, not to be pursued for their own sake, but merely as part of the path toward controlling the mind and overcoming attachment. Indeed Śākyamuni Buddha had achieved the highest of these states in his studies with his teachers Ālara Kālama and Uddaka Rāmaputta before his attainment of enlightenment. Such states are acquired in the pursuit of a firm concentrative ability which acts as a foundation upon which to base the practice of higher vision or insight (*vipaśyanā; lhag mthong*). In the last chapter we noted the inseparability of wisdom and ethics for the Buddhist enterprise. Following this we may suggest that it is primarily concentrative meditation which aids the affective realignment of the personality while insight meditation is concerned with the overthrow of ignorance or delusion.[6]

Insight meditation is the practice of discursive reflection while mental stabilisation is present. The object may be Buddhist doctrine, such as selflessness, impermanence or emptiness, or one's present ongoing experience. Within this latter mindfulness, there is no narrowly focused object of attention, rather, one takes present awareness as the wide focus, paying attention to the moment to moment flow of sensations, feelings and thoughts arising and ceasing, without being captured by them. Whatever occurs is to be received with bare attention, with a mind that is receptive rather than reactive. Heidegger's *Gelassanheit,* the "letting-be" that allows for presence would seem, perhaps to be somewhat similar. As he says: "The first step ... is the step back from the thinking that merely represents – that is, explains – to the thinking that responds and recalls."[7] This is in contrast to representational and calculative thinking, the thinking that is logical, conceptual, grasping and reifying, which perpetuates what he terms the "technological" outlook implicit in the activity of "framing". Heidegger's concept of *Andenken* or *Besinnung* (usually translated as meditative thinking or remembrance) for the "thinking that responds" perhaps relates most nearly to the non-dualistic, non-conceptual insight or wisdom that is the goal of meditative practice. Seeing in such a careful and receptive way breaks through stereotyped reactions, and gives rise to a deconstruction of mental functioning, fostering first awareness of, then release from, persistent and compulsive mental habits. From these observations emerge realisations about the nature of the mind, and mindfulness becomes insight. In terms of the twelvefold cycle of dependent origination one can become aware of, and finally interrupt, the patterns of habituated conditioning.[8] Continued practice of Buddhist meditation will lead to experience of insight into the reality of existence with its three marks of selflessness, impermanence and suffering.

There are three particularly important sutras in the Tripitaka relating to mindfulness; the most famous of them all is the *Satipaṭṭhānā Sutta* found in both the Pali Majjhima and Dīgha Nikāyas.[9] In this sutra the Buddha expounds on the Four Foundations of Mindfulness; mindfulness of the body, mindfulness of the feelings, mindfulness of the mind and mindfulness of the objects of the mind. Mindfulness of the body starts with the breath; with conscious breathing, so mind and breath become one. Then, with following the breath and breathing with awareness of the whole body, mind and body are brought into harmony, and through harmonisation of the breath both mind and body are calmed. Awareness of the body is practised in all positions and actions and the parts of the body are contemplated and mindfully observed. Through observation of the four elements present in the body, the interrelationship of the body with the world is contemplated, followed by contemplation of the impermanence of the body. In all these contemplations one is advised to notice the process of coming-to-be and ceasing-to-be in the constituents which comprise the body.

In the mindfulness of feelings the practitioner is encouraged first to identify feelings as to whether they are pleasant or unpleasant, then to consider their roots, whether in the body or mind, thus watching the process of becoming and ceasing of the feelings. Thirdly, mindfulness is brought to the mind itself; to perceptions (*samjñā*), dispositions (*saṃskāra*), and consciousness (*vijñāna*). Again the practice is to observe the arising, presence and disappearance of the mental phenomena, illuminated by mindfulness.

Finally mindfulness of the objects of mind looks at the five hindrances (desire, anger, dullness, agitation and remorse, and doubt),[10] the five aggregates and the six sense organs and objects in terms of their arising, ceasing and interdependence. Finally attention is drawn to the seven factors of awakening, of which the first is mindfulness itself, followed by investigation of phenomena, energy, joy, ease, concentration and letting go.

The *Ānâpāṇasati Sutta,* also from the *Majjhima Nikāya*, which Thich Nhat Hanh translates as The Sutra on the Full Awareness of Breathing, unites the four foundations of mindfulness with greater emphasis on awareness of the breath. One distinct result of mindfulness of the breath is its success in bringing mind and body together in the present moment. The *Theranama Sutta* emphasises the teaching of the Buddha regarding living in the present.[11]

> "Do not pursue the past
> Do not lose yourself in the future.
> The past no longer is
> The future has not yet come.
> Looking deeply at life as it is
> in the very here and now,
> the practitioner dwells
> in stability and peace."[12]

Through such meditation practice the meditator learns to quieten the mind, stand back from and disidentify with, the contents of mind, taking up a witness position towards them.

Such mindfulness as taught in these sutras strips experience of all accretions of memory, conceptualisation and habituated reactions; it deconstructs it into its components so we may better see their coming-into-being, ceasing, impermanence and interdependence. Such practice leads to experience of "in the seen there shall be just the seen, in the heard there shall be just the heard,"[13] as recommended by the Buddha; the appreciation expressed by Zen Buddhism as "when you are sitting, just sit, when you are eating, just eat."

Furthermore, though it may well be outside the personal experience of all but the most committed practitioner, there is another aspect of mindfulness and meditation practice of immense importance. Meditation is the path to nondual awareness, and it is through such practice that one can *realise* in the truest sense of the word, the unconditioned. Nondual awareness is free from the incompleteness of difference inevitably attached to any knowledge of content expressed linguistically or conceptually. Nondual awareness is not concerned with capturing an object but with experiencing the presence of attention to the clarity and non-obstruction of mind itself.[14] What is discovered is not a totality of knowledge but a presence of attention that holds and illuminates the connection between the subjective silence, the spaciousness of consciousness revealed through mindfulness and the objective absence that is emptiness. It is beautifully described by Ann Klein: "the ocean of one's focused attention remains a coherent dimension amid all its waves of deferred differences."[15] What lessons are there here for psychotherapy?

Lessons for Psychotherapy

The Therapists' Perspective

Firstly let us look from the standpoint of the training of psychotherapists. Rather than putting meditation practice forward as a therapeutic technique for clients, I would contend that perhaps its chief value for psychotherapy lies in its use in the training of therapists. As the description of the Sutra on the Four Foundations of Mindfulness shows, such meditation exposes our habitual thoughts, feelings and attitudes. Whatever cognitive theory and practical techniques are necessary in the training of psychotherapists, a prime requirement is that the therapist has done her own work with her own experience, and has explored and familiarised herself with her own mind states to the point where she is comfortable with them. Meditation is a supreme method for becoming aware of and understanding the number, quality, impermanence and change of mental states, and of building up the necessary balance to enable one to ride one's experience without being imprisoned in uncontrolled reaction. Having become comfortable and relatively unshockable in their own mental world, psychotherapists are enabled to extend that same ease to their clients. The basic task of psychotherapy is to enlarge a person's living space; to expand their sense of self by integrating the parts that are hidden or defended against, or seen as alien. To do this, first these alien areas must be brought to awareness, and then made friends with and accepted. Thus the charge they carry, of fear or anger or whatever, is defused and the energy released. Writer and therapist John Welwood sees the major point of overlap between meditation and psychotherapy in the practice of developing this sense of *maitri* or friendliness towards our own experience.[16] In mindfulness we can learn to be with our experience, to make space for it in a non-reactive way, seeing and watching what arises and neither suppressing nor indulging and exaggerating it. It is a way of learning to be with whatever comes up, of learning to be with the unknown, and to be comfortable with not knowing, which is at first not at all comfortable, yet is of inestimable use in the therapeutic encounter. Mindfulness meditation is a tremendous resource in training psychotherapists; in developing such friendliness to oneself and openness to experience as it arises, rather than as one would wish it to be. As John Welwood says: "Meditation is a direct experience of how change is more dependent on how we *be* with ourselves than anything we *do* to try to improve ourselves."[17] The very being of unconditioned presence is what allows for healing.[18] Indeed the concept of *maitri* is fundamental to the Naropa Institute psychotherapy training in conjunction with that of Basic Sanity. This mindfulness is in no way an escape from phenomenal reality, but a means to engage us more fully in reality as it presents itself, without the distortions of emotions and expectations which prevent us from responding fully and flexibly to whatever occurs. It is not an escape from the ego but a means of using the ego to observe its own workings and experience itself without distortion, thus becoming able to respond to and integrate whatever may face it, rather than being restricted by defensive structures, and rigid identifications. It is, in fact, ego as working sense of self rather than self concept, as discussed in chapter four.

As research has shown that it is the presence of the therapist rather than their overt theoretical stance that is of value in the therapeutic situation, it would seem that an important emphasis in the training of therapists would be placed on presence, the way therapists are within the therapeutic encounter. Yet this is frequently a part of training which is insufficiently addressed. As an experienced supervisor of therapists writes: "One of the frustrations I have encountered in supervising over the last twenty-five years is that the typical supervisee's focus is on what to do with the patient, as contrasted with how to *be* with the patient."[19] He said that in all his extensive years of American graduate school, internship and psychoanalytic training he never had direct supervision on how to be with a patient, and feels that his supervisees, in turn, while speaking of the importance of establishing rapport and maintaining a working alliance with clients, have been taught little about the subtler qualities of relatedness. He has found meditative techniques to be of great use in teaching supervisees how to be in the therapeutic encounter, and how to respond to clients rather than to impose upon them their own need to do.

Mikulas also refers to the value of meditation practice for therapists, noting: "Through concentration and mindfulness training, the therapist learns to quiet her/his mind, so she/he can really listen without evaluating and categorizing. She/he learns how to get out of her vantage point and, to some extent, see, feel, and think from the client's vantage point."[20]

Similarly a meditative training may teach therapists how to remain in unknowing, being open to what occurs, rather than constraining themselves and their clients within the limits of theory and resultant expectation. To be truly comfortable with unknowing is so far from any state valued within all but a few of the most contemporary academic, technical or medical trainings, or even in daily life, that it needs some practice, which meditation practice may offer. Both the Core Process and Contemplative Psychology therapy trainings use Buddhist meditation training as this resource, to encourage trainee therapists to experience different mind states as they arise, and to learn to be with them, rather than attempting to evade them or change them through doing.

Dubin speaks of an important component in the establishment of rapport as being a centring in the heart as a centre of experiencing which transcends purely intellectual levels. The development of designation and conceptualisation enable us to think abstractly, but also remove us from the immediacy of perception. Learning to focus attention and still the chatter of conceptualisation allows us to contact experience once again in its direct immediacy, and to respond to our experience from a more inclusive level of consciousness which can observe cognitive operations without being caught up in them.[21] Again, to achieve this level of openness and receptivity requires discipline and the ability to transcend one's usual egocentric concerns. Such discipline and ability may be acquired through a meditation practice.

Meditations like those discussed above have an immense value also in that they ground us in our bodies, and through awareness of breath bring body and mind into harmony. Simple grounding exercises paying attention to the breath and the body may be invaluable in psychotherapy. More complex exercises, such as those of yoga or the Tibetan *Kum Nye* exercises presented to the West by Tarthang Tulku take this aspect of therapy further, and may be of value both in training of therapists, and for clients themselves.[22]

There are also specific meditations which may be beneficial for specific purposes, helping to generate healthy mind states conducive to healing. The formal *Maitri* meditation is one that promotes the generation of friendliness and compassion towards oneself, one's friends, one's enemies and all sentient beings. John Welwood describes his frustration in studying Rogerian therapy in graduate school since: "I was never taught *how* to develop 'unconditional positive regard' for the client. I was told this was essential and it sounded good to me, but it was just assumed that I should be able to feel this way toward anyone who walked into my office."[23] Similarly the practice of exchanging self for other fosters the development of compassion; the fostering of positive attitudes and the combating of negative ones.[24] Another specific form of meditation is visualisation. Within Buddhism this is mostly found in the Tantric practices of the Vajrayāna; in the visualisation and impersonation of deities whereby the practitioner becomes merged with the deity and the world becomes the realm of the god. Similar uses of the imagination and guided meditations may be used in a therapeutic setting. This is particularly found in Roberto Assagioli's Psychosynthesis.[25]

Meditation and the Client

If a formal sitting practice is primarily for the therapist, a general fostering of mindfulness in action is primary for the client. I personally, do not believe that psychotherapy should be confused with teaching formal meditation practice. Although Buddhism is a rich source for good psychotherapeutic practice as I am arguing in this study, there are differences also which I would like to consider later. Therefore I consider that psychotherapists would be well advised not to give formal meditation practice to clients, thus confusing the roles of therapist and teacher.[26] I would suggest that clients who wish for this, or those for whom it is considered desirable, seek formal meditation instruction elsewhere.[27] In some cases and in some circumstances, meditation may be definitely counter productive to psychological health. As we have noted before, meditation training traditionally begins on a firm basis of ethical behaviour and mental health. Without these, it is very possible to confuse pre and trans-egoic states as discussed in chapter four.

Having said that, mindfulness and awareness are at the heart of therapeutic work. The aim of therapy is to bring awareness, and in its wake space and choice, to the conditioned and reactive responses with which we greet new experience. Mindfulness encourages us to ground our experience in awareness rather than in accustomed forgetfulness through which we lose touch with ourselves and our experience and our environment. Karen Wegela of the Naropa Institute has made a therapeutic practice out of transforming mindlessness practices into opportunities for mindfulness. She writes of mindlessness practices as those usually unconscious habits we use to disconnect mind from body and present awareness, citing fiddling and addictions as ways of escaping presence.[28]

Mindfulness brings us into the present moment which, as Thich Nhat Hanh reminds us is "the only moment we can touch life."[29] This can help to heal alienation from ourselves, our experience and our world, and can re-introduce lived meaning. Thich Nhat Hanh is perhaps the finest contemporary teacher of the benefits and transformative power of mindfulness. His writings constantly describe the healing power of bringing awareness to our mind states, particularly negative states such as anger. By staying in mindfulness with the state itself, and not allowing our conditioned reaction which is to shift immediately from the feeling itself into elaborations of the story surrounding it and the people involved in its arising which in turn evoke more negative thoughts and feelings, we may observe the initial state with mindfulness and attention which brings calm. This first stage is sometimes termed "bare attention"; perhaps, more precisely, it is attention to the bare feeling or state, to the very anger or joy or disquiet itself, divorced for a while from its story and from other emotions such as guilt, justification or judgement which we frequently build onto that first feeling, and from our subsequent identification with those added emotions. The very fact of acknowledging the core state, paying attention to it without accretions of judgement or guilt, and without identifying with it, allows us to observe it, calm it and ultimately will transform it. As Thich Nhat Hanh describes it:

> "Our mindfulness has the same function as the light of the sun. If we shine the light of full awareness steadily on our

> state of mind, that state of mind will transform into something better. The point of meditation is to look deeply into things in order to be able to see their nature. The nature of things is interdependent origination, the true source of everything that is. If we look into our anger, we can see its roots, such as misunderstanding (and ignorance), clumsiness (or lack of skill), the surrounding society, hidden resentment, habit (or our conditioning). These roots can be present both in ourselves and in the person who played the principal role in allowing the anger to arise. We observe mindfully in order to be able to see and to understand. Seeing and understanding are the elements of liberation which allow us to be free of the suffering which always accompanies anger. Seeing and understanding bring about love and compassion . . . our anger is a field of energy. Thanks to our mindful observation and insight into its roots, we can change this energy into the energy of love and compassion – a constructive and healing energy."[30]

A Western approach to mindfulness is found in the Focusing technique of Eugene Gendlin which we considered in chapter two. Gendlin maintains that practising mindfulness can open us up to the "felt sense", a non cognitive experience that is not purely unconscious or beyond awareness, but of which without practice we are unaware. He likens this to an animal's ability to respond and act from a sense of the whole situation, both the external circumstances and stimuli, and its own structured set of physiological and behavioural processes. The aim of his technique of focusing is to develop this body-based awareness and openness to experience on an intuitive and somatic level that is the body's pre-cognitive response to the meaning of the whole situation, its response to both internal and external stimuli, of which we are rarely consciously aware. Bringing this into consciousness may in itself bring about change and transformation. It is another example of enactive embedded experience. In both Buddhist meditation and Focusing the division between what is conscious and unconscious is portrayed as a matter of breadth of focus rather than structural division.[31] For Gendlin emotion implies narrowed focus whereas felt sense is received by states of wide, open focus giving an unclear response to the total context and relationship. Gendlin teaches a step by step programme to help one contact the felt sense, the body's response to the whole circumstance beneath our conscious experience[32]. He recommends first clearing a space to focus on present awareness or a specific problem, secondly listening to what arises, whether bodily sensation or emotional tone. Then one should try to "get a handle" on this experience; some word or phrase which reflects the tone of the felt sense, e.g. "sharp", "sticky", "fearful", etc. Going back and forth between the statement and the feeling, one changes the statement if a more appropriate one arises, attempting to make the match ever more resonant. One, then asks what is the relation between this statement and the problematic. At this stage one should be wholly receptive to whatever arises. In actuality, this very meditative staying with the experience, and not being drawn away from the experience itself, by conceptual diffusion and storylines, is often enough for a definite shift in feeling, and some insight to arise These messages can then be translated into cognitive terms, but in first listening to the meaning that the body holds, we may discover a different perspective on the problem.

Gendlin does not mention meditation in his explication of Focusing and the felt sense, although I suggest that what he is advocating comes close to techniques of meditation, particularly in the following: "We need a new conceptual pattern for our concept of 'felt sense', on which has the more basic unity preceding the inner/outer split, the self/other split, the affect/cognition split and the acting/speaking split."[33] This, surely points towards non-conceptual direct knowledge or insight. Gendlin does, however, as mentioned earlier, compare the felt sense to Heidegger's concept of *Befindlichbkeit*, mood or affectedness or attunement.[34]

Another Western attempt to explore meditative states is that of Mihalyi Csikzentmihalyi, who since the 1970s has been attempting to reformulate methods of controlling consciousness, and mind training according to the contemporary Western cultural climate.[35]. He see his work as an exploration of states of "optimal experience" he terms "flow". A state which he claims occurs when the information coming into consciousness is congruent with its goals, and rewards are intrinsic within the action. One of the chief factors of the flow experience is the merging of action and awareness, so that, while there is no loss of self or of consciousness, what is lost during this state of optimal experience is any consciousness of the *concept* of self. Such experience is autotelic, or self-rewarding, carried out and experienced for its own sake, as an end in itself, never as a means to some different end. According to Csikzentmihalyi, the fulfilled and self-regulating self is one that can transform potentially chaotic experience into flow. He suggests that there are four states necessary to achievement of this; setting goals, becoming immersed in the activity, paying attention to what is happening and learning to enjoy or letting go. Results of such achieved experiences of flow show many of the qualities often connected with meditation. For example, his researches into deep flow experiences in rock climbing mention terms such as "one-pointedness of mind", "merging of action and awareness", "timelessness", "happiness", "integration of mind and body", and "oneness with nature".[36] Such states occur in an experience of unity with some other – musical instrument or tool, person or the natural world. Csikzentmihalyi notes that if evolution leads to ever greater complexity, complexity itself is the result of both differentiation and integration. He points out that in recent history vast advances have been made in the differentiation of consciousness and individual separation, and suggests that future complexity may consist in development of the skills of integration. This is again the theme of the step beyond egocentricity, much repeated in contemporary discourse and central to Buddhism.

Meditation in the Therapeutic Encounter

Perhaps the most important aspect of the meditative state in psychotherapy lies in its extension to a way of conducting the therapeutic encounter; a way of being for the therapist with a client. For as research has shown, it is within the interaction between the person of the therapist and the person of the client that change and healing occur.[37] Medard Boss relates that Freud saw the therapeutic relationship, as the "focal point of therapy, – the very core of therapeutic action, its basis and arena, whether or not the people taking part in it are aware of its therapeutic significance."[38] In view of what has been discussed above relating to the interdependence of self and other, knower and known, it should make sense that a meditative state (or a state of wide-focused unfixed attention as far as possible from the normal, close-focused state of reification), is a state best able to penetrate into the intermediate state of relationship.[39] One of the Buddhist psychotherapy trainings refers to this as Joint Practice. Its founder, Maura Sills has written: "Core Process Psychotherapy is simply a joint enquiry into relationship. It seems that if one can abide in the immanent experiential moment, no suffering arises. Our reactive relationship to experience is the vehicle for confusion and ignorance with its concomitant suffering."[40]

Freud wrote of the necessity to suspend the critical faculty during psychoanalysis, encouraging analysts "to suspend ... judgement and give ... impartial attention to everything there is to observe."[41] He advocated a state of 'evenly suspended attention'.

> "For as soon as anyone deliberately concentrates his attention to a certain degree, he begins to select from the material before him; one point will be fixed in his mind with particular clearness and some other will be correspondingly disregarded, and in making this selection he will be following his expectations or inclinations. This however is precisely what must not be done."[42]

When emotions and mental states are treated with such bare attention to whatever arises, stripped of identification and reaction, they are transformed. Such attention, of itself, is healing. The acquisition of and tolerance for such bare attention, the attainment of the witness state, is a skill which needs some cultivation and one which is of great value in psychotherapy.

John Welwood has compared this with meditation, and I consider that his description is worth quoting at length:

> "In the therapy situation, the client's problems or emotions are like the thoughts that arise when you are sitting. You, the listener, provide the space which coming back to the breath allows in meditation. You have to fully respect and bow to the form – the client's real problem – listen to it and take it in. If you don't do that, there isn't a connection between the two of you that can effect healing.... The transformation that happens between two people in therapy is similar to what may take place inside a single person in meditation. In mindfulness practice, as painful thoughts and emotions arise, we note them, bow to them, acknowledge them, then let them go and come back to the breath, which is a concrete manifestation of open space. This process of going into and out of form in meditation is what allows transformation to take place ... the great challenge of working on oneself is in bringing our larger open awareness to bear on our frozen karmic structures ... Our large awareness usually gets buried or stuck in problems, emotion, reactions, or else it may try to detach and fly away into the sky. But a third alternative is to stay with our frozen structures and transform them. That is the core of practice, I believe, in both psychotherapy and meditation."[43]

Similarly in an interview, a teacher of meditation speaks of his experience of teaching a meditation class for therapists from three perspectives. The first is the general human one, "the second was the advantage for the therapist of being in a meditative state while they conduct therapy. Such a state creates the attentional focus and emotional dispassion that is a good therapeutic milieu ... The third thing I taught them was that *some* clients, but of course not all, could be guided by the therapist into a meditative state, talking about their issues and doing their therapy *within* the 'witness state.'"[44]

Ann Klein's description of the alternation between analytical and stabilising orientations of meditation in the context of the cultivation of compassion could stand as a presentation of the method of a Buddhist inspired psychotherapy by merely replacing compassion as the focus with whatever mind state occurs as the client's focus of attention. First she speaks of reflecting cognitively on the nature of compassion, then: "If in the course of reflection one taps into a strong feeling of compassion, one stabilizes oneself on that feeling. (This is not to deny that analysis is also a form of experience, but to emphasize that there is a shift from *reflecting on* compassion to *experiencing* it.) When a feeling of equanimity, love or compassion arises, one simply stays with that feeling until it fades away, whereupon one can refurbish it by recalling instances of, or supporting reasons for, compassionate connectedness."[45] Thus we can see how the meditative model reveals a way whereby the conceptual may connect with the non-conceptual; a way of being that moves freely back and forth between experience and reflection, reason and emotion, conceptual and non-conceptual domains.

Some recent experiments carried out in Italy with EEG tests has shown that in altered states the brain waves of different individuals become remarkably synchrononised.[46] This research, carried out using a device designed to measure levels of synchronisation in EEG patterns between the left and right brain hemispheres in one person, as well as synchronisation between different persons, indicates that in states of deep meditation there is significant increase in the synchronisation of the left and right hemispheres, and that also when two people meditate together their respective EEG patterns also become synchronised. Such research would support the experiential suppositions that a joint mindful or meditative state is one in which deep communication, healing and insight are most likely to occur. Different descriptions are to be found from different approaches which however seem to describe similar states. Freud speaks of "evenly suspended attention" while Krishnamurti describes it as "choiceless awareness." In the words of Humanistic psychotherapist John Rowan the essence of it is "a kind of deliberate unfocusing ... openness to one's own experience as well as that of the other in a context of action."[47] The aim of the therapist, as practised by meditators, is to suspend intentional thinking, but to remain aware of experience in the present moment.[48]

Conclusions

An enormous amount of research into meditation has been carried out in the last few decades. It is beyond the scope of this work to review it here.[49] Broadly speaking the results have been very varied and inconclusive. Perhaps the differences in meditative techniques and in the aims and expectations of the meditators themselves, and the emphasis on short-term outcomes and inexperienced meditators have militated against successful or conclusive results.[50] Another suggestion is that the approach to research on meditation has been too divorced from its theoretical background.[51]

However experientially, mindfulness meditation has been found to be of great value in the training of psychotherapists, allowing them to gain a familiarity with and flexible control of their own mind states, so that they can be with them and with their clients with *their* mind states in as open and non-judgmentally receptive a manner as possible. In the therapeutic encounter the therapist will foster mindfulness and awareness allowing emotions and thoughts to arise into consciousness and helping to bring the client into touch with their inner life. They will offer therapy as joint practice, a meditation shared in which the therapist is guide and protector helping the client to explore, in a protected space, issues which might be overwhelming if faced alone and unprotected. The gain for both meditator and therapy client is the achievement of awareness of the frames and lenses that we place between us and the process of experience; the ability to see the structures we have erected in a vain attempt to control the flow of process, so that we may be able to loosen or transform them. We cannot control the flow, but if we can have some control over our minds, we can move flexibly with the waves whatever the wind, and experience flow ourselves. As Śāntideva said:

> Where would I find enough leather
> With which to cover the surface of the earth?
> But (wearing) leather just on the soles of my shoes
> is equivalent to covering the earth with it.
>
> Likewise it is not possible for me
> To restrain the external course of things;
> But should I restrain this mind of mine
> What would be the need to restrain all else?"[52]

The amount or extent of mind restraint and reframing however will vary between Buddhism and the therapeutic project. For, as discussed in the next chapter, the goals for psychotherapy and for Buddhism are in some respects very different.

Part Three

Fruition

Goals and Implications

CHAPTER SEVEN

Goal

"Walking in the great monotony
no music now or harmony
only the naked life-sense
and the wind of silence
eros and logos here conjoined
long dark-blue sea and quiet sand
a gull's wing makes a lonely sign
in the night of meanings: a dawn."[1]

What are the goals of psychotherapy and of Buddhism? Can they be compared? I would suggest that the goals and the results of Buddhism and psychotherapy are, in fact, both comparable and similar qualitatively, though different quantitatively. The quality in question is that of liberation, liberation from confinement, ignorance and grasping through the cultivation of awareness, clear perception and experience. For Buddhism the liberation sought is no less than *nirvāṇa;* ultimate truth and ultimate liberation from *saṃsāra*, the realm of conventional or confining truth and all its dependent suffering. In psychotherapy the goal is narrower. It is a more or less conditional freedom, ranging from freedom from specific ills, which cause particular areas of suffering or constriction, to an open-ended attempt to push back the constraints to our human potential.

To some, perhaps, it seems unsuitable to compare the two enterprises, one concerned with the absolute and transcendent, the other firmly based in the relative and confining. The present Dalai Lama has been one of the most consistent advocates of the use and possibilities of Buddhist mind training within contexts other and lesser than those of the traditional Buddhist path. In his address to the Oxford Union in 1991 he stated: "Just as I believe it myself I often mention to others that it is possible for people to adopt various Buddhist meditative techniques or mental trainings without being a Buddhist ... After all, adoption of a specific religion is the business of the individual whereas the techniques of training the mind can remain universally applicable."[2] Elsewhere he has also written with regard to Buddhist mind training: "The primary aim ... is the attainment of enlightenment, but it is possible to experience even mundane benefits, such as good health by practising them."[3] He gives two reasons for the importance of understanding the nature of mind; firstly for its importance in the understanding of *karma,* and secondly for the crucial part states of mind play in the experience of happiness and sadness.

One may also take a developmental view seeing a distinction between different categories of liberation; a worldly or psychological liberation of self achievement, and a sacred liberation with a transcendent goal, suggesting that some degree of the first is a prerequisite for the latter.

> "Liberation in the profane and personal realm has as its goal the health and the liberation of the soul or the awareness. This health is psychologically oriented ... and this constitutes the precondition for any further forms of liberation." ... "The more ignorance can be transformed into knowledge, the more wisdom and awareness can be actualized. This is the primary goal in Buddhism, prior to the asking of any transcendental questions. The more unconscious contents can be raised from the unconscious and the more consciousness can be increased, the more independence from the dangers of unconscious processes then develops, reducing dependence on drives and libidinous fixations. This is the task of Western psychology."[4]

From a different school of psychotherapy, Padmal de Silva has written widely comparing the behaviour modification methods of Early Buddhism to those of contemporary behavioural psychotherapy, arguing that Buddhist teachings contain many useful strategies for behavioural and cognitive modification, and show that the Buddha was concerned with his followers' daily lives as well as their ultimate liberation.[5] Even within Buddhism itself, the very process of liberation may be termed psychological, based as it is upon exploration of existing mind states, starting from contemplation of their unsatisfactoriness in order to facilitate an ever-increasing understanding of what may be more healthy.[6] For as well as the Buddha's instructions to individuals concerning behaviour, Buddhism in its total philosophy of interdependence and emptiness, and its methods of promoting insight provides a rich resource for liberation to any degree. Even within a psychotherapy confined within personal history, an awareness of interdependence and the ultimate emptiness of separated and permanent essence may be helpful and liberating.

The Buddhist Goal

Comparison of the transcendental and relative gives rise to discussion concerning two differing approaches within Buddhism itself – whether its goal is liberation *from* the world or liberation *within* the world. Within the canonical texts support for both approaches may be found. In transcendental, otherworldly mode salvation is sought away from the natural cyclic world of death and finitude. Support for this position can without doubt be found in Buddhism, particularly in Early Buddhism, and in Theravāda, with exhortation to leave the civilised world, and enter the forest to contemplate the horrors of the body and attain liberation or *nirvāṇa* from the samsaric world of suffering.[7] The definition of *nirvāṇa* is difficult, and entire books have dealt with this subject alone.[8] For this approach, nirvāṇa while not a locus like the Christian heaven is definitely utterly transcendent. Discussion of this view often rests upon the verses:

> "Monks, there is a not-born, a not-become, a not-made, a not-compounded. Monks, if that unborn, not-become, not-made, not-compounded were not, there would be apparent no escape from this here that is born, become, made, compounded.
>
> But since, monks, there is an unborn .... therefore the escape from this here that is born, become ... is apparent ...[9]

There is, however, evidence for the alternative view, for an immanent transcendence, liberation *within* the world, even within the early canon. It may be pointed to in the Buddha's steadfast refusal to spend time in consideration of theoretical and philosophical concerns, as shown in the Mālunkyaputta sutta, and in the indeterminate questions which the Buddha refused to adjudicate upon, all of which have an otherworldly bent. He was, without doubt, concerned with conduct in this world, leading to entrapment within the confines of the conventional and ill-perceived In the Rohitassa sutta in his response to the seer Rohitassa who had unsuccessfully walked continuously for a hundred years in search of the end of the world where "one does not get born, nor grow old, nor die, nor pass away, nor get reborn", the Buddha declared: "It is in this very fathom-long physical frame with its perceptions and mind, that I declare, lies the world and the arising of the world, and the cessation of the world, and the path leading to the cessation of the world."[10] In a note to his translation of the Rohitassa sutta, Ñāṇananda describes the position of the one who has attained enlightenment:

> "The emancipated one is 'in the world' but not 'of the world.' For him the world is no longer the arena of a life-and-death struggle in which he is sorely involved but one vast illustration of the first principles of impermanence, suffering and not-self – of the separative (*nanabhavo*), privative (*vinabhavo*) and transformative (*annathabhavo*) nature of all existence."[11]

In the *Dhātuvibhanga sutta* of the *Majjhima Nikāya nirvāṇa* is equated with Truth. "O bhikkhu, that which is unreality is false;

that which is reality, Nibbana, is Truth. Therefore, O bhikkhu, a person so endowed is endowed with this Absolute Truth, For, the Absolute Noble Truth is Nibbana, which is Reality."[12] If *nirvāṇa* is truth, then what is truth? In chapter three we saw that the absolute truth is that all phenomena are dependently arisen, and that they are empty of inherent or essential reality or absolute substance. The realisation of the absolute truth is to see things "as they are", without the ignorance that sees them and ourselves as independent and substantial with its concomitant desiring and grasping. The extinction of ignorance and desire is thus the extinction of suffering which is *nirvāṇa*. Thus there may be, perhaps, a middle path between liberation *from* and liberation *within*. Understanding itself is liberation – thus liberation from the confines of human nature occurs through understanding that nature.[13]

This coincides with the Mahāyāna view which we saw expressed by Nāgārjuna, that *saṃsāra* and *nirvāṇa* are not essentially different, they are different perspectives.

> Life's no different from nirvana,
> nirvana's no different from life.
> Life's horizon is nirvana's horizon.
> The two are exactly the same.[14]

As Joan Stambaugh has noticed in relation to Dogen: "...spirituality does not have to be turned into anything metaphysical beyond this world. Dogen can show that there are unimaginable dimensions of this world right there if we will only open our minds to them."[15] Stambaugh suggests that the approach of Nāgārjuna is primarily logical, while that of Dogen is experiential and phenomenological. Both teach that *saṃsāra* and *nirvāṇa* are related, and each in some way depends upon the other; within the relative realm of ordinary existence the ultimate can only be pointed to with language which is of necessity itself conventional and confining.

> Without conventions,
> you cannot reveal the sublime.

> Without knowing the sublime,
> you cannot nirvana."[16]

In the Mahāyāna and the Vajrayāna there is more support for the view of liberation within the world[17] . This view sees the problem not as the problem of world in itself, but rather with our response to it; not with impermanence and finitude itself, but with our egocentric fear of it. Thus, rather than escape from the world, the attempt is to find a balance within impermanence.[18]

Even the "unborn", quoted above with reference to the transcendent view, can carry another interpretation if compared with the following words quoted by Tsong Kha pa in his commentary to Nāgārjuna's *Mūlamadhyamikakārikā*: "Whatever arises from conditions is unborn". Here Tsong Kha pa is concerned with stating the identity of dependent origination and emptiness, and the non-identity of emptiness and non-existence: "'Contingently arising' means 'empty of inherent existence.' 'Emptiness' does not mean 'the absence of functioning reality'."[19] The absolute truth is definitely revealed as the perception of the emptiness or dependent origination of all phenomena. The view is that of an immanent transcendence.[20]

This interrelationship of transcendence and immanence is emphasised by Nishitani Keiji in his great exploration of emptiness as an escape from nihilism in *Religion and Nothingness*. As he states:

> "... the field of emptiness is a field of absolute transcendence, a transcendence of time and place, of causal necessity, and of the very world-nexus itself.[21] But this absolute transcendence is at the same time an absolute immanence. Saṃsāra-*sive*-nirvāṇa, it has been noted, is true saṃsāra and true nirvāṇa; but nirvāṇa, the absolute far side, only becomes manifest as saṃsāra, which is the absolute near side. The field of true emptiness becomes manifest only in unison with that dynamic nexus of being-doing-becoming in time, or rather *as* time."[22]

This more immanent approach to liberation is more compatible with contemporary psychotherapy, and is, I would agree with Rita Gross, who has given much consideration to these two modes of freedom *from* and *within* the world: "the dominant emphasis of Western Buddhists, if not of Buddhism throughout the world today."[23] It is more in conformity with the contemporary postmodern world, with a post-patriarchal Buddhism.[24] In terms of the Bakhtinian tripartite model, if the first stage is that of immersion in the natural cosmos, the second is that of the division into good/bad, life/death, body/spirit of the individual life cycle and a transcendent liberation, and the third or dialogic approach reinserts the human figure into the cosmological environment, in a non-hierarchical, non-egocentric transcendent-*sive*-immanent discourse. Liberation *from* the constraints of ordinary human being is only achieved *through* understanding of that human condition.

Goals in Psychotherapy

Within the wide field of psychotherapy with its many schools there are large differences in the quantitative goals of different therapies. They range from behavioural or cognitive retraining to overcome specific phobias and problems, to wide-ranging 'life-changing' therapy seeking increased potential, and to attempts, co-terminous with religious quest, to expand the self beyond the personal in awareness of belonging to a greater whole. However, here too, the aim is always that of freedom from some confinement through the achievement of a larger meaning. People seek psychotherapeutic help because they feel behaviourally, cognitively or affectively confined by patterns of perception or action that seem beyond their conscious control. The goal is to free themselves from a set of automatic, unconscious or uncontrolled reactions and identifications to a less pre-ordained, more flexible openness and responsiveness to ever-changing situations.[25] Psychotherapeutic projects address the tendency of human beings to close down with defensive structures in the face of the responsive openness or transparency which is the goal to different degrees both of Buddhism and psychotherapy.[26]

Behavioural and cognitive therapy has, in general, specific targets and aims, the instigation of new and more adaptive behavioural patterns, leading to a greater degree of control and choice. As the goals of psychoanalytic work, Freud spoke of exchanging neurotic misery for ordinary unhappiness, and the ability to love and work, as well as the replacement of the uncontrolled id by the ego and superego. Such goals, or perhaps their later interpretation rather than the founder's intention, have been criticised as leading to social conformity and adaptation to conventional norms, at the expense of individuality. In response to this, the goals of Humanistic psychotherapy are, in general to support and expand the sense and potential of the self, and to explore the real and genuine self, rather than the false self of conformity. In existential terms the aim is freely-chosen authenticity. In terms of Wilber's Spectrum model, it is the achievement of the integrated body/mind centaur stage. Transpersonal psychotherapy would extend the boundaries of self further to include spiritual needs and altered states of consciousness.

In its furthest reaches Existential and Humanistic therapy may be hard to distinguish from Transpersonal. James Bugental, an Existential Humanistic psychotherapist, speaks of therapeutic goals in terms of different levels ranging from deficiency levels with aims of increased coping efficiency to "Being levels of therapeutic growth goals" which involve facing existential anxieties, freeing oneself from identification with a particular self image, and even transcendence. He defines transcendence as the "going beyond" of such usually unthinkingly accepted dichotomies as good/bad, right/wrong, I/other, life/death, in a manner that does not discard the comparisons but sees them in a more inclusive perspective. The same may be said of all the levels of therapy; they are not discarded but seen in wider perspective. Bugental writes of an ever-enlarging sense of identity distinguished into "me" as an object of perception, "the self" as self-concept abstracted out of many perceptions of one's "me" and finally "I": "I-*process* is a term to designate the subject of one's being, the beingness of a human life."[27] Of this he speaks in terms familiar to Buddhist discourse: "When I begin to realize that my truest identity is as process and not as fixed substance, I am on the verge of a terrible emptiness and a miraculous freedom." and: "We begin to realise that the world which has been the solid foundation of our being is equally a construction of our awareness." and again: "we are the process of being aware, not the content of the awareing."[28] Such aims bring one at the least within the sphere of the Buddhist goal.

To explore similarities in the concern of both Buddhism and psychotherapy with liberation, I believe it is useful to enter into the sphere of metaphor. Throughout the discourse of both Buddhism and psychotherapy certain metaphors recur constantly. The central ones, from which almost all others radiate are those of space and light. At the centre, the point of origin or of no-origin, and of goal, there is unlimited space, mind or awareness. From this progressive distinction, rigidification and conceptualisation spread out. Both Buddhism and psychotherapy speak constantly in terms of loosening structures of thought, of seeing through discrimination, and obstructions, of deconstructing our perception which is clouded with conceptuality, emotions or defences. H. Guenther writes of the relationship in terminology between Buddhist *rDzogs chen* and Medard Boss' *Daseinsanalyse*. He compares the concepts of "opening-up" and "illuminating" from *rDzogs chen* to Boss' terms: "world openness", "clearing" and "world disclosing." In terms of both systems conceptual mind or, in Tibetan *sems,* is a constriction and narrowing from the viewpoint of Being as a whole. According to Boss, such constriction is most conspicuous in mental patients, and Guenther points out that from the viewpoint of *rDzogs chen* we might all be listed as mental patients.[29]

Similarly the authors of a recent book on the psychology of religion liken the psychology of religious knowing to that of personal exploration in therapy, and write: "The great quest for both personal and religious insight requires openness .... Once the necessary space has been created, we need to learn attentiveness that is broad sustained and penetrating."[30] The work of psychotherapy is to shed light on the implicit concepts and beliefs that often unconsciously lie behind our explicit actions. It is to bring awareness to these areas, that we may explore them without fear, in a safe place, releasing the charge of the hidden fear or anxiety, liberating the energy confined in their resistance for more helpful actions, allowing us more space for choice, and some degree of control. A suitable conception of our relationship with the world is also necessary to estimate what control is desirable and possible. Perhaps in the words of the Serenity prayer: "God grant me the serenity to accept the things I cannot change, the courage to change the things I can, and the wisdom to know the difference."[31]. The aim is suppleness and flexibility that can ride with the wave, part way between drowning and becoming as a water drop within the wave, that beautiful metaphor of the ultimate Buddhist practice. For there is no doubt that the complete aim of Buddhism is quantitatively different from that of psychotherapy.

Contrasts

The quantitative difference between Buddhism and the psychotherapies lies in the extent of the awareness, meaning and liberation which is sought. Obviously the more restricted the goal of the therapy the further it is from comparison with the total Buddhist endeavour, and the more open-minded the aim, the nearer. Yet however open-ended the psychotherapy, Buddhism stretches further to goals of total perfection, total awareness, total freedom from all cognitive and emotional afflictions, in short to enlightenment. It aims for a thorough transformation from the egocentric vision of the ordinary man or woman to an understanding of the interconnection and emptiness of all life, leading ultimately to the Bodhisattva's vow to abstain from personal liberation until all beings are liberated.[32]

While it is a contention of this work, as stated in chapter four during discussion of views of the self, that, in fact, much psychotherapy is held back in its contemporary relevance by its confinement to the egocentric individual, and that it is the task and challenge of a contemporary psychotherapy in the postmodern world to transcend these egocentric limitations, yet there is no denying that there is a great difference in the degree to which Buddhism, and even the most aware psychotherapy, promotes non-egocentrism. For Buddhism the extinction of ego-centrism encompasses the extinction of both possessive craving, conceit and the false view of self. As psychologically explained by Bhikku Ñāṇananda in a note to his translation of the *Rohitassa sutta* which we mentioned earlier:

> "The culmination of the 'not-self' attitude is the eradication of the conceit, '(I) am': '. . . the percipient of 'not-self' attains to the eradication of the conceit 'I am', which is Nibbana here and now,' (*Anguttara* V 358). The removal of the subtle conceit, 'I am' (*asmimana*) is tantamount to a destruction of that delusive superimposed frame from which all measurings and reckonings of the world were directed through the instrumentality of the sense-faculties, and by which the mass of relative concepts in the form of sense-data were so organized as to give a picture of 'the world' with 'self' mirrored on it. What we call the normal functioning of the five external sense, is but the outward manifestation of the notion 'I am'".[33]

A psychotherapeutic project would agree with the idea of the picture of world with self mirrored on it. It would advocate awareness of the imposed self, and if it found this dysfunctional, would attempt to facilitate a more appropriate, or even a more flexible sense of self, but would rarely, if ever, pursue non-self to the same extent as Buddhism.

In part this is the result of a further contrast, a distinction of focus in the different approaches to the individual. Buddhism is concerned pre-eminently with the structure of mind rather than its contents, tending towards the universal rather than the particular. For Westerners problems of identity pertain to matters of choice, style and individual personality, whereas for Buddhists they are concerned with mental processes and structures which are built up upon open awareness. Thus liberation for Buddhists is from identification with any conception of self per se, and from the view of a world constructed and seen from such a self-centred perspective. Whereas psychotherapeutically, identification with a specific position may be seen as individually limiting, but normally only in terms of exchanging such identification for another more healthy or adapted position.

Psychotherapy, though influenced by theoretical overviews, focuses on the particularities of the individual story and symptoms.[34] And, as mentioned before, the cultural background and ideas of the self are very different. Here, perhaps is a particular arena, where more than ever, a dialogue rather than a domination of either view or a direct mapping of Buddhism onto Western psychotherapy is useful, and a balance of universal and individual is helpful. However, in a contemplative approach, while the individual elements may be heard and attended to, without either being grasped too tightly nor rejected, they may be seen in a wider context as well, allowing for an understanding of the ultimate metaphoricity or emptiness of all identification.

There are, certainly, dangers in confusing Buddhism and psychotherapy, and these must not be overlooked. In chapter four, during discussion of the self, notice was taken of the dangers of the transpersonal approach without adequate concern for the intra and interpersonal. This is especially important where one is dealing with systems of thought which originate from very different cultural assumptions concerning individuality and selfhood from those to which we are accustomed in the West. At the first cross cultural meeting between the Dalai Lama and other spiritual teachers and western psychotherapists, His Holiness was astonished by the notion of lack of self esteem. A positive sense of self (though not, perhaps, the individualised one of western standards) is assumed as the starting place for the Buddhist path. The alienation, emptiness (in the western sense of privation) and longing so familiar to western psychotherapists is not familiar to the Tibetan outlook.

We have noted earlier Wilber's description of what he terms the pre/trans fallacy, Engler's developmental views, and also John Welwood's concern about spiritual bypassing.[35] Psychiatrists Robin Skinner and Nina Coltart both write of their concern about this possible confusion. Skynner speaks of the ways in which knowledge gained from spiritual practices may be used as an escape from growth, or may, in fact, be used to support and strengthen limited and narrow views. Referring both to Skynner and Welwood, Nina Coltart points out the need for a healthy sense of personal identity before attempting any kind of self-transcendence, suggesting: "For a Westerner to proceed healthily on the spiritual path which may lead to self-transcendence and loss of 'the fortress of I', there needs must *exist already* a stable strong sense of personal identity – not necessarily a happy one."[36] From the opposite pole, Welwood himself points out the danger of trying to psychologize spiritual teachings, turning them into mere mental health techniques and minimising their profound *alternative* views of the world.

Having considered these similarities and differences between Buddhist and psychotherapeutic goals, I should now like to consider some implications of a Buddhist inspired psychotherapy within our lived experience.

CHAPTER EIGHT

Implications

So far, in relation to the ground of our enquiry, starting from the foundations of experience and meaning, we have considered first Western therapies, then Buddhist philosophy with an emphasis on those doctrines which I consider to be most central for a Buddhist influenced approach to psychotherapy. Next, considerations of the self within Buddhism and within various contemporary Western discourses, have revealed many similarities in view, yet some Western difficulties in affectively coming to terms with this view. In relation to the path, the instantiation of views, we have considered the ethical stance and meditation practices of Buddhism in relation to a contemporary psychotherapy. The aim and the goals of psychotherapy and Buddhism have been compared and contrasted, and seen, I hope, to be compatible in terms of aim, yet contrasted in terms of the extent or breadth of that aim. I would, therefore, like now to look at the implications of the views and path of Buddhism for psychotherapy, considering them in the context of contemporary discourse and of human lived experience which is the arena of psychotherapy. What exactly can Buddhist discourse provide for psychotherapy?

To facilitate consideration of the implications of a Buddhist contemplative approach and its relevance to contemporary Western discourse and to our experience, I intend to present this in terms of the three *maṇḍalas,* or dimensions of being of body, speech and mind, a traditional Buddhist tripartite division encompassing an overlapping approach, which I hope will reveal the areas of interest, and do so in ways which will facilitate an overcoming of the traditional dualistic distinctions of mind/body, subject/object and figure/background. These three, gates of our action and interaction, form our horizons of experience and meaning. Guenther has described them as the three gates "through which the enworlded individual goes our to meet his enworldedness."[1] In Western discourse there are distinctions comparable to these, body, speech and mind. Heidegger writes of the *existentiales* of "affectedness", "telling" and "understanding"[2]. Mark Johnson speaks of "embodiment", "imagination" and "understanding". Geoffrey Samuel uses the terms "body", "culture" and "mind" to stand for states of underlying relatedness, saying: "These states are descriptions of patterns of relationships, both relationships among human beings and relationship between human beings and their natural environment. In other words they are states of the entire human ecosystem."[3] In earlier Western discourse the concept of human nature was also delineated in a tripartite model of spirit, soul and matter or body. The Nicene Council in 787 reduced this to the more familiar dualistic one of spirit or mind, and body or matter. As noticed earlier such a dualistic distinction, accompanied by a move away from embeddedness in the natural world, has simultaneously placed value on spirit at the expense of body.

In Tantric Buddhism a distinction is made between the words used to describe ordinary perception and awakened perception. Thus ordinary body/mind, speech and mentation are designated by the terms *lus, ngag, yid/sems*, while the gates of transformed perception; embodiment as interaction (which Guenther terms "*gestalt* dynamics"), speech as communicative capacity, and mind as spirituality or resonance are designated by the honorific terms *sku, gsung, thugs*. The description of mind as spirituality or resonance encompasses the idea of mind as interdependence and our participation in being as a whole, in a manner reminiscent of Heidegger's "openness to Being". Here, in each dimension, we find both an everyday pathological relation and the potential for a transformed one. The former is closed, encased in reification and distinctions such as body/mind, subject/object and individual/world; the latter is open, permeable, dynamic and interdependent.

These three, body, speech and mind, are aligned also with the three Buddha bodies, Dharmakāya, Saṃbhogakāya and Nirmāṇakāya. These three are described somewhat differently by different Buddhist schools and approaches. Following Herbert Guenther's interpretation of Tibetan Vajrayāna, the *kāya* or body may be taken as a structure of experience, *sku* the word used for the transformed experience of embodiment is the word used to translate the Sanskrit *kāya*. Although experience is a whole, yet three aspects of it can be discerned; which he terms immediate-intuitive, mediating-reflective and factual aspects.

The Dharmakāya is the "hidden source of man's being", the body of mystical experience, the wisdom of things as they are, accompanied by joy. The Saṃbhogakāya, sometimes translated as the "enjoyment body", encompassing concepts which will reoccur in our discussion of speech, is a "structure of sensuous elements of imagery which are felt to give knowledge, and in the contemplation of which we feel to have come nearer to knowledge." Perhaps the most difficult realm to delineate, it is the realm of inner perception, of ideation and imagination; in Western terms, I believe it would be home to such concepts as the Platonic Ideas and the archetypes of the collective unconscious.

Nirmāṇakāya is the body of form, which on the level of nescience and division from true nature, a sentient being believes to be her real body. Traditionally this varies according to the six realms[4]. Stephen Batchelor describes the doctrine of the threefold Buddha body as describing three stages in the process of unfolding from formlessness to form; from the silent depths of experience (dharma body) through ideas and words (enjoyment body) to embodiment in action (form or emanation body). The dharma body, being formless, is never depicted, the enjoyment body at the level of ideas and images is depicted in the form of idealised Buddha figures, and the emanation body alone is individualised in the aspect of ordinary humans.[5]

It seems necessary to me that if we are to maintain our balance in a world which both Buddhist and contemporary Western discourse tells us is compounded, impermanent and outsideless, that we ground ourselves first within embodiment.

Embodiment

> *"When walking, just walk.*
> *When sitting, just sit.*
> *Above all, don't wobble."*
> – Yun-Men

> *"How wondrous this, how mysterious.*
> *I carry fuel, I draw water."*[6]
> – Layman P'ang

Traditionally Eastern and Western approaches to embodiment are quite distinct. In the West that tradition has been for a mind/body dualism, with some bias towards the mind as the stronger and more important part. In contrast in the East there are many traditions which espouse a view of mind/body oneness. This profound initial difference has important consequences. Arising from this first distinction in the view of mind and body is a vastly different approach to philosophy and science. In the West these disciplines have developed separately, with science focusing on the physical world as external nature, and mostly ignoring the relationship between mind and world. In the East traditional science and philosophy has taken as its starting point the lived human body, and from this focus investigated the relationship between microcosm and macrocosm. A further difference resulting from the different approaches to the relationship of mind and body is shown in attitudes to training. The Western assumption is that training proceeds from mind to body. In the East views of mind/body oneness are the foundation for methods of self-cultivation which affect, train and transform the mind through the body. Another implication of these differing approaches is found in the different relationship between theory and praxis. In the East praxis has always taken priority over theory. Not so in the West. In Greece, the *theiros*, the spectator was considered to possess the overview of the gods, the position of privilege over the mere actors and participants. The original *theiros* was the ambassador who travelled to neighbouring city states to observe their religious rites and dramas to bring back home what might be considered of value. Professor of Philosophy Mervyn Sprung explores this Greek adherence to the sense of life as theory, and the resultant supremacy of the intellect in his most recent book. He believes that in the postmodern era: "Philosophy as the pursuit of one reasoned truth, is not longer possible", and seeks for what he terms a "vivial" understanding based on sensory and behavioural experience in contrast to a purely intellectual or theoretical approach.[7]

In the West today, there is both movement away from theory towards embodied experience and praxis, as evinced in the views discussed above, and a contradictory movement shown in formalism and in the reading of world as text.[8] As should by now be obvious, this work is interested in and strongly upholds the trend towards a view of mind/body oneness, and finds in the Eastern philosophy a sense of the value of embodied experience as mediating between self and world, subject and object. Arising from, and strengthening this view, methods of self-cultivation may be, as we have seen, of immense value to psychotherapy, which explains their growing popularity and acceptance in the West. I would thus like to consider views of embodiment in Buddhism and in contemporary Western discourse which attempt to bridge the division of mind/body, subject/object.

Embodiment in Buddhism

The dimension of body in Buddhism embraces more than we normally consider as body, encompassing the mind/body continuum in its sense-based experience including its interaction with the environment. As we have already noted, Tibetan Vajrayāna distinguishes between body in its exoteric ordinary sense and its transformed esoteric sense which Guenther translates as "*gestalt*". Transformed thus, the dimension of embodiment is not our commonly shared world but a manifestation of sheer energy through light, colour and sound. A description from a recent work on Tantric Buddhism which continues Guenther's pattern of analysis, beautifully expresses both of these:

> "embodiment ... is understood to be not a 'soul' in a 'body' but rather a multilayered mind/body continuum of corporeality, affectivity, cognitivity, and spirituality whose layers are subtly interwoven and mutually interactive. This nonessentialist self is seen not as a boundaried or static entity but as the site of a host of energies, inner winds and flames, dissolutions, meltings, and flowings that can bring about dramatic transformations in embodied experience and provide a bridge between humanity and divinity."[9]

Within Buddhism we can find both a path of renunciation working within the normal shared world, and the path of transformation, imaginatively creating through visualisation and physical praxis, an alternative reality. Within the first, one uses the ordinary body and world to engage in ethically positive actions, maintaining the body as a support for meditation. Although there is a strong ascetic and world renouncing strain within Buddhism accompanied by meditation on the dissolution and disgust of the body, yet there is also much evidence for a balanced appreciation of body and world as the very foundation of practice. Śākyamuni Buddha himself failed to reach enlightenment after years of ascetic practice and bodily neglect. It was only after accepting nourishment from Sujata that he reached enlightenment preaching thereafter a "middle way" between asceticism and indulgence.

In Tsong Kha pa's commentary to Nāgārjuna's *Mūlamadhyamikakārikā,* there is a discussion of *samvṛti* or relative and conventional truth. There, Tsong Kha pa, quoting from Candrakīrti's *Madhyamakāvatāra*, gives the criterion for acceptance as conventional truth, not as we would today, as legitimised by conventions of belief or practice, but as legitimised through embodiment.

> "For the world whatever is apprehended by six unimpaired senses is considered true. Everything else stands as false for the world."[10]

Both subject and object of conventional truth are judged in relation to "consciousness of one of the six senses which is without the fault of a temporary cause for deception."[11] Internal faults which cause deception are given as eye diseases, external causes as mirror images, echoes and mirages.

The preliminaries for Tantric practice state repeatedly the necessity for appreciation of our human rebirth as being the only foundation for gaining enlightenment. "A human form fully endowed with all the liberties and opportunities to study and practise the Dharma is extremely rare and precious. It is the vehicle through which you will attain Enlightenment or, if you are not careful, a lower rebirth."[12]

The *sūtras* considered in chapter six in connection with meditation reveal a firm grounding in embodiment. The first establishment of mindfulness is the body.[13] The first exercise is awareness of breathing, which Thich Nhat Hanh calls "conscious breathing". This awareness of breathing acts as a link which unites body and mind and brings them into the present. In psychotherapy this is a most simple and useful method of bringing clients and indeed also therapists into the present moment, alert and awake to their embodied experience which includes sensation, expression and thought.[14] In the *Satipaṭṭhāna Sutta* this awareness of breathing is used to establish awareness of body and mind. The object of awareness is no longer the breath alone but body itself united with the breath.

> "Breathing in, I am aware of my whole body,
> Breathing out, I am aware of my whole body.
> Breathing in, I calm the activities of my body,
> Breathing out, I calm the activities of my body."[15]

Awareness of breath is followed by mindful observation of the positions of the body; walking, standing, sitting, lying and in action. This observation continues with closer attention to the individual parts of the body. In his commentary to this sutra Thich Nhat Hanh continues the use of breathing to accompany each step of observation. "Breathing in, I am aware of the hair on my head, Breathing out, I know that this is the hair on my head", as he says that breathing consciously helps us to dwell more easily in awareness and sustain our mindful observation. The body is then considered in its interrelationship with the universe in terms of the elements, earth, water, fire and air, of which it is composed. Such considerations emphasise our participation in the interdependent, non-self, unborn and unending nature of all that is. This contemplation is followed by the nine contemplations on the impermanence of the body, and here we find evidence of devaluation of the body, for the images suggest decay, putrefaction and impermanence. Yet in his contemporary commentary Thich Nhat Hanh suggests a different perspective. Such contemplations which he feels should only be practised by those in good mental and physical health who have conquered desire and aversion, rather than teaching hatred of our bodies and the world, should help us to see how precious life is; that it should not be wasted nor should we ignore its impermanence, but hold it lightly and freshly value it in the present moment.

In each of these observations there is a refrain:

> "This is how the practitioner remains established in the observations of the body in the body, observation of the body from the inside or from the outside, or observation of the body both from the inside and from the outside. He remains established in the observation of the process of coming-to-be in the body or the process of dissolution in the body or both in the process of coming-to-be and the process of dissolution. Or he is mindful of the fact, 'There is a body here,' until understanding and full awareness come about. He remains established in the observation, free, not caught up in any worldly consideration."[16]

Thus, as Thich Nhat Hanh points out the teachings of impermanence, selflessness and dependent origination may be realised directly through these practices of mindfully observing the body.

In her most recent work Ann Klein suggests that Buddhist mindfulness practices (citing particularly the Foundation of Mindfulness in the body) may help to provide what she terms "visceral coherence" in contrast to the narrative coherence of self sought for in the West. Such an embodied coherence is free of dependence on language with the attendant difficulties which the following chapter will address. It serves to mediate between mind and body and even, Klein suggests, between conditioned and unconditioned, providing a different way of being in the world. As most clearly stated in her own words:

> "The unconditioned is most ideally accessed by pure nonconceptual mindfulness and concentration, whereby one becomes grounded in one's own physical and mental experience. This grounded mindfulness collapses the mind/body opposition ..., suggesting the possibility of an *embodied* groundedness, one that takes its certainty and steadiness as much from a specific way of holding mind and body as from ideas or ideals. *The difference between embodying an idea and thinking it is subtle, but crucial.*"[17]

This echoes Sprung's words about the middle way: "It is the practice of wisdom, not a means to it. It embodies knowledge, but is not a knowing."[18] Such an embodied stance or posture is of the greatest possible relevance for psychotherapy.

It is in the writings of the twelfth-century Japanese monk Dogen that we find the most lived and most poetic expression of embodied practice. Dogen writes of the transformed world as the Body of the Buddha, relating such stories as that of Su Tung p'o who, enlightened by hearing the sounds of streams flowing at night, wrote the following verse of enlightenment:

> "The sounds of the valley streams are His long, broad tongue;
> The forms of the mountains are His pure body.
> At night I heard the myriad sutra-verses uttered
> How can I relate to others what they say."[19]

Although it reaches the limits of poetic expression and points to inexpressible mysteries, Dogen's teaching is grounded in the body of the world and the human. "What faith has he who does not know the body which is the spring pine, or the true reality which is, just as it is, the autumn chrysanthemum? How can he ever cut off the roots of birth and death?"[20] He also wrote manuals of practice concerning dress and rules for the kitchen. Furthermore in keeping with this Dogen preaches the oneness of practice and realisation. "In the Buddha Dharma, practice and realization are identical. Because one's present practice is practice in realization, one's initial negotiation of the way in itself is the whole of original realization ... As it is already realization in practice, realization is endless, as it is practice in realization, practice is beginningless."[21] Masao Abe suggests that this dynamic oneness of practice and attainment is mediated by the realisation of impermanence as Buddha nature; that attainment (Buddha nature) as ground, and practice (becoming a Buddha) as condition are nondualistically identical in the realisation of impermanence as Buddha nature which reveals the nonsubstantiality of attainment and the emptiness of Buddha Nature.[22] The implication of the oneness of practice and realisation is the simultaneous realisation of the identity of means and ends. In Western life the teleological approach has been largely unquestioned. This alternative approach does question such purposive living, and indeed reveals it as one of the major causes of the separation not only of means and ends, but thereby of experience and meaning. If we live always in search of future goals, we are never within our embodied experience.[23] And it is just this immersion in immediate experience with no "self" outside of this, that Francis Cook suggests is indeed for Dogen authentic self; an authentic self which is "self-transcendence, – not world-transcendence."[24] Paradoxically the more tightly the inauthentic self, which sees itself as separate from its experience, is grasped, the more there is alienation from everything seen as "not-self". If the authentic self is immediate and relational experience, the felt immediacy of things, there is no separation from experience and things, and, as we have seen earlier, "to forget the self is to be authenticated by the myriad things"; which is enlightenment. Thus authentic selfhood points to a profound way of *being in the world*.

Body in Contemporary Western Thought

Within contemporary Western thought, where attention is paid to the body in new ways, what is found is a collapsing of old distinctions and dichotomies, pre-eminently those of body versus mind, subject versus object, and of the objectivist view of the world as some pre-existing reality, about which there can be a correct "God's eye" view, of which our knowledge is a more or less correct representation. Such a view, as we have discussed, is being challenged by more interconnected and enactive accounts of the production of 'reality' as a combined effort and result of the very knowledge whereby we grasp it. These views have been more prominent in Continental than in Anglo-American philosophy. Over the last century there has been the constant theme of a search to bridge the gap between body and mind, man and world, particularly exposed by the phenono-menlogical project. We can point to Husserl's lifeworld, Heidegger's *Dasein* and Merleau-Ponty's *flesh* as attempts to convey the intertwining of the visible and the invisible. Heidegger's presentation of *Dasein* may be seen as a major signpost for such views, with its emphasis on being-in-the-world, and the precedence of existence over essence. However such emphasis on existence and experience has paradoxically mostly remained a purely intellectual emphasis. Merleau-Ponty was the one philosopher to take note of scientific research and psychology and to discuss being-in-the-world from the point of view of the interface of the physiological and psychic. Such exploration presents the human being in a different light to the traditional view. It presents both mind and body, and also subject and world as abstractions of "presence", and reinstates the embodied subject in process as one that is never finally distinct and cut off, but always already intentionally related to world. Such a conception of the human subject implies similar revision of world. In this light the dynamic lived relation of subject and world is revealed as pre-objective and pre-reflective. For such a view, development implies the emergence of subjectivity and personality from the pre-personal existence of the body, with such development occurring against a background of the pre-reflective interaction of being-in-the-world, and in dialogue with world and others.

From a more ecological perspective, David Abram in his book *The Spell of the Sensuous* builds upon the work of Husserl and Merleau-Ponty to argue for attention to embodiment in order to explore and rediscover the participatory nature of perception. His work is a plea to understand and to realise this in the deepest sense, so that we may rediscover our interdependence with world to the benefit both of humankind and the world we are fast destroying.

Heidegger suggested, as discussed earlier, that the first step away from the metaphysical tradition of reflection and representation and our forgetfulness of Being should be "the step back from the thinking which merely re-presents to the thinking which responds and recalls."[25] In a trilogy of books, David Levin has interpreted Heidegger's attempt to delineate the thinking which responds in terms of pre-reflective experiential dimensions of embodiment, thus uniting meaning and experience as discussed above in the preamble to chapter two.[26] The three titles themselves explain the different foci of this exploration; *The Body's Recollection of Being* explores the lived experience of gesture and motility, while *The Opening of Vision* continues the discussion in the field of vision, discovering a psychopathology in the contemporary approach to the visual dimension which Levin connects to nihilism, and against which he advocates a radically different vision, one which would structure the figure/ground, subject/object distinction in a new way. The third and final book in the trilogy, *The Listening Self*, addresses the potential for hearing in a way which encourages greater self-awareness and a different relation to Being. Each of these books addresses what Levin sees as the pathologies of the different senses expressed in their contemporary ways of embodiment, and considers these pathologies as both constituent of and resultant from the nihilism of the age. Levin advocates a new embodied responsive way of experiencing which could give rise to a different more open, more interactive response to Being. His argument is influenced both by Heidegger's concept of *Gelassenheit* or releasement and by Buddhism, particularly Zen, in its concern with non verbal, non-reflexive experience of "direct pointing at reality."

Another philosopher Mark Johnson, as we saw earlier, has upheld the importance of embodiment through the work he started in conjunction with linguist George Lakoff.[27] They first studied the way our life and language is formed by the structures of our imagination, the "metaphors we live by."[28] They discovered that such imaginative structures emerge from our embodied experience; that the categories and concepts we use to understand our world, and the forms of imagination which create them grow out of our bodily experience. Johnson suggests that there can be no meaning without the structures and patterns that establish relationship. These organising patterns and structures he calls "image schemata." "An image schemata is a recurring, dynamic pattern of our perceptual interactions and motor programs."[29] They are *gestalt* structures by means of which our experience manifests coherence and order.[30] An example of this would be the verticality schema. The experience of verticality, an up/down orientation is repeated in endless daily perceptions and activities, starting with our felt sense of standing upright. The verticality schema is the abstract structure of such verticality experiences, images and perceptions, and this experientially based structure is then imaginatively extended to an ever-widening field as we project patterns of experiences from one domain of experience onto another different domain. This is the task of metaphor, and for Lakoff and Johnson metaphor is not merely a linguistic term, but a fundamental structure of cognition whereby our experience is ordered and understood.[31] Thus the verticality schema is extended in order to understand quantity; "more" is "up", prices "rise", less is "down", prices "fall".

For Johnson, experience is far richer than the prevailing view of objectivism would have us believe. It "is to be understood in a very rich, broad sense as including basic perceptual, motor-program, emotional, historical, social and linguistic dimensions",[32] all those encompassed within the body, speech, mind model. Embodiment, our embodied experience (body) provides the physical level for the metaphorical projection of imagination aided by language (speech) which informs the conceptual, social and historical dimensions of life (mind)[33]. Thus meaning and experience are united: "our understanding *is* our mode of 'being in the world.'" It is the way we are meaningfully situated in our world through our bodily interactions, our cultural institutions, our linguistic tradition, and our historical context."[34] Such a view overturns that of meaning as being a conceptual and propositional representation of, and operation on, an external ahistorical reality, free of bodily constraints and of value. In its place we have a constructivist theory of understanding that emphasises embodiment as the foundation of meaning and reason, and the importance of imagination in extending and projecting spatio-temporal experience into abstract spheres. Understanding is not a reflection on prior experience, it is rather the very way we have that experience. It is the result of our body, speech and mind which together meld to make our world what it is. Later reflections on experience rest on this more basic understanding.

Much contemporary research concerning embodiment is resulting in the collapsing of the mind/body duality, challenging both philosophy's neglect of body and science's neglect of mind or consciousness. These works suggest a stance that follows neither dualism nor monism according to earlier models.[35] Exemplifying this middle track, the philosopher John Searle recently wrote: "Mental phenomena are caused by neurophysiological processes in the brain, and are themselves features of the brain ... Both consciousness and intentionality are biological processes caused by lower-level neuronal processes in the brain, and neither is reducible to something else."[36] Varela too, has written; "*Le moi cognitif est sa propre implementation, son histoire et son action sont d'un seul bloc.*"[37]

Neurobiologist Gerald Edelman whose work was considered in chapter four in relation to contemporary views of the self, is in agreement with the work of Lakoff and Johnson, and is currently searching for a biological theory of brain function and evolution which will describe *how* symbolic idealised cognitive models of language arise as the result of mechanisms of perceptual and conceptual categorisation. His theory too is concerned with the embodiment of mind, and is founded in principles of evolution applied to neurophysiology, a theory he terms the Theory of Neuronal Group Selection (TGNS).

Edelman distinguishes between what he calls primary consciousness and higher consciousness. Primary consciousness arises from developments of the cortical system which link it to the limbic system and from the development of a new kind of memory based on this linkage, which categorise responses in different brain systems according to the demands of value systems in the limbic brain stem. Phenomenal experience for a primary consciousness arises from the interaction of ongoing value-free perceptual categorisations with value-laden memory, before those perceptual events contribute further to the alteration of the memory. Primary consciousness is the precondition for the evolution of any higher-order consciousness. It is individual, continuous and intentional yet changing in concert with both world and internal signals. However, it is limited to a small interval of present time, described by Edelman as a "remembered present." Also, says Edelman, "it lacks an explicit *notion* or a concept of a personal self, and it does not afford the ability to model the past or the future as part of a correlated scene."[38] Higher consciousness, which rests upon the base of primary consciousness, requires the development of a symbolic memory which allows for the construction of a socially based concept of self and the ability to model the world in terms of past and future. For its full evolution it requires the emergence of language which we will consider in the next chapter, but prior to this Edelman considers a model of self-nonself interaction has to evolve and a socially constructed selfhood be added to the previous stratum of biological individuality. Once the self is developed, initially through social, secondly through linguistic interactions, world is developed; a world of both inner and outer events which requires naming and intending. The difficulty of understanding the self arises, according to Edelman, because of the very limits of embodiment, since the forms of embodiment that lead to consciousness are absolutely unique according to the body and individual history of each individual. Thus embodiment is the basis of our individuality. "The extended TGNS purports to explain how embodiment of mind takes place and thus connects cognition to biology. It provides a consistent basis for explaining how meaning arises from embodiment as a result of referential interactions."[39]

As noted earlier, Varela, Thompson and Rosch in their recent groundbreaking book *The Embodied Mind* bring together recent Western approaches to cognitive science, everyday lived experience and Buddhist traditions of mindfulness. In their own words: "What we are suggesting is a change in the nature of reflection from an abstract, disembodied activity to an embodied (mindful), open-ended reflection. By *embodied,* we mean reflection in which body and mind have been brought together. What this formulation intends to convey is that reflection *is* not just *on* experience, but reflection *is* a form of experience itself – and that reflective form of experience can be performed with mindfulness/awareness."[40] So embodiment is not seen as discussion of mind/body relation but as the lived foundation of our actual experience, attention to which may transform that very experience. Varela, Thompson and Rosch suggest that psychoanalysis is the discipline most familiar to Westerners that comes closest to this open-ended approach to knowledge in its idea that the "very conception of mind and of the subject who is undergoing analysis is understood to change as the web of representation in which the self in entangled is slowly penetrated through analysis."[41] It is the intention of this current work to expand this statement and to relate it to other forms of psychotherapy than psychoanalysis alone. Indeed Varela, Thompson and Rosch state that what they feel traditional psychoanalytic methods lack is the very mindfulness/awareness component which has been central to this discussion.[42]

Varela and the other thinkers discussed above, espouse a constructivist and enactive approach to cognitive science which describes how knowledge of self and world are inseparable from our bodies, our language and our social environment. Knowledge arises from ongoing interpretation that in turn arises from our capacities for understanding which are rooted in the structure of our biological embodiment and are lived in the realms of language and culture. Neither world nor self exist in isolation, nor are they non-existent Both the enactive approach to cognitive science and Buddhism wish to affirm the everyday lived world, although they propound views of self and world that are, at least initially, unfamiliar. Above all they suggest a different approach to the dualities of body/mind and subject/world.

All the new Western studies of consciousness point to a precognitive, preconscious and hitherto largely ignored, sense of embodiment. In twentieth-century studies Michael Polanyi's "tacit dimension", Edelman's "primary consciousness", Searle's "background" and Merleau-Ponty's "habitual body" and "intentional arc" of vision, comprehension and mobility attempt to present the dialogue between body-subject and world. Such a different way of experiencing embodiment not as physical object but as a mode of experiencing and ordering world may reflect the Tantric distinction between the transformed, even deified aspect of body as *sku*, rather than *lus*.

Conclusion

Thus, we have seen that Buddhist views on embodiment, while somewhat different from those prevalent in the West up to the present time, are found to be far more compatible with those presently arising from contemporary Western research. They also underlie practices instantiating mindfulness of conventional embodiment and also an enhanced imaginative view of ideal embodiment, supported by tantric visualisation and ritual. These views have further important implications for contemporary psychotherapy. Embodiment may play a part of particular importance as a grounding against total relativity. If the ahistorical and transcendental, or merely intellectually supported, grounds of earlier metanarratives have been found lacking, what is left to defend us from incoherent relativism? Our common human embodiment and structure of understanding may be such a ground as long as it is not seen as an unchanging or transcendent one. We have noted Ann Klein's discussion of Buddhist mindfulness practices, citing particularly the *Satipaṭṭhāna Sutta*, to provide what she terms "visceral coherence" grounded in the body, as opposed to the narrative coherence that is dependent upon language and convention. We have also noted both Sprung's references to embodiment with regard to Madhyamaka and his contemporary essay into a "vivial" philosophy grounded upon lived experience.[43] Whereas both absolutism and nihilism lead us away from embodied experience, the middle way reinstates it as the locus for realisation. As Johnson describes, between the two extremes of foundationalism and relativism lies "an intermediate domain of embodied understanding."[44]

Such conscious embodiment may be the foundation of an interactive rather than a purely objective or subjective stance towards the world. As we have discussed, awareness and appreciation of embodiment increase a feeling of connection with the world. A sense of groundedness on the earth and awareness of breathing, the exchange of inspiration and expiration emphasises connection, and fosters feelings of belonging. Such feelings founded in physical sensation can become powerful antidotes to alienation and nihilism, and the ground for a difffering way of being and interacting. An everyday way of rootedness starts from physical embodiment within the world. In terms of psychotherapy, healing differences in our experience of the world may be fostered through simple practices promoting a sense of groundedness, and expanding and loosening breathing. Series of exercises have been set out by several of the somatic therapies mentioned in chapter two, and also exist within many Eastern spiritual disciplines. in addition to the meditation practices considering earlier.[45]

Speech

"Yet the wanderer brings back
from the mountain slopes to the valley
not a handful of earth, unsayable, but rather
a hard-won word, unalloyed, the golden and blue
gentian. Are we perhaps here *in order to say: house,*
bridge, fountain, gate, jug, fruit tree, window?
At most: column, castle? . . . but to say, *understand,*
oh to say so, *more intensely than the things themselves*
ever intended to be.

Here *is the time for the sayable,* here *its home.*
Speak and acknowledge."[46]

Speech is a specifically human response. The ability to speak is that which distinguishes the human being from all other sentient beings. A popular Buddhist definition of man is "the being who speaks and understands meanings." For the Greeks it was *zoion logon echon*, "living being having the capacity for discourse."[47] Suzanne Langer suggests that "it is the power of using symbols – the power of *speech* – that makes him lord of the earth."[48]

As one of the three gateways of being, speech stands for signification, relationship, communication and imagination. Speech is the foremost method of communication between people, it is the coin of dialogue, the basis for symbolic representation and culture. In its turn it arises from prelinguistic embodiment and enaction, and it includes the world of imagination. Language structures not only our communication but also our categorisation and grasp of our world. It is now being considered as fundamental both to our being-in-the-world, and to the construction of the world we inhabit. As John Searle points out: "The world divides the way we divide it, our main way of dividing things up is in the language. Our concept and experience of reality is a matter of our linguistic categories."[49] However this is not always adequately realised. The traditional realistic and objectivistic perspective on speech comes from considering it as providing merely a representation of pre-existent reality, a faithful representation of an objective world. Both Buddhism and much recent Western discourse, philosophic and scientific, oppose this view, and present speech as being constitutive of reality as dynamic interaction between embodied subject and world.[50] From these perspectives two views of speech are frequently presented, first as ordinary talk, and second as transformed speech, aware of its imaginative and creative role. Not everything to be considered falls neatly into this distinction but there is a recurring contrast between the everyday and what might be aspired to, beautifully described by Carol Gilligan as "the difference between a voice that is an open channel – connected physically with breath and sound, psychologically with feelings and thoughts, and culturally with a rich resource of language – and a voice that is impeded or blocked."[51] One of the main blockages of the open voice is the conception of self, which we have discussed at length (chapter five), but which we will reiterate here is closely connected to language.

Speech in Buddhism

Speech may be distinguished in two parts: ordinary speech which in terms of the two truths, is relative or confining, and transformed speech or *mantra*, a resonance of reality. The realm of ordinary speech is the realm of the confining, in terms of the three natures of Yogācāra, the realm of *parakalpita*. It must be "seen through" to its actual transparency. Unfortunately we tend to take it as real in a more constricting way, as some unshakeable link between word and object, believing that the world must of necessity be divided as our language divides it. For the Tibetan Mādhyamika commentators ordinary language is *ming tsam*, mere name, and much of the most detailed study is engaged in the analysis and deconstruction of ordinary speech and its categories. Madhyamaka backed by its exposition of emptiness, utterly rejects the conventional views of language as true and essential representation of pre-existent reality, advocating that language should be seen through, and revealed as a matter of convention. The actual existence of each thing is a matter of its dependence upon other things and its imputation by a consciousness. Designation is a linguistic act. Nothing is self existent, decontextualized. For the Mādhyamika:

> "Our words are like the reflection of a face in a mirror – there is no real connection between the reflected image and the face, but the image nevertheless serves a specific purpose for the person using the mirror. Similarly, our words bear no intrinsic connection with our epistemological and ontological problems and the language used to express these problems, but nevertheless these words of ours can serve to realize a specific purpose. They can be understood to express something that is not susceptible to expression in the language of objective facts."[52]

From the standpoint of the path of renunciation, speech in the formal framework of grammar and designation is conventionally to be used in ethically right speech – abstention from untruth, abusive language, unkindness and idle talk, and ultimately to be seen through. Emptiness is used to see through the conceptual diffusion and differentiation *(prapañca)* of language as discussed earlier. Emptiness itself must be actualised and experienced, being, as Huntingdon points out: "amenable to interpretation only as the expression of an entire form of life."[53] Thus language is seen as conventionally existent and functional, but ultimately to be seen through. It is confining if accepted literally as a representation of reality, which is only known through the filter of language and conceptuality. In this fashion language involves taking the stance of the observer in relation to our own action, and separates us from direct experience. Mindfulness and meditation are the practices which enable us to see this perceptual process, and see the occurrence of the first split between self and world.

In the path of transformation, speech is not only to be used ethically and seen through but also to be transformed. It encompasses not only speech itself but all the energy of breath which supports it. Transformed speech is mantra, the archetypal expressive energy which gives birth to all individual things. It is described by Guenther as "utterance as originary disclosure."[54] This compares interestingly to the non-Buddhist description of Eagleton noted earlier: "the place where reality 'un-conceals' itself."[55] The difference between confining and liberated speech lies in its degree of closure or openness to world. This in turn is regulated according to what extent it is ruled by primary ignorance nescient of the three marks of impermanence, unsatisfactoriness and non-self. The result of such nescience is reification under the domination of a fixed self.

Transformed speech is aligned with the Saṃbhogakāya or enjoyment body. This relates not only to spoken language itself but to the supreme mode of communication representing all the processes of the articulation of meaning and the unconcealing of reality. It mediates between the inarticulate domain of wisdom, the supreme reality, the dharma-body and the everyday world, the embodiment in action of the emanation-body. In this sphere of ritual practice, Buddhism uses speech in ways rarely found today in the West. Speech is seen not only as the carrier of conceptual communication but in the somatic form of resonance and the imaginative form of visualisation. At such times, chanting of *mantra* or texts in a certain manner evokes physical and mental effects which may be more important than their conceptual message. Here, the sound and resonance are valued for themselves. Ritual chanting with its somatic vibration, rhythmic breathing and correct posture produces a palpable physiological effect. Visualisation practices are concerned with the evocation of ideal worlds and deities and accompanied by bodily and spiritual identification with them on the part of the practitioner. However, all such practices are always accompanied by an understanding of the essential emptiness and endless metaphoricity of all processes. They embody the middle position in the unfolding of the formless into form, the realm of ideation and archetypes, mediating between the formless realm and our realm of samsaric desire.

Between the two, much of the writings of the great Tsong kha pa is concerned with attempts to reconcile conventional analytical cognition with realisation of ultimate emptiness. For the dGe lugs pa school, following Tsong kha pa, ultimate nondual realisation may be reached *through* analytic cognition, there is no incommensurability between them. Analytic understanding is seen as a necessary, if not sufficient cause for enlightenment, which necessitates the internalisation of the understood meanings through the means of meditation. As José Cabezon describes the process: "Ultimately, words find their fulfilment in the set of transformative experiences known as *realizations*."[56] Other schools see this somewhat differently, the best-known examples being the gnomic utterances of Zen, attempts to shake the mind out of its conceptual frames, and the distinction made between the pointing finger and the moon.

Contemporary Ideas of Speech in the West

In the West philosophical and scientific enquiries in this century have led to considerations of speech in a far broader sense than that of mere vocal representation of a separate and untouchable reality. The search for a different approach is again to be found in Heidegger's work, particularly in his later writings. Here Heidegger stated that we are within language rather than being its controller, saying on several occasions: "Language is the house of Being."[57] He sought a transformation of speech; the "saying of a turning." Such a transformation is again concerned with man's openness to Being, with the hearing of silence, the "ringing of stillness" (*das Geläut de Stille*), as he described it, which is the language of Being.[58] Such a transformation is, as one of his commentators points out: "more a matter of hearing differently than speaking differently."[59] Heidegger sees the change as being from a position of mastery to one of receptivity, renunciation and commemorative thinking; to placing ourselves "within the grant of language." For him it is a transformation from speech to Saying, in which to say means to let appear, to show.[60] Such showing is prior to the arising of signs in the showing. As humans we belong within the Saying. Such Saying displays the shift from a standpoint of subjectivity and the division of subject/object. "Thus our saying – always an answering – remains forever relational. Relation is thought of here always in terms of the appropriation and no longer conceived in the form of a mere reference."[61] Access to appropriation or event (*Ereignis*) is through experience[62] and we dwell in *ereignis* only in so far as we are appropriated by language. In our fallen or everyday manner of speech, far from dwelling in language, within Saying as the House of Being, we use speech which merely designates.

For Levinas also, speech is response. Here, however rather than response to Being, it is a question of response to the other. For Levinas the beginning of language is in the face, which in its silence calls you.[63] Language is the face of being addressed and responding. "The relationship between the same and the other is language."[64] This relationship, the face to face, which is the beginning of language is a relation which can never form part of totality since language does not – or true language does not – consist in invoking the other as merely a being represented in my thought, a figure of my egoism, but as a revelation of alterity irreducible to the subject/object relation. Thus, again, true language is event rather than representation. The response is also for Levinas an ethical event, and, for him, as he constantly reiterates, ethics rather than ontology is first philosophy. The ethical task is to free what gets in the way of open response to the alterity of the other.

Levinas uses the model of the Saying and the Said to explain how the ethical response signifies within language. The Saying is openness to the other, the event of acceptance of the other's alterity and my refusal to attempt to reduce it to the Same. It is the act of address. In contrast, the Said is a statement, or proposition, the content or meaning of words. There is a noticeable similarity between this, Heidegger's distinction between dwelling in the Saying and using speech which designates, and Bakhtin's distinction between speech and utterance. For Bakhtin too, utterance is always a response – a response to language and to existence which is always already there. It is a participative and liminal act, an interface between what is actually said and what is unspoken, the extraverbal horizon of speech

The paradox is that the moment the Saying is put into words it enters the domain of the Said.[65] The logic of transformed Speech which encompasses Saying within speech is not that of either/or. Here we encounter again a logic similar to that first encountered in the Prajñāpāramitā literature, in the Diamond Sutra: "Subhuti, what are called wholesome actions are in fact not wholesome actions. That is why they are called wholesome actions."[66] It is the logic found in the eight negations of Nāgārjuna, and the six propositions of Fa Tsang. It is a logic of non-duality, found more recently in the work of Nishida Kitaro and perhaps, as we shall see in the double readings of deconstruction, in intertwining and in chiasm.

Thus, in Heidegger, Levinas and Bakhtin there is a twofold approach to speech: that of the everyday and that revealing a wider, enriched perspective. In different form this also appears in the work of Wittgenstein, the philosopher perhaps most closely associated with language in twentieth century Continental philosophy, and also the one most commonly considered in contemporary comparison with Nāgārjuna. His work has even been employed as a contemporary hermeneutic in revealing their meaning.[67] In his early work, the *Tractatus*, Wittgenstein showed that the problems of meaning in life transcended the limits of language. Claims about self, death and the meaning of life are outside what can be meaningfully said: "What we cannot speak about we must pass over in silence."[68] And it is silence which plays the part of an enriched or transformed speech in the *Tractatus*. In *Prototractatus*, an early version of *Tractatus* Wittgenstein stated: "My work consists of two parts: – the one presented here plus all that I have *not* written. And it is precisely this second part that is the important one. . . . In short, I believe that where *many* others today are just *gassing*, I have managed in my book to put everything firmly into place by being silent about it."[69]

In his later *Philosophical Investigations* Wittgenstein explored further the way language is embedded in forms of life. His project was a therapeutic one; to allow the fly to escape from the fly bottle, as we noted earlier[70], and to allow us to cease doing philosophy having brought ourselves into agreement with the way things are.[71] One of the chief causes of disharmony according to Wittgenstein, is the "bewitchment of language." We become caught in a belief in the reification of words, and the objective truth of the world as presented in language. In opposition to this, Wittgenstein presents us with a realm of language games, founded not on absolute privileged transcendental standards, but each dependent merely on a context of conventional cultural and historical criteria; meaning as usage rather than meaning as representation. Understanding this, that everyday language is, in Buddhist terms, merely conventionally true, may release us from its iron grip.

We have stated that Wittgenstein's philosophy is therapeutic, or in Rorty's terms edifying. One of his commentators has noted that Wittgenstein himself compared philosophy and psychoanalysis in that they both undertake to effect change in life through change in understanding or perspective that brings one into harmony with one's life.[72] Wittgenstein considered Freud's project however as philosophical rather than scientific, and criticised it for its aspiration to science. Perhaps it is to Freud's initial desire for scientific respectability that we should turn for the origin of psychotherapy's lack of engagement with philosophical foundation, upon which we commented in chapter one.

On the surface Jacques Derrida appears more concerned with the deconstruction of ordinary speech than the positing of a transformed speech. However Simon Critchley proffers a persuasive interpretation for a reading of Derridean deconstruction as an ethical demand. He describes deconstruction in terms which sound somewhat familiar to those conversant with the concept of *śūnyatā*: "All ontological statements of the form

'Deconstruction is x' miss the point *a priori* for it is precisely the ontological presuppositions of the copula that provide one of the enduring themes of deconstruction."[73] Instead, Critchley presents deconstruction as a method of textual practice, a double reading, "that is to say, a reading that interlaces at least two motifs or layers of reading."[74] The first is a commentarial interpretation of the text according to its intended meaning. The second is a destablization of this; the opening up of alterity within the intended meaning, which in some fashion contradicts or destabilizes it, as emptiness destabilizes the conventional view of reality.

Derrida shows that in the lack of a direct relation of signifier and signified, the sign is a structure of difference, defined as much by what it is not as by what it is. Thus meaning is only to be found in the spaces between. Every sign carries a trace of that other which is absent, a certainty forever deferred. This echoes the Buddhist description of language-based inference as operating in a negative or exclusory manner.[75] As we have noted, the method of deconstruction may be compared to that of Madhyamaka Prāsangika, a *reductio ad absurdum* in which a text or proposition is found to fail in its own terms, as the criteria which it uses are reflexively turned against itself. Derrida critiques the belief in self-presence and the search for any transcendental signifier which corresponds to any transcendental signified, essence or truth in a manner which is reminiscent of Nāgārjuna's critique of self-inherent being. For a deconstructive reading, both self and world can be read as text.[76]

Such Continental philosophy as that mentioned above is, and has been, much exercised with the realm of speech and provides a critique of the objectivist view of the world. It has, however, rarely been conjoined to any scientific projects, with the exception of the work of Merleau-Ponty and Lacan, and currently Varela and colleagues.

Lacan's writing, as described in chapter two, is centrally concerned with speech. As we saw, Lacan believed that the unconscious itself is structured like a language. He considered entrance into the symbolic world both as *the* major developmental step, and one which involves a misunderstanding of the nature of self. Lacan's concept of speech encompasses both apparently consciously controlled speech and the realms of the unconscious, where, following Freud, the subject is not in control of the text. However for Lacan the emphasis is on the truth and rightness of the unconscious. Critchley has compared Lacan's distinction between *enonciation* (the act of speaking) and *enoncé* (the formulation of this act into a statement) with Levinas' distinction between Saying and Said. Thus his work may bring together traces of both Freudian and Buddhist ideas, the link being that of language. The opening up of the unconscious may be seen as a potential enrichment of speech, but the restriction of *enonciation* into *enoncé* is the restriction of the conventional or confined, under the control of a misperceived self.

Those approaches within cognitive science which have applied a non-objectivist stance to, and as a result of, their researches, are those to which we have continually turned. A recurring observation of such works in relation to speech concerns its action in the expression and strengthening of self concept. They note the way in which languages are implicitly imbued with the view of the human self as an independent, autonomous actor expressed in personal narrative. Within the world of language we can also live at one remove from embodied action as in self-consciousness we identify our self as the observer of our actions. In a recent work psychologist Guy Claxton has pointed to the privileging of, and identification with, consciousness as self to the exclusion of the unconscious.[77] The unconscious here is not the Freudian unconscious as repository for the repressed nor the Jungian collective unconscious, but the background network of unacknowledged processes from which consciousness emerges as part of a continuous spectrum.

Edelman delineates the arising of higher-order consciousness upon which speech depends from primary consciousness which in turn arises from non-conscious perception. Lakoff and Johnson, as we discussed earlier, show that the idealised cognitive models upon which language rests rely on concepts of embodiment occurring in bodily activity prior to language. Language is symbolic, based on cognitive models and image schemata grounded in bodily functioning which are imaginatively extended through metaphor and metonymy. Thus concepts initially become meaningful in terms of embodiment and function, and something is said to be true when understanding of a statement fits with one's experience. Again, we find, that there is no God's eye view of absolute truth in isolation from embodiment and social interaction. Our view of what exists is determined by our means of knowing. [78]

Jerome Bruner also suggests that linguistic capabilities rest upon pre-linguistic support; which he calls protolinguistic representations of the world which exist prior to language in a context of praxis, and reach their full realisation only with language.[79] These he describes as a set of predispositions to construe the world in a certain way, and to act upon these construals. This is comparable to the image schemata of Lakoff and Johnson. Bruner argues that it is a drive to create narrative that determines the way in which grammatical forms are acquired by a young child, as a means of making sense of their own actions and human interactions. He mentions four features of narrativity: concern with people and their actions, readiness to mark the unusual and ignore the usual, linearalization and maintenance of sequence and a narrative voice or perspective. It is this last which fosters and strengthens the sense of self. The feature of linearity is reminiscent of the linear mode discussed by Margaret Donaldson (see chapter four). Donaldson clearly points out how different cultures foster and support the development of different modes. As noted earlier she advocates consideration of Buddhism for its support in developing the value sensing modes and the means for changing modes at will. Western culture has tended to overvalue the intellectual, the logical, rational and linear modes.

The influence of language in the construction of the separated self was discussed in chapter four. Abram has most carefully plotted the effects of language in the development of that self in its increasing separation from participation in world. Following Merleau-Ponty Abram sees perception as arising as reciprocal exchange between the living body and its animate environment. From this sensorial field, language arises as a "profoundly carnal phenomenon, rooted in our sensorial experience of each other and of the world."[80] For Abram living speech is a vocal 'gesticulation' whose meaning is inseparable from the sound and rhythm of the words. For human beings, a second, more abstract layer of conventional meanings, divorced from the 'felt significance' carried by this expressive, gestural speech through its tone and resonance, has replaced it with a code, severed from any sensuous dimension. He traces this rupture from the end of pictographic and the inception of alphabetic writing. Learning to read and to write with the alphabet gave rise to a new reflexive sense of self. As we noted in chapter four Abram describes how the Homeric meaning of *psyche* as the invisible breath of life came, after Socrates and Plato, to denote that internal aspect of self that is able to turn away from the everyday sensory world towards the intelligible Ideas. This later became further reduced to the rational abstracted intellect, losing its transcendental perspective. Having attempted to show that language is a profoundly bodily-based phenomenon sustained through relationship with the animate landscape Abram's intention is to reawaken awareness of man's recipricosity with the total environment, and reinvigorate language:

> "Planting words, like seeds, under rocks and fallen logs – letting language take root, once again, in the earthen silence of shadow and bone and leaf."[81]

In the foregoing discussion of both Buddhist and contemporary Western discourse in relation to the domain of speech and communication, we have repeatedly found a distinction between everyday speech and a potentially transformed speech, and a widened appreciation of the unacknowledged and underprivileged prelinguistic foundations of speech. I would now like to explore ideas of speech from two different perspectives which may show some overlap. The first is speech from the point of view of imagination and metaphor, which we have briefly discussed in terms of prelinguistic modes. Secondly I would like to speak of speech in terms of a feminine voice.

Imagination and Metaphor

There is another kind of speech, or more precisely a condition of speech which determines to a large extent what we can say or think, that is analogic, creative, participatory and consciously metaphorical. Lakoff and Johnson have shown the importance of imagination in extending the symbolic use of language from prelinguistic embodied action. Yet imagination is not, or no longer, in general considered as part of the Gate of Speech, which is more often considered solely as the domain of the logical, sequential and literal. Heidegger criticised ordinary speaking as exhausted metaphor: "everyday language is a forgotten and therefore used-up poem, from which there hardly resounds a call any longer."[82] Yet he pointed to its far richer potential: "Language is the precinct (*templum*), that is, the house of Being. The nature of language does not exhaust itself in signifying, nor is it merely something that has the character of sign or cipher."[83] This is the transformed conception of speech to which Buddhist tantra and contemporary discourse point, and which is ordinarily ignored.

Johnson states definitively:

> "*there can be no meaningful experience without imagination*, whether in its productive or reproductive functions. As productive, imagination gives us the very structure of objectivity. As reproductive, it supplies all of the connections by means of which we achieve coherent, unified, and meaningful experience and understanding. We are talking here about operations of the imagination so pervasive, automatic, and indispensable that we are ordinarily not aware of them. Nevertheless, our ordered world, and the possibility of understanding any part of it, depends on the existence of this synthesizing activity".[84]

As we have seen in the previous discussion, language may perhaps be described as the top layer of what may be called "speech", which would then include its prelinguistic foundations described in different ways by different authors. Together they create meaning. This idea is to be found as early as the eighteenth century when John Locke stated: "sensible ideas are transferred to more abstract significations, and made to stand for ideas that come not under the cognizance of the senses."[85] Imagination as shown by Johnson is the relation between the prelinguistic and the spoken, and only through recognising the interactional character of imagination which partakes both of the somatic and the rational, can we hope to understand the nature of meaning.

Abram's work reflects this same belief, and Baar's recent research into consciousness would seem to support this, reinforcing the importance of the somatic or sensate foundation of meaning. As he recently noted: "The most moving poetry, the most enduring encounters with others, join the abstract and concrete levels of experience."[86] He describes images and inner speech as internally created sensations, and suggests the possibility that many abstract concepts are accessed by means of images, or through inner speech. As Sports Psychologists know, imaginary practice has been found to aid outer performance. Similarly in Trauma therapy imaginitive recreation and completion of traumatic events have been found to bring healing. The advantage of metaphor is that is connects abstractions and image to a solid grounding in perception.

To see through everyday language and reconnect with its transformative, creative and open dimension, not merely with its descriptive properties, we need to be able to recognise this metaphorical character, which we are usually only aware of in artistic or religious discourse. Writer Jeanette Winterson speaks beautifully of this in relation to art:

> "Art is large and it enlarges you and me. To a shrunk-up world its vistas are shocking. Art is the burning bush that

> both shelters and makes visible our profounder longings. Through it we see ourselves in metaphor. Art is metaphor, from the Greek, *meta* (above) and *pherein* (to carry) it is that which is carried above the literalness of life. Art is metaphor. Metaphor is transformation."[87]

Philosopher Richard Rorty also notices the invitation to transformation: "A metaphor is, so to speak, a voice from outside logical space ..." It is a call to change one's language and one's life, rather than a proposal about how to systematize either."[88]

In Buddhism a large part of the practices of Tantra are concerned with creative imagination and the conscious vision of the metaphorical quality of both everyday and transformed reality which is made possible by their foundation in emptiness. In the development phase the practitioner imagines themself as a fully enlightened Buddha inhabiting a *maṇḍala* of a luminous Buddha realm. The initial act of all such practices is the recitation of a *mantra* whereby the practitioner acknowledges herself to be ultimately of the nature of emptiness.[89] Then follows the imaginative creation of themselves as an enlightened Buddha. Finally this vision is dissolved into emptiness, the practitioner returning to the world empowered with remembrance of it as an enlightened realm. The Tibetan term for this creation of oneself as a Buddha is *bdag bskyed*, literally self-creation. Such practices empower the practitioner not only by imitation of a transformed state, but also by seeing through the solidity of the everyday.

All of this resonates closely with the work of psychotherapy. In chapter four I quoted at length from Lakoff and Johnston: "A large part of self-understanding is the search for appropriate personal metaphors that make sense of our lives. ... In therapy, for example, much of self-understanding involves consciously recognizing previously unconscious metaphors and how we live by them."[90] It is necessary to see the metaphors we live by, both culturally accepted and personal, to understand them as metaphors, to re-cognise and reconnect with the creative imagination that gave rise to them, and thus to understand that they are not written in stone, and may be recreated and reinterpreted in order to construct new narratives, new metaphors and new meanings for old experiences, which are more in tune with current experience. All of which can only come into being within emptiness, the lack of a permanent and unchanging essence. This lack of a permanent unchanging self is, as Stephen Batchelor has described it: "not a blanket denial of personal identity but the opening to a creative enhancement of who one is and how one performs in the world."[91]

In a most individual work, Owen Barfield described as idolatry the manner in which we first experience phenomena as representations, then relate to them non-representationally as objects in their own right, existing independently of human consciousness. He advocated another use of imagination to enable us to consciously see through representations. "To be *able* to experience the representations as idols, and then to be able also to perform the act of figuration 'consciously' so as to experience them as participated; that is imagination."[92]

Barfield's work has been commented upon and continued by Archetypal Psychology.[93] Archetypal Psychology also constantly calls for a deliteralization of language and valuation of metaphor, and suggests that this should be achieved through personification, and attention to the image. It is another attack on representation or objectification from a different perspective.[94] Archetypal Psychology calls for an imaginative revisioning of speech, a new "angelology of words."[95] Another Archetypal psychologist suggests that imagination has the potential to be the Western model of release from the delusions of ego.[96] He suggests that imagination *is* soul or anima, thus linking the themes of transformation of speech, the importance of the imagination and the feminine voice.

The Feminine Voice

Here I would like to speak of, and perhaps in, the feminine voice, for this has been, as yet unacknowledged as an important voice in the dialogue. It has been mentioned overtly only in discussion of the French feminist analysts in relation to Western psychotherapies. In a wider, less defined, more feminine way this voice pervades both this work, postmodernism and the practice of psychotherapy. To define feminism I would agree with the definition given by Alice Jardine: "Feminism, while infinite in its variations, is finally rooted in the belief that women's' truth-in-experience-and-reality is and has always been different from men's, and that it as well as all its artefacts and productions have consequently been devalued and always already delegitimized in patriarchal culture."[97] The feminine voice is however, not essentially restricted to gender, and is, I contend, as important and necessary for men as for women. It is a voice that until recently has been a subtext in Western discourse which has sprung from a milieu embodying the masculine and the patriarchal, against the background of which the feminine voice can only be seen as 'other'. Hence the feminine has too often been heard only in its difference or deviation from the masculine norm. Alice Jardine in her fascinating study of the feminine voice in contemporary discourse describes this thinking as "the master narratives' own non-knowledge", what has eluded them, what has engulfed them. This other than themselves is almost always a "space" of some kind over which the narrative has lost control, and it is this space which subverts the metanarratives of Truth, Representation, Reason, the Subject. To describe the transformation of the feminine at the interior of such narratives, she suggests the neologism "*gynesis*". This is the different way of speaking heard by Carol Gilligan in the study of a specifically feminine approach to morality, which she entitled *In a Different Voice*.

What is the feminine voice? Perhaps, as we saw, it is easier to define it in terms of what it is not – in contradistinction to the voice of patriarchy that is logical, hierarchical and masterly, concerned with identity, separation and independence. The feminine is more aware of and concerned with difference than with identity, with relationship grounded in a background of interdependence. It is context-dependent and dynamic, unhappy with absolutes and closure, with frozen hierarchies and fixture.[98] It is embodied rather than oriented towards spirit and/or mind, and it is, as described in the Yang/Yin symbology of Taoism, receptive, more concerned with being than doing. Doing entails goal-directed action, technology, progress, individuality and ego, embodied in images of the phallus, the blade. Being entails openness, receptivity, responsivity, play, context and the transpersonal, embodied in images of the container; Riane Eisler's chalice, the womb, the *choros*. Naturalist Terry Tempest Williams speaks of it poetically:

> "I see the Feminine defined as a reconnection to the Self, a commitment to the wildness within – our instincts, our capacity to create and destroy; our hunger for connection as well as sovereignty, interdependence and independence, at once. We are taught not to trust our own experience.
>
> The Feminine teaches us experience is our way back home, the psychic bridge that spans rational and intuitive waters. To embrace the Feminine is to embrace paradox. Paradox preserves mystery, and mystery inspires belief."[99]

This is absolutely *not* a suggestion that these attributes of the feminine should displace those of the masculine. What is necessary, for both men and women, and indeed for the cosmos, is a re-cognition and rehonouring of the feminine, long ignored in a patriarchal world. The state of the environment shows the ravages of past imbalance, ecology speaks in a feminine voice. So frequently do individual clients who present themselves in therapy. Pushed to succeed, unable to care for ourselves, how can we show compassion for others?

A middle way, an androgynous way is called for, in which dialogue is engaged between the masculine and the feminine, in which space is made for the hitherto "alterity" of the feminine. For the feminine has been mistrusted and misvalued within patriarchal discourse, seen as ambiguous, uncontrolled, multivalent, elusive, illusive, both valuable and fearful. The belief that "Women are to nature, as man is to culture"[100] has left the feminine as something threatening, and uncontrolled. We find this clearly exemplified in Tibetan myth/history, where the land of Tibet is seen as a demoness tamed by the placement of Buddhist rites. The feminine here is the "pre-existing primordial chaos, the chaos which is a female being. Then the chaos is conquered and she becomes the stuff of which the world is fashioned."[101]

For Levinas the feminine is also alterity and equivocation.[102] The feminine displays equivocation in that it occurs as a kind of withdrawal, a speech which expresses silence, an interiority and privacy which yet has implications in terms of the outer world, a double movement Levinas likens to the relationship of voluptuosity to fecundity. Levinas' presentation of woman as alterity is not carried out in the light of secondariness, or of difference from the prior masculine, but rather in the prioritisation of alterity and exteriority. In her equivocation she embodies plurality which escapes the totality of the Same. It is also important to note that the division of gender is not rigid for Levinas, but that each individual partakes of both masculine and feminine.[103]

Western psychotherapy was patriarchal in its origins. Freud today stands as the epitome, both as individual and symbol, of the patriarch. His standards are those of the masculine, against which those of the feminine are measured. If the feminine differs from such masculine norms, such difference can only be read in terms of privation. Perhaps this is most clearly seen in his consideration of the formation of the superego in women, which he believed could only be seen as deficient due to women's' difficulty in achieving resolution of the Oedipal complex.[104] This masculine bias has continued with Lacan and his privileging of the phallus as the symbol of entry into the Symbolic world. Despite arguments for a distinction between the symbolic phallus and the actual penis, and that Lacan's presentation is descriptive rather than prescriptive, it is obvious that such terminology, and the thinking behind it, tends to uphold the dominance and priority of the masculine.

I would concur with a therapist writing recently that psychotherapeutic work of all theoretical styles has been significantly impaired by the dominant imbalance between masculine and feminine principles.[105] Her suggestions for a psychotherapy grounded in the feminine principle echo or travel hand in hand with the approach suggested in this work, though the former is uninfluenced by Buddhist thought. "The core feminine experience is one of being immersed in the living world, one link in an infinite chain."[106] Again: "A feminine approach to the therapeutic work begins in ... a place of not-knowing, or experiencing focused on Being rather than Doing. ... This receptive approach believes everything the patient needs is inside his own psyche: the issue is to mobilize and actualize the patient's own health rather than to cure him."[107] Such is the heart of the approach presented here in the framework of the Buddhist doctrines – of dependent origination as the foundation of interconnection and interdependence, of Buddha nature as foundation for intrinsic health, of emptiness as foundation of unknowing[108]- and of its practices of mindfulness and meditation to instantiate such understanding and to enable therapists to foster and develop receptivity and the ability and courage to rest in unknowing. Thus it would appear that the feminine voice is implicitly, if not always explicitly, framed within the Buddhist doctrine.

To speak overtly of the feminine voice in Buddhism, I can do no better than to point to a recent study, and merely here, summarise its arguments and immense research on this topic. In *Buddhism After Patriarchy* Rita Gross has sought for the feminine voice in Buddhism in the past, and strongly suggests how it may be strengthened to give rise to a truly androgynous Buddhism for the future. She finds that the dharma itself is neither male nor female, although there has been, and continues to be a serious gap between vision and practice, wherein practice has been largely androcentric. Basing her arguments upon what is expressed explicitly in the second turning of the wheel, and implicitly in the first and third turnings, she finds that no Buddhist teachings provide the basis for gender privilege, and that they are, in fact, more compatible with feminine than patriarchal interpretations. Just as I have seen Buddhism and psychotherapy as comparable attempts to explore how fixed and conventional patterns of mental constructs impede liberation, so Gross has compared Buddhism and feminism; seeing the primary patterning which creates the duality of self and other in the operations of patriarchy, following Simone de Beauvoir's now classic definition of woman as "other". The feminine has not only been defined as other, but also as lack according to Lacanian analysis.[109] It is perhaps interesting here to speculate imaginatively and reinterpret this idea of the feminine as lack in accordance with David Loy's writings which we have considered on several occasions above, in which he compares a sense of lack to *śūnyatā*, and to remember that Prajñāpāramitā, the personification of the wisdom of emptiness, is always female. Such imaginative comparison sheds light on the distinction between lack as privation, and the lack of emptiness which is no lack.

Gross advocates an androgynous reconstruction of Buddhism embodying the teaching of the third turning of the wheel speaking of non-dual suchness, and the principles of masculinity and femininity. Practically she appeals for a revaluation of the sangha or community as the embodiment of feminine values of commitment, communication and relationship. Her approach to Buddhism, as that of this work, is biased towards the idea of liberation within the world, rather than liberation from the world. In this light she, as also I, argue for a reconceptualisation of the sacredness of everyday activity, a call for the re-enchantment of body and speech.[110]

Conclusion

A psychotherapy in tune with contemporary thought and inspired by Buddhism will need to have a particular relationship with Speech. Strangely despite the centrality of language, the fact that psychoanalysis is "the talking cure", careful consideration of speech itself rather than the contents of speech within psychotherapy has been rare, usually the work of individuals, as we have seen in the case of Lacan and Hillman. Buddhist ideas may help us consciously to address and thus transform our experience in ways compatible with contemporary Western explorations. Both Buddhism and contemporary discourse distinguish between an everyday speech, and a potentially transformed one. They point out the impoverishment of the former, and its dangers. Everyday language bewitches us into believing that it presents a true picture of a reality that exists absolutely in isolation from us. This in turn leads to objectification, the perspective of the narrator and egocentricity. It is necessary to deliteralize, to see through the enchantment of language, realising how it acts as a filter through which we come to experience. The point is not to remove this filter, in some attempt to regain direct experience, but to become aware of it in its contingency, metaphoricity and creativity. Language and expression need not to be withheld but to be liberated, seen through and consciously used metaphorically. Buddhism, particularly Madhyamaka nominalism brings awareness to speech as convention, essential for use, but not essential in nature. [111]

Then we may come to understand the possibility of a transformed relationship with language. The way towards this will entail a revaluation of language's foundation in prelinguistic embodiment and practice and of the importance of imagination and metaphor, and of what I have called the feminine voice. Incorporation of these may lead to a speech which will liberate rather than confine, a transformed voice expressing relationship, communication and resonance with the whole. Instead of a speech which is in thrall to the self system, which reinforces the divisions between body and mind and self and world, a transformed speech of openness and transparency can release the divisions and reinstate the interconnection and interpenetration of self and other, expressive of resonance with the whole, that is the dimension of Mind.

Mind

"You never employ the world aright, till the Sea itself floweth in your veins, till you are clothed with the heavens, and crowned with the stars."[112]

Mind in Buddhism has a wider connotation than that commonly given it in Western discourse.[113] Although there are individual differences according to different schools, the term refers more to the container of our experience than to the contents of our cognition.[114] It has been described as "our subjectively lived environment"[115], the medium through which we know the objective world, and which, as we have seen, provides the potential for shaping it. Mind is the relationship with world that, in its open form expresses resonance with the whole, which is described by Guenther as "spirituality".[116] It expresses the inseparability of what is more usually in the West divided into mind and body, reason and emotion. In its restricted form it is ego-centred mentation, confined within the deferral of language and the cognitive sphere. Earlier, I have discussed Buddhist psychology and models of mind and identity, here I would like to take the wider view of mind as the horizon of our experience and consider the implications of Buddhist philosophy and practice relating to this widest dimension of experience, in the context both of psychotherapy and recurrent contemporary themes from Western discourse which make up the universe of ideas which we currently inhabit. Three themes in particular have recurred throughout this exploration and are, I suggest, central both to our personal experience and to the changing ideas which make up our current horizons. These are the three linked themes of Interrelationship, Non-egocentricity and Nihilism.

Interrelationship

In chapter three exploration of the Buddhist teachings concerning the emptiness of self-sufficiency or essence in both selves and phenomena revealed that this was the corollary of their dependent origination. Thereby everything arises not in isolation, but in dynamic dependence upon other phenomena or upon a cognizing mind. In contemporary Western discourse too, from very different perspectives, we have found this emphasis upon interdependence and interaction both in philosophic and scientific fields. Heidegger's *Dasein* brought enquiry to bear upon our "enworldedness" with its *existentiales*, and Merleau Ponty's phenomenology of perception researched into the interconnection of subjectivity and world.[117] Merleau Ponty quotes Husserl's assistant, Eugene Fink's formulation of the phenomenological reduction, the suspension of those presupposed positions which are normally taken for granted, as "wonder" in the face of the world.[118] He suggests that in order to see the world truly and grasp it as paradoxical, we must first break with our familiar acceptance of it; first deconstruction, then reconstruction through attention. "True philosophy consists in relearning to look at the world."[119] This is perhaps the basis of Varela, Thompson and Roschs' plea for the uniting of enactive Western cognitive science with Buddhist mind training; that such mindfulness and meditation may change reality, re-awakening strangeness. As Merleau Ponty stated: "phenomenology's task was to reveal the mystery of the world and of reason."[120] Surely this echoes words from a very different philosopher: "It is not *how* things are in the world that is mystical, but *that* it exists."[121]

Both Buddhism and many twentieth century philosophers (and indeed, scientists) seek for, and reveal an interdependence of objectivity and subjectivity in our lived experience, our incarnate subjectivity, our being-in-the-world. To Merleau Ponty the conventional view of experience of the body is discovered to be the degeneration of lived experience into representation: "not a phenomenon but a fact of the psyche."[122] He argues for a return to experience: "to be a consciousness or rather *to be an experience* is to hold inner communication with the world, the body and other people, to be with them instead of beside them. To concern oneself with psychology is necessarily to encounter, beneath objective thought which moves among ready-made things, a first opening upon things without which there would be no objective knowledge."[123] Being-in-the-world for Merleau Ponty is not, as for Sartre, an exile, rather it is interconnection.

Merleau Ponty's tragically terminated later work re-emphasises this interconnection, in his concept of the chiasm or intertwining of the visible and the invisible, the intersection of "brute being" and "flesh". That last term expresses our primordial bond with reality or "what is"; our openness upon "what is". It expresses his attempt to encompass both the active and the passive aspects of the lived body which is both visible and seeing, and our relationship with the flesh of the world of which we participate, of which we are an articulation.

Greatly inspired by Merleau-Ponty's work, Abram, as we have seen, supports a call for awareness of our sensory-based embodiment embedded in its situation, which may inspire a speech aware of such connection. These views for enriched body and speech are grounded in his view of interdependence, the participatory unity and interchange of perceiver and perceived, subject and object.

Both Relativity Theory and Quantum Mechanics have overturned the sequential-order reality of Newtonian physics and the mind/body split of Cartesian philosophy which for so long formed our conceptual horizons. The resultant theories of indeterminacy, relativity, process and mutual implication, let alone chaos and superstrings are theories with which the ordinary person has not yet come to terms, yet which greatly alter our understanding of 'reality'. Further emphasising interrelationship and interdependence, Nobel prize winner Ilya Prigogine's work has been concerned with what he calls dissipative structures, which he claims are characteristic of living systems, being their ability to be continuously replenished and reconstituted through their exchanges with their environments. Such exchanges of energy and matter allow them paradoxically to remain stable notwithstanding changes in their constituent parts as a result of such exchanges and of changes in their environments. James Lovelock's Gaia theory sees the earth as such an organism, capable of regenerating itself in exchange with its environs.

In the interdisciplinary field of cognitive science the work of Varela, Thompson and Rosch, so often mentioned, also displays a comparable paradigm shift from a world of cognitive processes reflecting an objective "real world" out there to an enactive reality surpassing strict subjective/objective division. The other major interdisciplinary field of Systems Theory approaches phenomena in terms of hierarchies of wholes interacting with their larger environments. Each whole in turn consists of lesser parts, the whole providing the environment. Features of such views are the complementarity of differentiation and integration, concepts of mutual causality, and thinking in terms of process rather than objects. For such an approach, objects or individuals seen in isolation are improperly reified parts of systems which are properly constituted of relationship. The great dualities of ordinary thinking: "matter and mind, body and consciousness are not ultimate realities. Rather they are conceptualizations to bring order ... into experience. They have no rigid metaphysical boundaries."[124] Again Neuroscientist Gerald Edelman believes: "The brain and the nervous system cannot be considered in isolation from states of the world and social interaction."[125]

Anthropologist and systems theorist Gregory Bateson proposed a theory of mind as a systems phenomenon characteristic of living things. Any system which displays certain criteria is able to process information and display mind. Thus mental characteristics are displayed not only by individual organisms, but also by social systems and ecosystems. For Bateson mind was immanent not only in the body but also in the pathways and relationships outside the body.

In psychotherapy, the developmental history outlined in chapter two displayed a widening of territory to include interpersonal relationships and even the transpersonal. Yet a really fundamental understanding of interrelationship in its wider or communal ramifications is clearly shown only in the work of a few individuals and therapies. R.D. Laing's work on schizophrenia as a disease of systems reveals such an understanding. It is based on another hypothesis of Bateson's; his concept of the double bind This describes the way in which an individual receives two mutually exclusive messages from one or more family or group members, e.g. loving words accompanied by unloving or threatening gestures. A "schizophrenic" response to such a twofold message, Laing suggested, was a "sane" response to a "crazy" situation. One area in which such work has had important results is the field of family therapy.

Stanislav Grof's work with perinatal or birth states, and altered states of consciousness resultant upon holotropic breathing or psychedelic drugs, has also enlarged the scope of psychotherapy, and our understanding of interrelationship. Yet despite these examples, despite the greater emphasis on the wider dimensions of therapy e.g. the spiritual perspective, and despite the changes noted above in philosophy and science, Petruschka Clarkson's previously quoted belief that adequate responses to such change are conspicuous by their absence still holds good.[126] She believes that the postmodern era displays too great change and chaotic complexity to respond to singular solutions, and lays down three requirements for all helping professions: "that we be willing to move with our times; we move with our art/science; and move with each other."[127] Perhaps such a willingness will also encompass the hermeneutic approach suggested by Cushman; the need to bring awareness to the horizons within which we move, the political and social background often ignored by psychotherapy. Also in reaction to psychology's closure to interrelationship and its concentration upon the isolated individual, Ecopsychologists are beginning to emphasise the embeddedness of man within nature and cosmos, of the individual with their environment.

Thus many voices from contemporary discourse now uphold ideas of interdependence which are in concert with the concept of dependent origination taught by the Buddha, and imaged so splendidly in the net of Indra. Such emphasis upon interdependence has a further implication; that of a shift of perspective, away from egocentrism.

Non-Egocentrism

In discovering the dependence of all phenomena upon each other, we discover also the dependence of the self. As discussed in chapter four, although such knowledge is intellectually current in almost all contemporary disciplines, we have not yet experientially come to terms with it. Since the time of Śākyamuni Buddha, Buddhism has presented its doctrines and practices to counter this emotional clinging to the self. In that chapter notice was also taken of the distinction between self and self concept. Similarly in his *Notes on Dhamma* Ñaṇavīra Thera delineates clearly between individuality and personality, the latter being synonymous with "being a somebody", "being a subject" and "selfhood".[128] He explains that phenomena can be significant without being "mine"; that they can be teleological without being appropriated.[129]

Such views may be substantiated from the canonical texts as we quoted earlier:

> "In the seen there will just be the seen; in the heard, just the heard; in the reflected, just the reflected; in the cognized, just the cognized. This is how, Bāhiya, you must train yourself. Now Bāhiya, when in the seen there will be to you just the see; ... just the heard; ... just the reflected; ... just the cognized, then, Bāhiya, you will not identify with it. When you will not identify yourself with it, you will not locate yourself therein. When you do not locate yourself therein, it follows that you will have no 'here' or 'beyond' or 'midway-between' and this would be the end of suffering."[130]

And in the eighth century Śantideva suggested: "In the same way as the hands and so forth are regarded as limbs of the body, likewise why are embodied creatures not regarded as limbs of life."[131] Such views are far from those of the egocentric individual.

From the Buddhist point of view egocentricity is the assumption of, and identification with, a representation of the unified self from whose perspective the world is represented and constituted, while in reality: "The eye (ear, nose, tongue, body, mind) is that in the world by which one is a perceived or conceiver of the world."[132] In ignorance of the dependent origination of everything including ourselves, we create a unified and reified self and identify with this fictional self, which becomes ever more opaque as we attempt to solidify it, defending it from a felt lack or loss. For Buddhism this sense of lack or deficiency arises directly from misperception, and is an unreal lack, a lack of something which never existed and never will exist, a permanent autonomous self. Once we realise such a reification is both unreal and unnecessary, the sorrow of its imperfection and impossibility dissolves. As we have discussed earlier, David Loy suggests that from the Buddhist perspective, this sense of lack is the prime object of repression. Going further I would suggest that for Buddhism both desire and lack are to be found to be empty or transparent, and egocentricity, with its positive pole of desire and its negative pole of lack, is revealed as a filter superimposed upon an interdependent, multi-centred world. Such a realisation of interdependence reveals the restriction and impoverishment of egocentricity, and dissolves the need for it, allowing us to see through both desire *and* lack.

In scientific terms, in a recent study psychologist Guy Claxton describes the development of what he terms the "Self System" in three layers.[133] The first layer is that of sensory patterns grouped according to experience, the second is the extrapolation of these from their context according to concepts, function and meaning. The third level is that of language with its further disconnection from personal experience. Instead of seeing ourselves as distributed over different systems, we identify with a verbal label. Claxton describes how, in the absence of life-threatening events and survival needs, this Self System may be connected to the survival system, such that threats to the labelled or nominal self are perceived and reacted as if they were very threats to survival.[134]

Following the narrative tendency we have already discussed, we also identify with the narrator perspective. It is Claxton's contention that the self with which we identify, the designated "I", the narrator of our life stories is identified only with our consciousness. Similarly, as noted earlier, Ann Klein has noted the fragility of the narrative coherence upon which we attempt to found our identity and suggested replacing it with a more securely founded "visceral coherence" fostered by Buddhist mindfulness practices. From the perspective of the narrator, unconsciousness is either relegated, to Freud's repository of repression or Jung's mythical archive, or ignored. Claxton argues that we should recognise how much of ourselves are unconscious, not merely in a special or mystical sense, but merely outside, beyond or before the control of the I with which we identify. Neural network models, such as those discussed by Edelman and Varela and Systems Theory approaches, reconnect conscious with unconscious, mind with world, and posit an ecological self, very different from an egocentric one.

Guenther defines transformed mind as spirituality or resonance. Claxton suggests that spirituality lies in a correct understanding of "world-body-brain-mind", and the illegitimacy of separating them.[135] Religious experience is the understanding of this, the removal of the Self-System with its illusion of separateness and autonomy from the working of brain-mind-world. Thus the accepted division of conscious/unconscious is found to be as fundamental and as questionable as that of body/mind and subject/object. If the hegemony of the self concept is loosened, experience may be received more directly *before* the assumptions, identifications and emotions of the self-system are stirred into it. Such a view is obviously compatible with that of Buddhist epistemology with its model of a first moment of clear cognition, prior to subsequent accretions and distortions. As we have seen based on the view, morality, meditation and mindfulness are the paths to health; firstly by dispelling ignorance and unconsciousness of the processes of the self-system; secondly by reconnecting with the unconscious experience outside of the self-system. A moral outlook intellectually vitiates the hegemony of the self and affectively opposes the strength of desire and aversion which support it. Mindfulness and meditation enhance this process. This follows the pattern seen before; first deconstruction, then reconstruction in attention to experience.

As the perspective widens from egocentrism and even from anthropocentrism, it is accompanied by a movement towards difference, plurality and multivocality rather than monologue and unity. Within Western discourse this trend is found in Bakhtin's concepts of dialogue and heteroglossia,[136] in Levinas' privileging of alterity, the face to face demand of the Other, even in *différance*, Derrida's double voice of deconstruction.[137]

One aspect of this is, as noted earlier, an awareness of the silence within the spoken – of the preconscious and prelinguistic foundations of language, that which evades and avoids the closure of totality, whether called ontology or logocentrism. Levinas even suggests that it is not only the said but also the "saying" that is equivocal.[138] Saying is a response to and responsibility for that which is prior, over which speech has no priority. Heidegger speaks of the prior pledge: "the realization that the true stance of thinking cannot be to put questions, but must be listening to the grant or *pledge*."[139]

A concern with difference, alterity and the traces of the irreducible are the marks of the postmodern, rather than unity and totality. This has important implications in terms of this project. It is not my intention to weld together Buddhism and psychology into a new totality, a new theory, but to initiate a multi-voiced discourse, allowing for resonance to arrive which partakes of these voices *and* of the silence and space between. If any external transcendent has been deconstructed and found wanting, perhaps there yet remains the trace, an immanent transcendent, only hinted at in Western discourse in *différance*, in alterity and equivocation, in the feminine, which evades the totality and unity of the same, but which is far more strongly upheld in Buddhism, in the unconditioned, in the emptiness which is indivisible from the conditioned and from the network of dependent origination.

Such polyphony and resonance calls for a different logic, different from either/or, and from synthesis. The traces of such a logic have recurred throughout this text. Most obviously in the eight negations of Nāgārjuna, echoed positively in the six positive positions expressed by Fa Tsang's Hua Yen treatises. It is to be found today in the world of technology in Fuzzy Logic[140], and maybe hinted at in Derrida's neologism *seriature,*[141] in the chiasm, the intertwining of Merleau Ponty,[142] and in the double structure of deconstructive reading. Crichley terms this latter, the logic of interruption,[143] the "interdependence of irreconcilable orders of discourse,"[144] and a relation or logic of supplementarity.[145] There is some commonalty between the intersection of the Saying and the Said and Nāgārjuna's statement concerning the identity of the limits of *nirvāṇa* and the limits of *saṃsāra*.[146] It is the logic of the intersection of incommensurable orders of discourse, a logic that is other than either/or.

Perhaps unsurprisingly the most overt and structured presentations of this logic in contemporary discourse come from Eastern sources. Nishida Kitaro propounded a paradoxical logic of contradictory identity, the "logic of the place of nothingness", a logic which exhibits a dynamic tension of affirmation and negation, presence and absence without synthesis.[147] For Nishida the existential self is to be found in that dimension where the individual negates the universal. He believed that Christianity portrays a transcendent transcendence, and Buddhism an immanent transcendence. This immanent transcendence has been a recurring theme in this work, and is that which upholds the Zen celebration of ordinary human experience, when it is released from the filter of egocentricity. The release of egocentric, and indeed anthropocentric, perspective reinstates us within a supportive network, releasing the anxiety which inevitably accompanies our misguided project of autonomous selfhood. Another Japanese philosopher Nishitani Keiji, founding his work upon Nishida's study of the "place of nothingness" and the Buddhist doctrine of emptiness, finds in this an answer to nihilism. For the concept of *śūnyatā* founded upon the conditional yet partaking of the unconditional, an absolute which is yet immanent, would not appear to have a direct Western counterpart.

Answer to Nihilism

The question of nihilism has been that of supreme importance since Nietzsche. It would thus perhaps, be appropriate to quote his own definition:

> "What does nihilism mean? *That the highest values devaluate themselves.* The aim is lacking; 'why' finds no answer. *Radical nihilism* is the conviction of an absolute untenability of existence when it comes to the highest values one recognizes; plus the realization that we lack the least right to posit a beyond or even an in itself of things that might be 'divine' or morality incarnate."[148]

For Heidegger, nihilism was negation of Being, and a concern with nihilism in some form or other has been a constant theme in twentieth century thought. Such a philosophic stance is related to the presenting disorders of psychotherapy. As noted earlier, the presenting problems of today's psychotherapy differ from those described by Freud. Hysterical paralyses are rare, far more common are cases of depression, loss of meaning and self esteem, and those relating to the breakdown of relationships unable to carry the unprecedented weight of expectation and value as makeweight to a world that otherwise seems empty. As David Levin points out in his introductory paper to a volume entitled *Pathologies of the Modern Self*:

> "We need to understand the social and cultural significance of these disorders. We need to understand them as historical manifestations of a nihilism that also takes place in the cultural and spiritual dimensions of human existence, where it feeds on a poisonous and debilitating crisis within the heart of humanism and consumes our narcissistic attention while cutting us off ever more decisively and fatefully from the being of the Self; from our humanity, and the very ground of our individuality."[149]

Here, Levin makes two important points: the influence of nihilism upon mental health, and the result of such primary nihilism, which is paradoxically a narcissistic clinging, first to ourselves, then to nihilism itself, and which becomes the very obstacle which cuts us off from health. For, according to the arguments of Buddhism and the proponents of every theory which upholds interrelationship, it is this clinging to self, and its concomitant separation from other, that provides both the initial problem and the fuel that feeds it. Thus we can see the connections between interrelationship, non egocentrism and nihilism. The dis-ease and insecurity which comes initially from concepts of separation, leads to clinging to the self concept and its narrative and metanarratives as separated and autonomous realities which, when found lacking, plunge us into nihilism. In turn, we then cling to the idea of nothing itself, reifying even that. The Buddhist answer is to let go of all clinging, to both being and nothingness, to find that all along we have been supported in interrelationship which has both conditioned (dependent origination) and unconditioned (emptiness) aspects. As we noted earlier, Ann Klein suggests that from a Buddhist perspective, the postmodern emphasis on the conditioned and multifarious nature of things, with its unwillingness to admit of any category outside the process of diffusion, is comparable to talking about dependent origination without emptiness. Certainly emptiness adds a dimension to psychotherapy as a source of unconditioned health and potential.

According to Nishitani Keiji, nihilism, or relative nothingness is a necessary step in the process of understanding and accepting emptiness, which is absolute nothingness. Nishitani's major work *Religion and Nothingness* has been described as "in a sense a modern hermeneutic of Zen Buddhism."[150] To Nishitani: "the overcoming of this pessimistic nihilism represents the single greatest issue facing philosophy and religion in our times."[151] He argues that in modern times the essence of human existence has become identified with self-consciousness,[152] paradigmatically exemplified in the Cartesian cogito, and that we see ourselves only according to the horizons of what he terms the "field of consciousness." He believes that it is necessary for mankind to move from this field of consciousness *through* the "field of (relative) nihility" to the "field of absolute nothingness" beyond all duality, which is *śūnyatā*. According to Nishitani, Western philosophy since Aristotle has been centred upon a conception of substance as a description of being. Although Kant's critique of this reversed the poles of the argument, substituting a subject-oriented standpoint, Nishitani conceives of both as operating in the field of consciousness, grounded in the presupposition of an objective-representational point of view entailing separation of subject and object, within and without. The ultimate aim is to attain to the position of the "in itself", which is neither subject nor substance, which may be realised only on the field of *śūnyatā*. From this standpoint of the "in itself", the substantiality of things emerges through being one with *śūnyatā*. "The standpoint of emptiness is altogether different: it is an absolute openness."[153] However to reach this position, the way out of the field of consciousness leads through the field of nihility before we can attain the field of emptiness.

The field of nihility – though in fact no field, since there is no place to stand – is an existential experience. In Western philosophy, Neitzsche, Heidegger and Sartre have engaged with this. However for Nishitani they have not pursued the problem far enough. For him, the step into the field of nihility is the moment of conversion from the egocentric or anthropocentric mode of being which asks what use things have for us, to an attitude which questions the purpose of ourselves. On the field of nihility, "existence itself then turns into a single great question mark. It becomes something of which we know neither whence it comes nor whither it goes, something essentially incomprehensible and unnameable."[154] Nishitani compares Cartesian doubt, which for him is under the sway of ego and within the field of consciousness, with the Great Doubt of Zen which brings us into the field of nihility.

The third step for Nishitani leads from this field of nihility, which he considers a relative nothingness, which is absence of being and still tainted with representation, to the field of *śūnyatā*, absolute nothingness which is one with absolute being. As Masao Abe describes:

"The conversion from the field of nihility to the field of *śūnyatā* is not a conversion from being to nonbeing or relative nothingness, but rather a conversion from relative nothingness to absolute nothingness which is dynamically identical with absolute being. The self-presentation of ultimate Reality through our existence is only possible when we overcome all possible representation and conceptualization, positive and negative, affirmative and negative."[155]

Beyond all relativity and representation, on the field of *śūnyatā*, form is emptiness and emptiness is form.[156]

Thus on the field of emptiness, phenomena are paradoxically reinstated as thoroughly 'real', since there is nothing more 'real' behind them. At the same time, as normally seen, they are illusory appearance. On the field of *śūnyatā, nirvāṇa* is no different from *saṃsāra*. This is the realm of the logic of non duality, wherein absolute truth and relative truth co-exist.[157] It is the realm of impersonal personality, in which: "In its being, we might say, the world worlds."[158] It is the mode of beings in themselves on the field of *śūnyatā*. The foundation of this is interdependence.[159] Nishitani reaffirms the total positive interdependence of Hua Yen, which he terms "circuminsessional." "That beings, one and all are gathered into one, while each one remains absolutely unique in its 'being', points to a relationship in which, as we said above, all things are master and servant to one another. We may call this relationship, which is only possible on the field of *śūnyatā*, 'circuminsessional.'"[160]

Furthermore, on the field of *śūnyatā*, wisdom and praxis coincide. The praxis, which originates in the field of *śūnyatā* is an "action of non-action" since it originates not from the ego, consciousness and intellect, but as a realisation of things in themselves. On the field of *śūnyatā* knowing is also a non-knowing knowing. Robert Thurman likens this non-knowing knowing which transcends consciousness, and which Nishitani terms "transconsciousness", with the nondual *prajñāpāramitā*, the perfection of wisdom displayed in the Mahāyāna literature.[161] Nishitani himself exemplifies this non-knowing knowing by the poet Basho's exhortation:

> "From the pine tree
> learn of the pine tree.
> And from the bamboo
> of the bamboo."

suggesting that we learn of each not by observation, but by entering into the very mode of being wherein the pine tree is the pine tree, the bamboo the bamboo, and from thence to look at pine tree and bamboo.[162] Here we are in the same locus as Dogen's statement that: "for all things to advance forward and practise and confirm the self, is enlightenment."

What this calls for is not just a new way of understanding, but one which is instantiated in action, in which, as we have seen, wisdom and praxis are nondual. Its foundation is in acceptance of interrelationship and non-egocentrism which leads to release of grasping at the conceptualisations and partiality which separate us from what is. It is necessary to let go of the different forms of grasping after grounds which appear as the usual answers to nihilism, even perhaps to accept that the journey into the field of nihilism itself is necessary. Heidegger would seem to be suggesting this also: "... (To) put in question our own being so that it becomes questionable in its relatedness to Being, and thereby open to Being."[163] Eventually grasping nihilism itself is to be let go. In acceptance and openness to absolute emptiness, beyond divisions of being and non being, we may return to things in themselves. The consensus of those who have written of such possibility point towards a realisation in praxis. To repeat some of the writers quoted earlier:

> "Giving grounds (must) come to an end sometime. But the end is not an ungrounded presupposition – it is an ungrounded way of acting."[164]
>
> "Finally we saw that these various forms of groundlessness are really one: organism and environment enfold into

> each other and unfold from one another in the fundamental circularity that is life itself."[165]
>
> "If each link of *pratītya-samutpāda* is conditioned by all the others then to become completely groundless is also to become completely grounded, not in some particular, but in the whole network of interdependent relations that constitute the world. The supreme irony of my struggle to ground myself is that it cannot succeed because I am already grounded in the totality."[166]

From such realisation may arise "an epiphany of one's entire form of life. No form of conceptual diffusion remains, and no questions begging for answers that reinforce a deep-seated resistance to acceptance that this life, as it is now lived, is the only arbiter of truth and reality ..."[167] We return thus, to embodied experience.

Having considered the implications of the views and practices discussed in terms of their implications for body, speech and mind, and their compatibility with contemporary Western discourse, can we now make some suggestions as to the possible form of a Buddhist inspired psychotherapy?

Part Four

Conclusion

CHAPTER NINE

Towards an Empty Fullness

"The death of the self of which the great writers speak is no violent act. It is merely the joining of the great rock heart of the earth in its roll. It is merely the slow cessation of the will's spirits and the intellect's chatter: it is waiting like a hollow bell with still tongue. Fuge, tace, quiesce. The waiting itself is the thing."[1]

It is perhaps paradoxical to attempt to bring this study to closure or finality; for to be true to its presiding orientation its concern has been, and must continue to be, to emphasise process, emptiness, interdependence and plurality rather than finality, totality or closure. Yet while accepting that any attempt at conclusion must be a temporary halt, an impermanent resting place, it would seem helpful to review some of the discussions above, and to see if, from them, we can draw any constructive suggestions as to the form a contemporary Buddhist-inspired psychotherapy might usefully take.

The central attraction of Buddhism for psychotherapy is its long concern with mind and with suffering, its analyses of mind states and its practices designed to instantiate health. It can offer to Western psychology not merely a description of mind but also methods of transformation and a definition of health which can help both to liberate the analytical approach from the psychology of sickness, the medical model of deficiency from which it arose, and to give theoretical foundation to the idea of intrinsic health espoused by Humanistic psychology.

We noted how the four noble truths, the framework of Buddhism, may be interpreted as analysis, diagnosis, prognosis and prescription, all centred on the experience of human life. The first truth, which is to be known, describes suffering, presenting it as existent and impersonal. The second concerns the cause of suffering, which is to be abandoned. The law of dependent origination describes causality in general. Consistently Buddhist analyses are concerned to show *how* processes arise, rather than to delineate *what* exists. The model of the five *skandhas* or aggregates presents a model of human identity, the construction of a self based on physical, emotional and conceptual components. This model demonstrates how this process of constructing identity is never free of emotional and cognitive dispositions and biases. The twelvefold model of dependent origination in relation to the human life cycle even more clearly shows the relationship between misperception and subsequent emotional attachment, whereby a rigid and unchanging identification with a self concept becomes the inflexible and egocentric centre of gravity from which the world is perceived or, even as we have described, "enacted" in every minute. For psychotherapy the task is first to understand how concepts become conceived as unchanging facts or objects, and then to loosen or delink the stages of that process, allowing for disidentification, space, choice and flexibility. Psychotherapy encourages awareness of the dispositions in order to see how a life statement or belief, chosen or imposed at one stage of life, need not be unconsciously or reactively reimposed at all subsequent occasions. It cultivates relationship rather than identification, flexible response rather than automatic reactivity, believing that the self is a process rather than a solid unchanging object. We are enabled to see the metaphoricity of our narratives, to hold our lives more lightly and see them as imbued with greater possibility if we do not identify unchangingly with one perspective.

The third truth assures us that there is a way of avoiding suffering, embodied in the fourth truth of the path of wisdom, morality and meditation. As the Buddha reinterpreted the existing doctrine of *karma* or causation in terms of intention, he both ethicised and psychologised it, making ideas of morality and psychology central to Buddhism. Unhealthy mind states harm the mind, just as physical trauma bruises the body. Unhealthy mind states unsettle the mind, setting up the reactive patterns of grasping desire and aversion, adversely affecting the equanimity that leads to the realisation that heals suffering. It is through mindfulness and meditation, both that the consequences of unhealthiness are noted, and that the mind is subsequently to be controlled. Thus the first necessity is to provide the calm space in which to witness how the mind works, and then to disidentify from these otherwise automatic reactive patterns and identifications which entrap us. Through mindfulness we can arrive at a more lived awareness of our embodiment, our language and the horizons of belief within which we live. We may further see how the grasping and identification of our individual mental processes separate us from understanding our interdependence.

The wisdom of the path is especially that of the broader view. We have discussed how Buddhism presents a complex causality of interrelation, a multi-level processual model which gives rise to an understanding of the mutual interdependence of all phenomena, their emptiness of permanent and isolated form or essence, which paradoxically leads to their restored meaningfulness within the dynamic process of the whole. As the hypostatized "gods" of earlier times have been weakened one by one, such an attempt to find meaning and coherence in change without reliance upon some reified transcendent outside our experience is of the greatest importance. In 1960 Abraham Maslow wrote that what our fast-changing world needed was a new type of human being that he called "Heraclitian": "people who don't need to staticize the world, who don't need to freeze it and to make it stable ... who are able confidently to face tomorrow not knowing what is going to come, ... with confidence enough in ourselves that we will be able to improvise in that situation which has never existed before."[2] Similarly another writer in the same field speaks of the "clarity and confidence *within* uncertainty that is needed."[3] Such views will not provide us with a permanent reified foundation dependent upon some fixed ideology but with a balance that will allow us to ride the wave. Indeed a current book of essays from a psychoanalytic perspective speaks of symptoms as "(failed) attempts at closure, at calling a halt to something. Like provisional deaths, they are spurious forms of mastery."[4] As the same author states elsewhere, such mastery is illusive, for "we are all beginners at contingency, because it is the only thing we can be."[5] Exactly as a recent work on Madhyamaka philosophy concludes: "We must turn the conversation from talk of resolution . . . to discussion of an insight or attention – a refined, purified love of *this world* – that never ceases to illuminate, destabilize, and simultaneously affirm differences which are themselves supported by other, suppressed forms of illusory differences."[6]

The Buddhist view of interdependence and emptiness of inherent nature coupled with mindfulness of conventional things in awareness of their conventionality allows us to go with contingency, beyond a limited version of self, soul, ego and even no-self. It underpins an open-ended search, a non-clinging to any ultimately deceptive and empty structure or theory. Each new model may be more or less meaningful, more or less useful, but in time may be outgrown and transcended. Only an attention to phenomena in themselves and a belief in the ultimate emptiness of all models allows for continuing growth and a paradoxical kind of balance in a world of impermanence, contingency and change.

Considering all the above, what may be the specific features of a psychotherapy for contemporary society deeply inspired by both the theory and practice of Buddhism? The details will depend on the form, or forms, of Western psychotherapy with which it is conjoined. The very psychological acuity of Buddhism is shown in the number of different therapies to which it has been linked. Therapists from all major schools have written of Buddhism and therapy[7]. Yet, from the Buddhist side, taking careful account not only of its practices such as meditation, but also of it central beliefs, certain general principles will stand out.

Firstly it can lead towards an open-ended exploration, without specific expectations and goals, attempting and daring to work with whatever comes up within a field of unknowing. The role of the therapist is to hold open this space of unknowing, the space of this emptiness for the client, and to stay with and in it with her. The Buddhist inspired therapist is always encouraged to hold the wider view – that beyond all the identifications and reactivity of the client, beyond even the Lacanian *méconnaissance* of self, there is the potential of the unconditioned, with qualities of emptiness, clarity and resonance. Perhaps paradoxically, this is also united with a mindful attention of experience and the things of the world as they are in themselves, an embodied grounding or visceral coherence that honours body, feeling and intuition equally with rational thought, loosened from their obedience to the demands of a self image.[8]

According to the idea of the two truths this bifocal vision will move between both perspectives, holding open the potential of the unconfined within the conventional and confined. For both are necessary. Very often it would seem that the therapist is working only within the relative, and it is easy to restrict the focus to this alone, but an intention to hold both truths brings breadth and depth to the therapeutic encounter. The relative truth of any situation is its facticity – as it presents in all its interconnections; its absolute truth, its core nature, is its transparency, its emptiness of fixed and unchanging essence – it *can* be worked with. These two perspectives are present in all situations, but because of identification, reification and rigidity we lose sight of the possibility of the unconfined. Perhaps it is the specific task of a contemplative psychotherapist to restore mindfulness to the unconfined aspects, even if in actual practice this may be only in intention. It does not call for an altered state of consciousness, rather an altered perspective; an embodied intention to bring the qualities of emptiness, clarity and compassion to the therapeutic encounter. It is an approach rather than an overt method.

As we have seen while considering the implications of Buddhism for psychotherapy in terms of body, speech and mind, such an intention pays attention to all the dimensions of our experience both as they are, and as they may be if our habitual reactions and restrictions are loosened. Thus, this bifocal vision may restore us to awareness of our embodiment, to a purified attention to phenomena for their own sake, to speech as metaphor, imagination and creativity and to mind as the enriched environment of interconnected potential.

From the view of interdependence arises also a broader, deeper and more interactive understanding of causality which results in a profound shift of focus from the isolated individual to a receptivity to the importance of relationship and context. Recently psychotherapy has been receiving a great deal of criticism from many quarters, both internal and external. Most of this is a response to its perceived narcissism, and lack of involvement in the wider world. James Hillman and Michael Ventura's recent work *We've had a hundred years of psychotherapy and the world is getting worse* is perhaps the best known example. As Hillman points out: "It took the last several decades for therapy to learn that the body is psyche, that what the body does, how it moves, what it senses is psyche. More recently, therapy is learning that the psyche exists wholly in relational systems. It's not a free radical, a monad, self-determined. The next step is to realize that the city, where the body lives and moves, and where the relational network is woven, is also psyche."[9] Similar themes are echoed in the works of Deep Ecologist and Ecopsychologists.[10] In fact this theme was noted years ago by Jung, who wrote as long ago as 1942 that: "Neurosis is ultimately bound up with the problems of our time and really represents an unsuccessful attempt on the part of the individual to solve the general problem in his own person."[11] Yet apart from R.D. Laing's attempt to see schizophrenia as a sane response to an insane world, the general view has been to isolate the patient or client in a personal world. We have also briefly considered Cushman's critique of psychotherapy's collusion in the development of the "empty self", and his call for a hermeneutic approach to psychotherapy, grounded in awareness of our political and social horizons. As hermeneutics began as a self-conscious discipline in the field of interpretation of sacred scripture, particularly that from other cultures, a Buddhist inspiration for a Western psychotherapy will both encourage and require a hermeneutic approach. A conscious awareness of its contextualisation and the dialogue between the different social and cultural backgrounds may lead to ever wider horizons, and even to conscious awareness of the perspectivity of *all* horizons.

The work of the psychotherapist is seen to be vitiated if limited to the sphere only of the personal with no acknowledgement of wider relationships. The view of dependent relationship may be applied to all the circles or *maṇḍalas* of existence, the personal, the interpersonal, the experiential, the social and the transpersonal. As a pebble sends out ripples in a pond, so the life stories of individuals may be seen as *maṇḍalas,* interlocking with other *maṇḍalas,* each interactive, interdependent and reflective as imaged in the net of Indra, thus linking an individual within the greater *maṇḍalas* of family, time and world. This view can lead us beyond egocentrism to compassion. This is an understanding of compassion interpreted not in terms of charity with its distinction between giver and receiver, but of resonance; resonance with others, with what is Other. For an understanding of dependent origination emphasises *inter*-dependence not *in*dependence and *inter* is the space between, not the space inside and leads to the middle way, the balance, whereas *in* standing in contradistinction to *out* evokes dichotomy and duality. Psychotherapy must inevitably focus on the *in,* but ignores the *out* at its peril. A view which upholds interdependence will help to save it from such dangerous ignorance.

Another important feature of the view of a Buddhist-inspired psychotherapy is its profound belief in the "basic sanity" or unconditioned core of each person, in their Buddha nature, essentially unhindered by the adventitious forms, veils and obstructions which personal life, history and experience have imposed on it. This discriminates between awareness as such and the structure of mind imposed upon it. Such an orientation provides for a different approach to one starting from a belief in sin, or a medical model of definitions of pathology. As we have noted the therapist will hold a bifocal view of confined and unconfined, of both the presenting problems and the suffering of the client *and* of their potential for health, the clear awareness of Buddha nature. Yet this is not conducive to egocentrism, for Buddha nature is *not* ego, or any personalised structure. As described by a Buddhist psychotherapy teacher: "It means dropping any particular fixed reference point, dropping the notion of possessor and possession."[12] The quality of Buddha nature is beyond description and words. Perhaps the closest we can approach to it is formless awareness, and it is characterised by those schools of Buddhism which allow for it to have characteristics at all, by emptiness or openness, clarity or knowingness, and compassion or resonance. Even such positive descriptions are avoided by the Mādhyamika who, believing that such description can only lead to hypostatisation, will only speak of *śūnyatā*. This orientation for the therapist leads to a different way of being with the client.

This different way of Buddhist-inspired psychotherapy is founded on the contemplative practices of mindfulness and meditation. All contemporary psychotherapies concur in the importance of the presence of the therapist and see the relationship with the client as central to the healing process. A suitable relationship is usually recommended to be warm and nurturing, though never collusive, and the presence that of attentive openness to the client unobstructed by too much contamination of theory and countertransference. However, there are few, if any, suggested methods of teaching presence and relationship – except for the practice of meditation. The practice of sitting with one's arising mental process, seeing thoughts arise, and witnessing them with welcome, without judgement, and letting them pass rather than becoming attached to them and their content or identifying with them, teaches the therapist a way of relationship with a client. It gives rise to a joint practice in which there is no highly defined power structure or rigid parameters of theory, and, if the therapist has done her own work successfully, little therapist contamination or aggression. For the client and their experience, the basic stance of such therapy is a belief in the healing potential of just "being with" difficult states of mind, paying basic attention to them devoid of accumulative judgement, story and identification, as we discussed earlier.

The emphasis of mindfulness and meditation in the training of psychotherapists in Buddhist-inspired therapy supports the belief that there is no ultimate undivided self apart from our experience, and that there is a distinction both between awareness itself and the structures normally imposed upon it; between the reception of experience and reaction to it. Such a foundation leads on to the further belief that healing and value lie in the present, in the ability to be as open as possible to our embodied experience, in a manner that is as clear as possible, free from defences or hindrances of grasping either in the positive form of attachment or the negative form of hatred and fear. Thus we are encouraged to touch and be with our own experience as directly as possible, as it arises in body and feelings, unfiltered by dispositions of expectation, conceptualisation and theory. We are encouraged just to be with the experience itself, without expectation, without judgement and without self-image, paying attention to the body, attention to the feelings, attention to mind and the objects of the mind, in themselves, in the present moment, noticing that if we do not identify with them, they are impermanent, never entirely continuously satisfactory and without an unchanging core or essential nature. This is the arena of the Buddhist-inspired psychotherapist; what is going on in the present moment of therapeutic encounter. For in being entirely present in the present moment, value can unfold and meaning be created. They will never be experientially present and alive elsewhere.

On this basis I would suggest that a Buddhist-inspired psychotherapy may well be less cathartic than others, offering a middle way between repression and continual expression; as practised in meditation, where thoughts are not repressed but allowed to arise, witnessed, then let go. In the words of Sogyal Rinpoche: "rather than repressing emotions or indulging in them, here it is important to view them, and your thoughts, and whatever arises, with an acceptance and generosity that are as open and spacious as possible."[13] A Buddhist inspired psychotherapy may have a slightly different intention from others. It does not set out to bring about change *per se*. It sees that what happens is outside personal control but that our reaction to events is both our responsibility and response-ability. Thus clients will be encouraged to be with their experience, noticing how they tend to identify with what they like and repress what they have been taught to dislike, or what they fear. They will be encouraged to cultivate ever more tolerance towards acknowledging all areas of experience with equanimity, to make friends with difficulty, and relax striving towards desires. Acknowledging such mind states need not necessitate acting them out, but they must be acknowledged and not repressed unheard. Increased awareness and friendliness to our experience, to ourselves, in itself will result in a changed relationship to the world we inhabit and create. Western psychotherapies often consider change in relation to the contents of mind, setting up an ideal of what we wish to change, or to be. From a Buddhist perspective such ideals only get in the way. Change occurs in our relationship with our arising experience. Bare attention to this, divorced from identification and reaction is in itself healing and the source of transformation.

As noted earlier, Thich Nhat Hanh teaches that the constant expression and re-expression of negative emotions will water the karmic seeds for a similar negative future. Rather than unremitting concern with past suffering he places great emphasis, as does the present Dalai Lama, on the cultivation of healthy mind states, of appreciation and joy in the daily events of life mindfully engaged in for their own sakes. Such an emphasis on positive emotions are more usually found in cognitive and behavioural therapies, and are often somewhat ignored elsewhere.[14]

Finally, as Ann Klein has described so well in her recent work on Buddhism and Feminism which, with its concern with the contemporary postmodern scene, I find most helpful and pertinent to this discussion concerning psychotherapy, it is through attention and its cultivation in mindfulness, that we may bridge the conceptual and the non-conceptual, mind and body, conditioned and unconditioned.[15] Perhaps through embodiment, "visceral coherence" or a "vivial sense", in the phrases of different writers, we may transcend the endless deferral and entrapment of language in an immanent transcendence which returns us to the world in a different posture.

Although it is outside the scope of this work, there is also a further possibility to consider concerning the relationship between Buddhism and psychotherapy. Buddhism changed its form in each new country and climate it came to, and I suggest that it is perhaps from the field of psychology that Buddhism will find many of its specifically Western clothes.[16] Certainly there would seem to have been more fruitful meetings between Buddhism and the contemporary sciences of mind than directly with philosophy or Western religion. The present Dalai Lama has been a firm advocate of such dialogue, well aware of the potential benefits of Buddhism to mental health in the West, and seemingly undismayed by such use of Buddhism, he wrote recently that:

> "There are two general areas for which dialogue or cross-communication between Buddhism and psychology could be very valuable. One is the investigation of the nature of mind itself, of the thought processes, conceptualization – simply straight investigation into the nature of mind. The second one is investigation of the nature of mind specifically in relation to therapeutic purposes dealing with people who are subject to some mental imbalance or dysfunction – how to bring them to better health."[17]

He continued to say that as the main objective of Buddhism is to eradicate the mental distortions, in particular those of attachment and anger, since these are the cause of much mental imbalance and dysfunction, Buddhism will have a secondary therapeutic side effect, and may well be of use to psychotherapy.

Similarly, after a recent meeting between His Holiness and a group of twenty two Western dharma teachers from all the major Buddhist traditions represented in Europe and America, to discuss the transmission of Buddhism to the West, the resultant declaration contained the following statement:

> "Teachers should also be open to beneficial influences from secular and other religious traditions. For example, the insights and techniques of contemporary psychotherapy can often be of great value in reducing suffering experienced by students. At the same time, efforts to develop psychologically oriented practices from within the existing Buddhist traditions should be encouraged."[18]

However, there are dangers in the meeting; on the one hand dangers of overromantising the East, and on the other a danger of orientalism or a covert political reduction to the norms and needs of Western society. To plunder Buddhism for decontextualised practices and psychological interpretations is both disrespectful towards Buddhism itself, and of little use to psychotherapy. To subsume Buddhism under psychotherapy would, I contend, be merely a vitiation. I hope that I have made explicit in the foregoing the distinctions between Dharma *as* therapy, and Dharma as a strong influence upon an integrated psychotherapy, and between dialogue and amalgamation. Again the Dalai Lama has spoken of the use of Buddhist practices outside their own context, suggesting that as long as such practices are presented as interpretations and not as *the* Buddhist interpretation, such borrowing is acceptable.[19] As mentioned above in the Introduction, such an interpretation, coming from adherence to Buddhism as a path of liberation rather than as an institution, would appear to be of relevance to the contemporary scene. For while I hope I have shown that the ideas and practices of Buddhism may be of immense benefit to a contemporary psychotherapy, its institutional forms as religion may be less so. For example the Tibetan language has no words for guilt or alienation, or concepts for lack of self esteem, and a psychotherapy without articulation of these would certainly be at a loss vis á vis a western clientele.[20] Freedom from cultural restrictions and the rigidifications of time, custom and dogma may even prove liberating to Buddhism itself, perhaps one could say, therapeutic.

The Dalai Lama's words would appear to give an authoritative encouragement to the exploration of Buddhist philosophy and praxis as an inspiration for a contemporary Western psychotherapy. I hope I have at least suggested some reasons why such an inspiration appears relevant and timely. *Au fond*, perhaps there is this particular compatibility between psychology and Buddhism because, as we cited earlier: "if one allows that philosophy's concern is with being, one must also recognise that the concern of psychoanalysis is with lack of being"[21] which brings us back to *śūnyatā* and dependent origination. Psychotherapy sometimes appears to forget today, that its inception springs from the discovery of the unconscious, and it is the unconscious that subverts all certainty, rationality and system. A philosophy that combines close attention to our experience and our stories with a belief in their ultimate contingency and lack of firm solidity would seem to be a fitting inspiration for a contemporary psychotherapy, an enriching source of new ways of description, aware of the non-duality of being and lack of being.

Notes

Chapter One – Introduction

1 A. Dillard, *Pilgrim at Tinker Creek*. p. 131.
2 In particular the works of William James who was a friend of Carus.
3 C.A. Rhys Davids, (trs.) *Dhamma-Sangani. A Buddhist Manual of Psychological Ethics*, introduction.
4 C.G. Jung, *Collected Works*, Vol. 11, para. 905.
5 E. Fromm, D.T. Suzuki & R. DeMartino, *Zen Buddhism & Psychoanalysis*.
6 A. Watts, *Psychotherapy East & West*. p. 11.
7 For example the Human Development Training Program, an eight-week intensive seminar offered several summers running by Tarthang Tulku at the Nyingma Institute, Berkeley, for professionals in the helping professions. See Gay Gaer Luce, "Western Psychology Meets Tibetan Buddhism" in Tarthang Tulku (ed.), *Crystal Mirror* III.
8 "But this doctrine is concerned with things of this life, and is not a matter of time; it bids man to come and behold, it guides him on and away, and should be known by the wise as a personal experience." *The Book of the Kindred Sayings* (*Saṃyutta Nikāya*), Vol. 1, p. 147.
9 T. Clifford, *The Diamond Healing*, p. 215.
10 S. Hamilton, "Passionlessness in Buddhism". A paper delivered at Wolfson College, Oxford, March 1994.
11 This was expressed in his presentation of the Louis H. Jordan Lectures in Comparative Religion 1994, "How Buddhism Began: the Conditioned Genesis of the Early Teachings," particularly in the first seminar entitled, "How, not what: *kamma* as a reaction to brahminism", later published as *How Buddhism Began*.
12 The Dhammapada (trs.) T. Byrom. London: Wildwood House, 1976, p. 3.
13 "Western philosophy has been more concerned with the rational understanding of life and mind than with the relevance of a pragmatic method for transforming human experience." Varela, Thompson & Rosch, *The Embodied Mind*. p. 218.
14 J. Hillman, *Blue Fire*. p. 73. *Dharma* is a central term in Buddhism, standing both for truth or teaching and for phenomena. It is glossed by

Walpola Rahula as "Truth, Teaching, doctrine, righteousness, piety, morality, justice, nature, all things and states conditioned or unconditioned etc."

15 Chokyi Nyima Rinpoche, *The Union of Mahamudra and Dzogchen*. p. 1.

16 See T. Kuhn, *The Structure of Scientific Revolutions*.

17 For changing views in Science and their relation to Buddhism see F. Capra, *The Tao of Physics*; J.W. Hayward, *Shifting Worlds, Changing Minds*; B.A. Wallace, *Choosing Reality*; in philosophy, C. Gudmunson, *Wittgenstein & Buddhism*; C.W. Huntingdon, *The Emptiness of Emptiness* and "A non-referential view of language and conceptual thought in the work of Tsong-kha-pa"; A.P. Tuck, *Comparative Philosophy and the Philosophy of Scholarship*; R. Thurman, "Philosophical nonegocentricism in Wittgenstein & Candrakīrti."

18 D. Cupitt, *The Time Being*. p. 2.

19 Lyotard used the term "modern" to designate any science that legitimates itself with reference to a metadiscourse.

20 "Postmodernism begins when the nihilism of the modern world is seriously perceived, and when the vision of reason that brought this world into being is no longer permitted to rule unchallenged." D.M. Levin, *The Opening of Vision*. p. 26.

21 J.-F. Lyotard, *The Postmodern Condition*. p. xxiv. This description itself has been criticised as legitimising the non-necessity of legitimation.

22 Neo-pragmatism, to differentiate itself from earlier American pragmatism, incorporates distinctly postmodern ideas of foundationlessness and fragmentation.

23 This term is specifically employed by Varela, Thompson & Rosch, whose views expressed in *The Embodied Mind* will be referred to below.

24 "A world that accepts the multiplicity of perception, the insubstantiality and contingency of reality, the disturbing, fragmented, elusive, indeterminate nature of the self, the pervasive confusion and anguish of human consciousness would seem to fit Buddhism like a glove." S. Batchelor, *The Awakening of the West*. p. 273.

25 The bivalent orientation of Western scientific thinking has quite recently been challenged by what is called Fuzzy Logic, a multivalued or 'vague' logic, based on a continuous matter of degree rather than exclusivity. A recent book on this subject points out that a map of those areas in which research on fuzzy logic is respected and widespread is closely comparable to a map of those areas in which Buddhist thought flourishes. Such thinking was largely rejected in the West until the results of its application in technological contexts became apparent. B. Kosko, *Fuzzy Thinking*. p. 72.

26 D. Goleman, *Mind Science*. p. 3.

27 M. Boss, *A Psychiatrist Discovers India*. p. 10.

28 *Ibid*. p. 88.

29 J. Macy, *Mutual Causality in Buddhism and General Systems Theory*; F.J. Varela, E. Thompson, E. Rosch, *The Embodied Mind*; G. Watson,

G. Claxton, & S. Batchelor, (eds.), *The Fly & The Fly Bottle*; L. Olds, *Metaphors of Interrelatedness*. p. 129; J. Pickering, "*Buddhism and Cognitivism.*"

30 S. Kvale, "Postmodern Psychology: A contradiction in terms?" p. 31.

31 C. Hampden Turner, *Maps of the Mind*. p. 14. Perhaps one should say the *early* Greeks. After Socrates, the term psyche began to change its meaning, moving from participation in the cosmos towards its current internal connotation, see below pp. 106 & 213. Also, Bettelheim has mourned the loss in the English translation of Freud's work which has replaced psyche with mind, with concomitant loss of meaning and value. See *Freud & Man's Soul*.

32 A.C. Klein, *The Great Bliss Queen*. p. 185 cites W. Ong as seeing this separation as the result of the change from an oral to a literary culture. In the latter feelings and experiences are considered to be the interior property of an individual, and if projected beyond this, will be projected onto other individuals, whereas in oral cultures feelings and experienced are more likely to be expressed and located in the wider space outside and around individuals in the world. Klein also notes Charles Taylor's view of this change occurring in the progression from a participatory world view to a mechanistic one. In the first: "Ideas are ontic, the basis of reality, for the second they are contents of mind." C. Taylor, *Sources of the Self*. p. 188. This progression may be mapped onto the movement from the first to the second Bakhtinian stages, and a prospective reintegration to the third. See below p. 13.

33 S. Kvale, "Postmodern Psychology: a contradiction in terms?" p. 53.

34 M.M. Bakhtin, *The Dialogic Imagination*. p. 280.

35 M. Holquist, *Dialogism*. p. 41.

36 S. Mumford, *Himalayan Dialogue*. p. 16. Mumford takes his model from Bakhtin's work on chronotopes, periods distinguished by the manner in which time and space are experienced, and by the degree of dialogic awareness, see M.M. Bakhtin, *The Dialogical Imagination*.

37 A contemporary image might be found in the infinite infolded recurrence of fractals.

38 R. Rorty, *Philosophy and the Mirror of Nature*. p. 12. & pp. 365–379.

39 "Thus, our cases of psychopathology cannot be understood outside an ontological field of interpretation in which we acknowledge our present historical experience of Being, our debilitating loss of conviction in the meaningfulness of living, our dreadful encounter with the possibility of nothingness." D.M. Levin, "Psychopathology in the Epoch of Nihilism" p. 26.

40 S. Gans speaking of Levinas refers to: "the between of human relatedness" in "Levinas & Pontalis". p. 85. Homi Bhabha speaks of: "the emergence of the interstices – the overlap and displacement of domains of difference . . . and the formation of subjects 'in between', or in excess of, the sum of the 'parts' of difference. . ." *The Location of Culture*. p. 2. He points out presciently that if the 'post' in postmodern or poststructural is to bear any meaning at all, it must not lie in the merely sequential meaning of 'post', but in a transformation of the

present into: "an expanded or ex-centric site of experience and empowerment." (p. 4). The very limits and fragmentation of the grand meta-narratives become the boundaries from which "something begins its presencing." (p. 6.)

41 R. Rorty, *Philosophy & the Mirror of Nature*. p. 370.

42 This comes from G. Deleuze & F. Guattari, *A Thousand Plateaus*, trs. B. Massumi, Minneapolis: University of Minnesota Press. 1986.

43 G. Samuel, *Mind, Body & Culture*. p. 12.

44 For example: R.Moacanin, *Jung's Psychology and Tibetan Buddhism*; M. West (ed.), *The Psychology of Meditation*; M. Epstsein, *Thoughts Without a Thinker*, and edited collections of essays from various viewpoints e.g. J. Welwood (ed.), *The Meeting of the Ways* and *Awakening the Heart*; N. Katz (ed.), *Buddhism & Western Psychology*; G. Claxton (ed.), *Beyond Therapy*; J.H. Crook & D. Fontana (eds.), *Space in Mind*.

45 In 1963 R.D. Laing considered the need for a firm primary theory for psychotherapy which would draw all practices and theories into relation with the central concerns of all forms of psychotherapy. He suggested that the fundamental requirements of such a theory are "concepts which both indicate the interaction and inter-experience of two persons, and help us to understand the relation between each person's own experience and his own behaviour, within the context of the relationship between them. And we must in turn be able to conceive of this relationship within the relevant contextual social *systems*. Most fundamentally a critical theory must be able to place all theories and practices within the scope of a total vision of the ontological structure of being human." *The Politics of Experience*. p. 40.

46 These are the training in Core Process Psychotherapy run by the Karuna Institute in Devon, England, and the MA in Contemplative Psychotherapy offered at Naropa Institute in Boulder, Colorado. Under the guidance of Akong Rinpoche at Samye Ling in Scotland a training for psychotherapists is currently beginning, and also in Denmark a training is starting with Tarab Tulku. It appears that these will differ from the two established trainings in their closer adherence to traditional Buddhist practice.

47 However, Karen Kissel Wegela, the Director of Naropa's Contemporative Psychology programme has recently published a book entitled "How to Be a Help and Not a Nuisance" which while not claiming to be a record of the training, does include much of the approach of it.

48 C.G. Jung, Collected Works, Vol. 11, para. 537.

49 "We find increasing acknowledgement of the fact that psychotherapeutic results are strikingly similar regardless of the theoretical framework followed by each therapist; that the personality of the therapist is more important than his adherence to a particular school of thought." G. Mora, "Recent American Psychiatric Developments". p. 32. Also R. Russell, *Report on Effective Psychotherapy & Legislative Testimony* and J. Norcross, (ed.), *Handbook of Eclectic*

Psychotherapy. For an overview of research on psychotherapy outcome see Stiles, Shapiro & Elliot, "Are all psychotherapies equal?".
50 This is certainly the case regarding both of the existing professional psychotherapy trainings.
51 This is why the two existing trainings are *integrative* Buddhist approaches to psychotherapy, a meeting of Buddhism and Western psychotherapies.
52 B. Stevens Sullivan, *Psychotherapy Grounded in the Feminine Principle*. p. 1.
53 R.D. Laing, *The Politics of Experience*. p. 45.
54 M. Boss, *The Existential Foundations of Medicine & Psychiatry*. p. 280.
55 M. Boss, Eastern Wisdom & Western Psychotherapy. p. 191.
56 H.H. Dalai Lama, *The Meaning of Life from a Buddhist Perspective*. p. 93.

Part One – Ground Theoretical Considerations: Preamble

1 T.S. Eliot, *The Dry Salvages*.
2 T.S. Eliot, *East Coker*.
3 C.G. Jung, *Collected Works*. Vol. 11, p. 334.
4 *Ibid*. p. 330.
5 V. Frankl, *Psychotherapy & Existentialism*. p. 74.
6 Eric Fromm referring to the difference in presenting symptoms from earlier (Freudian) times, spoke of "Inner deadness.... The common suffering is the alienation from oneself, from one's fellow man and from nature; the awareness that life runs out of one's hand like sand and that one will die without having lived; that one lives in the middle of plenty and yet is joyless." *Psychoanalysis & Zen Buddhism*. p. 26.
7 T.S. Eliot, *Dry Salvages*.
8 J. Campbell, *The Flight of the Wild Gander*. p. 186.
9 R.M. Rilke, "Worpswede" p. 89.
10 J. Campbell, *The Power of Myth*. p. 5.
11 Chogyam Trungpa, *Transcending Madness*. p. 180. Cf. "It is not *how* things are in the world *that* is mystical, but that it exists." L. Wittgenstein, *Tractatus Logico-Philosophicus*. 6.44. As psychiatrist Robin Skynner writes of his own experience: "... I am most alive, closest to the source and meaning of my existence, when I am open to my immediate experience, receptive to what it can teach me and vulnerable to its power to change my being. In this moment, when I am sure of nothing, I am yet most deeply confident of the possibility of understanding ... The next instant I have lost this movement, this freedom, this life constantly renewed seeking to preserve some experience, like a butterfly gassed in a bottle and pinned to a board, losing in the process everything that made me wish

to capture it in the first place." "Psychotherapy and Spiritual Traditions." p. 30.

12 J. Campbell, *The Flight of the Wild Gander*. p. 188. A psychotherapist writes: "The power of analysis, like the point of life is the experience itself, not the endpoint." B.S. Sullivan, *Psychotherapy Grounded in the Feminine Principle*. p. 100.

13 R. Kurtz, *Body-Centred Psychotherapy, The Hakomi Method*. p. 142.

14 J. Campbell. The Flight of the Wild Gander. p. 189.

15 Note "The reality of man and of his world proceeds from livingness, not from anything that mind as a formulatedness of livingness can codify, for objectified knowledge is always removed from truth." H. Guenther, *Tibetan Buddhism in Western Perspective*. p. 59.

Chapter Two – Western Psychotherapies

1 G. Manley Hopkins, "No Worst, there is none." *Poems & Prose of Gerard Manley Hopkins*. p. 61.

2 R.D. Laing, *Knots*. London: Tavistock. 1970. p. 9.

3 In writing of Freud I am writing from familiarity with the English translation of his work. Bruno Bettelheim in *Freud and Man's Soul* critiques the English translation, in particular, that of psyche as mind or mental rather than as soul, thus impoverishing the field of psyche, and cleansing it of emotional, spiritual and motivational connotations. Similarly he argues that the use of "ego" rather than "I" is both limiting, and more importantly, divorced from direct experience. "I" includes bodily awareness in a way that "ego" does not.

4 S. Freud, *New Introductory Lectures on Psycho-Analysis*. Standard Edition, Vol. XXII, p. 77.

5 See for example, H. Lerman, *A Mote in Freud's Eye*.

6 H. Guntrip, *Psychoanalytic Theory, Therapy and the Self*. p. 133.

7 The first version of this paper was delivered at the fourteenth International Psychoanalytical Congress held at Marienbad in August 1936, an English translation appearing in 1937. For a discussion of Lacan's theory, see below, p. 37.

8 D. Winnicott, *Playing & Reality*. p. 111.

9 As Winnicott explains: "A baby is held and handled satisfactorily, and with this taken for granted is presented with an object in such a way that the baby's legitimate experience of omnipotence is not violated. The result can be that the baby is able to use the object, and to feel as if this object is a subjective object, and created by the baby." D.W. Winnicott, *Playing & Reality*. p. 112.

10 *Ibid*. p. 114.

11 *Ibid*. p. 117.

12 *Ibid*. p. 2.

13 *Ibid*. p. 54.

14 See P. Cushman, *Constructing the Self, Constructing America*. p. 186.

15 H. Kohut, *Self Psychology and the Humanities*. p. 74.

16 H. Kohut, *The Restoration of the Self*. p. 22.
17 *Ibid*. p. 68.
18 H. Kohut, *Self Psychology and the Humanities*. p. 10
19 H. Kohut, *The Restoration of the Self*. p. 63.
20 H. Kohut, *Self Psychology & the Humanities*. p. 119
21 See F.J. Levine & R. Kravis, "Psychoanalytic Theories of the Self:. Contrasting Clinical Approaches to the New Narcissism" in P. Young Eisendrath & J. Hall, (eds.) *The Book of the Self*.
22 M. Heidegger, "Building Dwelling Thinking." *in Poetry, Language, Thought*. p. 146.
23 M. Sarup, *Jacques Lacan*. p. 13. It is important to note that the term "desire" takes a different meaning in Lacanian discourse from that it plays in either Buddhist or Freudian contexts. The same term, used by Levinas, will be discussed in chapter four.
24 See Lacan, *The Four Fundamental Concepts of Psycho-Analysis*. p. 211. Such language,though unusual, may be, I believe, less so when viewed from a Buddhist perspective. Perhaps it would not go too far to suggest that from such a perspective Lacan's exclusive either/or might be avoided through the nonduality of emptiness and dependent origination. Discussion of these follows in the next chapter.
25 *Ibid*. p. 36.
26 *Ibid*. p. 94.
27 Quoted by Sarup, *Ibid*. p. 68.
28 *Ibid*. p. 64.
29 J. Lacan, "The Mirror Stage." in Écrits. p. 4.
30 M. Sarup, *Jacques Lacan*. p. 66.
31 *Ibid*. p. 105.
32 According to fable, an angry Zeus split the original androgynous four legged creature in half, since when the two parts have been struggling to rejoin one another and regain their original spherical whole. See also J. Lacan, *The Four Fundamental Concepts of Psycho-analysis*. pp. 195–6, 205.
33 M. Sarup, *Post-Structuralism & Postmodernism*. p. 24.
34 D. Cornell, *The Philosophy of the Limit*. p. 172.
35 J. Kristeva, *In The Beginning Was Love*. p. 4.
36 J. Kristeva, Powers of Horror. p. 4.
37 J. Kristeva, "Freud and Love: Treatment and its Discontents" in *The Kristeva Reader*. p. 258.
38 *Ibid*. p. 257.
39 J. Kristeva, *In the Beginning was Love*. p. 8. This lack could, I believe, be correlated in Buddhist terms with the idea of lack of inherent nature. Elsewhere Kristeva speaks again in terms which bring to mind Buddhist concepts concerning lack of inherent being within dependent origination and our ignorance of this: "From Plato on, *Being* is already *true being; esse verum* as the scholastics were to put it. The strategy of this formulation becomes clearer; the subject of enunciation has foreclosed his real 'natural' dependence as well as his symbolic debt to the other." J. Kristeva, "The True-Real." p. 219. For

discussion of inherent nature and dependent origination see below, chapter three.

40 *Ibid*. p. 9. This too may, perhaps, be compared to a Buddhist acceptance of conventional or confined truth merely as conventional or confined, see below, chapter three.

41 L. Irigary, Je, tu, nous Toward a Culture of Difference. p. 20.

42 See below p. 217.

43 W. Dryden "Albert Ellis: An efficient and paassionate life" in *Journal of Counselling & Development* 67 p. 545 quoted in Corey. p. 323.

44 M. Boss, "Martin Heidegger's Zollikon Seminars."

45 M. Boss, *Existential Foundations of Medicine & Psychiatry*. p. 159.

46 H. Dreyfus, *Being-in-the-world*. p. 25.

47 M. Boss, *Existential Foundations of Medicine and Psychiatry*. p. 146.

48 H. Dreyfus, *Being-in-the-world*. p. 180.

49 R. May, *The Origins & Significance of the Existential Movement in Psychology*. p. 18.

50 These are termed "*existentiales*" (Dreyfus) or "*existentialia*" (Boss) and denote the structure of Dasein, the basic aspects of Dasein – understanding, affectedness, telling and falling. Detailed discussion of these lies outside the scope of this work, but affectedness (*befindlichkeit*) has been introduced into the domain of psychotherapy through the work of Gendlin, see below pp. 53 & 162. For discussion of *existentiales* see Dreyfus, *Being-in-the-world*, chapters 10–13.

51 M. Boss, *Psychoanalysis and Daseinsanalysis*. p. 234.

52 L. Binswanger, "Existential Analysis and Psychotherapy". p. 144.

53 For an excellent review, see E.W.L. Smith, *The Body in Psychotherapy*.

54 S. Freud, *The Ego & the Id*. p. 16.

55 Dreyfus translates befindlichkeit as "affectedness" in lieu of any more appropriate word but explains: "What one needs is an English word that conveys *being found in a situation where things and options already matter*." *Being-in-the-world*. p. 168. Perhaps interestingly from a Buddhist perspective, another translation offered is that of 'dispositions', which we will see in the following chapter is the term frequently used to translate *samskāra*, one of the aggregates of the self according to Buddhism. This is suggested by R.J. Dostal, *The Cambridge Companion to Heidegger*. p. 155.

56 E. Gendlin, *Focusing*. p. 10.

57 See below, chapter six.

58 F. S. Perls, *Gestalt Therapy Verbatim*. p. 16.

59 A. Maslow, *Towards a Psychology of Being*. p. iii.

60 F. Vaughan, "Transpersonal Psychotherapy: Context, Content, and Process." in Walsh & Vaughan, (eds.), *Beyond Ego*. p. 182.

61 C.G. Jung, *Collected Works*. Vol. 9 part 1, para. 88.

62 C.G. Jung, *Collected Works*. Vol. 11, para. 497.

63 A. Jaffé, *The Myth of Meaning*. p. 79.

64 *Ibid*. p. 80.

65 C.G. Jung, *Collected Works*. Vol. 8, para. 400.

66 "The coincidence in time of two or more causally unrelated events

which have the same or a similar meaning" (C.G. Jung, Collected Works, Vol 8, para 849).

67 J. Hillman, *Archetypal Psychology*. p. 26.

68 J. Hillman & M. Ventura, *We've Had a Hundred Years of Psychotherapy and the World's Getting Worse*. See also P. Cushman's critique of psychotherapy for its lack of historical and political contextualisation in *Constructing the Self, Constructing America*.

69 R. Assagioli, *Psychosynthesis*. p. 22.

70 See various anthologies of articles e.g. J. Welwood (ed.), T*he Meeting of East & West* and *The Awakening of the Heart*; F. Vaughan & R. Walsh, (eds.), *Beyond Ego*; D. Goleman, *The Meditative Mind*; G. Claxton (ed.), *Beyond Therapy*.

71 F. Vaughan & R. Walsh, "The Art of Transcendence: An Introduction to Common Elements of Transpersonal Practices." in *Journal of Transpersonal Psychology*, Vol. 25, no. 1, 1993. p. 1.

72 S. Grof, *Beyond the Brain*. p. 341.

73 W. James, *The Varieties of Religious Experience*. p. 519.

74 W. James, *Principles of Psychology*, quoted by Vaughan & Walsh (see note 65.)

75 *Ibid*. p. 401.

76 *Ibid*.

77 W. James, "Does 'Consciousness' Exist?" in *Essential Writings*. p. 172.

78 W. James, *Principles of Psychology*. p. 290.

79 W. James, *Does Consciousness Exist?* in *The Essential Writings*. p. 181.

80 G. Corey, *Theory & Practice of Counselling & Psychotherapy*. p. 425.

81 See E. Gendlin, *Focusing-Oriented Psychotherapy*. Part 2.

82 E.g. In Psychoanalysis, Fromm, Epstein, Engler, Coltart; in Cognitive-Behavioural, De Silva, Mikulas, Kwee. Transpersonal psychotherapies followed so closely upon the heels of the Humanistic school, and took on so many of their forerunners' principles that Humanistic therapists with a Buddhist influence, almost, by definition are likely to be considered under the Transpersonal division, where we find Welwood, Wegela, Walsh and others.

83 From *No Boundary* by Ken Wilber. ©1979 by Ken Wilber. Reprinted by arrangement with Shambhala Publications Inc., 300 Massachusetts Avenue, Boston, Ma 02115.

84 K. Wilber, "Psychologia Perennis" in Vaughan & Walsh. (eds.), *Beyond Ego*. p. 76.

85 D. Loy, *The Nonduality of Life & Death*. p. 157.

86 A fine discussion of the human situation from this perspective is to be found in R.J. Martino, "The Human Situation & Zen Buddhism", a paper initially presented at the conference on Zen Buddhism & Psychoanalysis, in Mexico in 1957, and published in its first version in Fromm, Suzuki & deMartino 1960. A revised edition of this paper appears in N. Katz, (ed.), *Buddhist & Western Psychology*. p. 167.

87 *Ibid*. p. 158.

88 M. Sarup, *Jacques Lacan*. p. 43.

Chapter Three – The Buddhist View

1 Dogen, "Given to a Zen Person who Requested a Poem."
2 J. Steinbeck, *The Log from the Sea of Cortez*. p. 99.
3 J. Pickering, "Buddhism and Cognitivism." p. 25.
4 *Ibid.*
5 Exposition of emptiness, dependent arising and the two truths will ultimately be founded on Tibetan presentations of Prāsaṅgika Madhyamaka based on Nāgārjuna's *Mūlamadhyamakakārikā*, with particular reference to Tsong Kha pa's commentary upon this work, especially chapter 24. (r*Tsa she tik chen pa'i rgya mtsho*. Varanasi.) See also E. Napper, *Dependent Arising and Emptiness* for a consideration of Tsong Kha pa's interpretation of Prāsaṅgika Madhyamaka, and a translation of part of his *Great Exposition on the Stages of the Path* (*lam rim chen mo*) concerned with his exposition of Madhyamaka philosophy.
6 Philologist K. Norman in the course of the inaugural lecture of the Bukkyo Dendo Kyokai visiting Professorship 1994 at SOAS, entitled "Buddhism and Philology," suggested that in spite of common usage, the four noble truths should be read as four truths *of* the noble one (i.e. the Buddha), or four truths *for* the noble ones.
7 I am indebted to a discussion with Stephen Batchelor pointing out this shift in focus which is discussed by Ñāṇavīra, *Clearing the Path*. p. 258.
8 The Buddha stated: "I say karma is intention; having willed, one acts through thought and deed." *Aṅguttara Nikāya* III. 415. Professor Gombrich states: "I do not see how one could exaggerate the importance of the Buddha's ethicisation of the world, which I regard as a turning point in the history of civilisation." R. Gombrich, "How, not what: *kamma* as a reaction to Brahminism." The first of the Louis H. Jordan Lectures in Comparative Religion 1994. SOAS. p. 12. This is now published as *How Buddhism Began*.
9 Majjhima Nikāya p. 283. PTS Vol. 1, p. 191. Citations from the *Majjima Nikāya* will be from the translation by Ñāṇamoli & Bodhi, from the *Digha* Nikāya translated by Walshe. All other cannonical citation will be from PTS editions, unless otherwise stated.
10 Nāgārjuna *Mūlamadhyamikakārikā* (MMK) XXIV. 40. trs M. Sprung.
11 Dalai Lama, *The Meaning of Life from a Buddhist Perspective*. p. 5.
12 Carl Jung's presentation of synchronicity may be considered as a lone Western attempt to find an acausal principle.
13 *Majjima Nikāya* p. 655, PTS ii. 32
14 *Ibid*. p. 355. PTS I 263.
15 *khor ba / rang dbang med par yang nas yang du skyes bar len par*. I am indebted to Stephen Batchelor for passing on to me this oral definition which he received from Geshe Rabten.
16 Interestingly contemporary Neuroscience would seem to uphold the Buddhist belief, suggesting that strong feelings such as threat or desire

may reduce the creativity of intuition, making consciousness narrower and coarser, creating tunnel vision, a concentrated focus more influenced by expectations and predispositions, but cut off from a view of the situaation as a whole. See G. Claxton. *Hare Brain, Tortoise Mind.* p. 131.

17 See H.H. Dalai Lama, *The Meaning of Life from a Buddhist Perspective.* p. 6.

18 *Dhammapada.* v. 279.

19 Nāgārjuna. MMK. trs. Inada p. 39.

20 *Ibid.*

21 Nagarjuna, MMK. 24.18 trs. S. Batchelor. I am greatly indebted to Stephen Batchelor for allowing me to use his, as yet unpublished translations.

22 In a similar fashion, Heidegger speaks of the world as representation: "Nature and History become the objects of a representation that explains.... Only that which becomes object in this way is – is considered to be in being.... This objectifying of whatever is, is accomplished in a setting-before, a representing, that aims at bringing each particular being before it in such a way that man who calculates can be sure, and that means be certain, of that being." M. Heidegger, "The Age of the World Picture." p. 127. So we get the world as picture which Heidegger calls the essence of the modern.

23 Tsong Kha pa, "The Three Principal Aspects of the Path." trs. Tsepak Rigzin in Dalai Lama, *Four Essential Buddhist Commentaries.*

24 Nāgārjuna, MMK 24 11. trs. S. Batchelor.

25 Thich Nhat Hanh, *The Heart of Understanding.* p. 3. Ann Klein points to another imaginative presentation of such interdependence in the writings of the non-Buddhist Jorge Luis Borges: " To say *the tiger* is to say the tigers that begot it, the deer and turtles devoured by it, the grass on which the deer fed, the earth that was mother to the grass, the heaven that gave birth to the earth." J.L. Borges, *Labyrinths: Selected Stories & Other Writings.* New York: New Directions. 1964. p. 171 quoted in A.C. Klein, *The Great Bliss Queen.* p. 135.

26 H. Guenther uses "openness" or "open-dimension" or "dynamic openness" or even "nothing" in various works, stating: "Śūnya ... is mostly translated by 'void', 'empty', and the noun Śūnyatā ... by 'insubstantiality'. Such translations are utterly wrong. Śūnya and śūnyatā mean 'nothing' in the sense of not standing for anything at all. Śūnyatā has nothing to do with the philosophically antiquated concepts of substance and its negation." *Tibetan Buddhism in Western Perspective.* p. 39, no. 6. S. Batchelor uses the translation "transparency" in his *The Awakening of the West.*

27 For discussion of such arguments see D.S. Ruegg. "The Jo nang pas: A School of Buddhist Ontologists according to the Grub mtha' sel gyi me long." JAOS 83, p. 73–91. 1963, and *La Théorie du Tathagatagarbha et du Gotra.* Paris: Ecole Française d'Extrême Orient 1969. Also S. Hookham, *The Buddha Within.*

28 See F. Cook, *Hua Yen Buddhism*. p. 2. A description of a "cosmology of wholeness" from a recent science book sounds very similar: "Things ... are not separate entities but the products of an interconnected whole. There are no simple causes and isolated effects; all things cause and determine each other. Everything that occurs, no matter how minute and local, is the outcome of all that has occurred before and is the ground for all that will occur thereafter. Reality is like a system of interacting waves. Rather than discrete things and independent events, there are but ripples upon ripples upon waves in this universe, propagating and interpenetrating in a seamless sea." E. Laszlo, *The Creative Cosmos*. p. 37.
29 Nagarjuna MMK. 24.19. trs. S. Batchelor.
30 *Ibid*. 18.9. literal trs. S. Batchelor.
31 *Ibid*. 24, 19-20 trs. S. Batchelor.
32 *Ibid*. 24. 10. trs. S. Batchelor.
33 A. Tuck, *Comparative Philosophy and the Philosophy of Scholarship; On the Western Interpretation of Nāgārjuna*. p. 91.
34 J. Low, "Buddhist Developmental Psychology." p. 120.
35 Tsong Kha pa in his commentary to Nāgārjuna's MMK ... p. 400 states: "*de dag spros las spros pa ni stong pa nyid kyis 'gag par' gur*" – "endless proliferations will be brought to an end by 'emptiness'". Elsewhere in the same work he states that the purpose of teaching emptiness is "to pacify proliferations which without exception grasp onto signs." Such signs or views may be compared to the patterns or response referred to above, and also to Heidegger's concept of *gestell* or enframing, the thought patterns of technology, in which things are always seen as means to other ends, or as functions of specific purposes. It is the contradiction to the receptive thought which responds, allowing Being to appear, or in Buddhist terms the meditative realisation that sees *tathatā*.
36 I. Calvino, *Six Memos for the Next Millennium*. p. 108.
37 *Ibid*. p. 124.
38 F. Varela, E. Rosch, E. Thompson, *The Embodied Mind*. p. 225.
39 M. Heidegger, *The Question Concerning Technology*. p. 154.
40 For adherents of the Yogacāra outlook the teachings of the third turning of the wheel are considered the final and definitive teachings of the Buddha, while for Mādhyamikas, and these include pre-eminently the Tibetan dGe-lugs-pa, the teachings of the second turning are definitive, while those of the third turning are considered to be in need of interpretation. Broadly speaking adherents of the Madhyamaka uphold a rang stong interpretation of emptiness, while those following the Yogācara presentation may take a gzhan stong view. See above, no. 24.
41 See J. Willis, *On Knowing Reality*. Introduction.
42 See above, no. 27.
43 For a detailed study, see A. Tuck, *Comparative Philosophy and the Philosophy of Scholarship*; M. Sprung, *The Lucid Exposition of the Middle Way*, translator's introduction; and C.W. Huntingdon, *The Emptiness of Emptiness*.

44 "Today, thanks to the crumbling of some traditional habits of thought and to the pioneering work of some Western philosophers – Nietszche, Heidegger and Wittgenstein to mention the best known – we can attempt once again and in fresh terms to learn what we may from Nāgārjuna and his school about the puzzlements and conundrums of human existence." M. Sprung, *Lucid Exposition of the Middle Way.* p. 3. Such interpretations are offered by F. Streng, C. Gudmunson, C.W. Huntingdon, R. Thurman and M. Sprung.

45 "If we see knowing not as having an essence, to be described by scientists or philosophers, but rather as a right, by current standards, to believe, then we are well on the way to seeing conversation as the ultimate context within which knowledge is to be understood." R. Rorty, *Philosophy & the Mirror of Nature.* p. 389.

46 J. Derrida, *Margins of Philosophy.* p. 13.

47 *Ibid.* p. 21.

48 A.C. Klein, *Meeting the Great Bliss Queen.* p. 137.

49 E. Conze, *Selected Sayings from the Perfection of Wisdom*; M. Sprung, *The Question of Being.* p. 129.

50 "Nihilism is a cultural epidemic that defines the spirit of our epoch. Thus, our cases of psychopathology cannot be understood outside of an ontological field of interpretation in which we acknowledge our present historical experience of Being: our debilitating loss of conviction in the meaningfulness of living; our dreadful encounter with the possibility of nothingness." D.M. Levin, "Psychopathology in the Epoch of Nihilism. p. 26.

51 L. Wittgenstein, *On Certainty* quoted in H. Dreyfus *Being-in-the-world.* p. 155.

52 L. Wittgenstein, *Philosophical Investigations.* 309. Cf. also another statement regarding the aim of philosophy: "The real discovery is the one that makes me capable of stopping doing philosophy when I want to. – The one that gives philosophy peace, so that it is no longer tormented by questions that bring *itself* in question. – Instead we now demonstrate a method, by examples; and the series of examples can be broken off. – Problems are solved (difficulties eliminated), not a *single* problem. There is not a philosophical method, though there are indeed methods, like different therapies." (ibid 133).

53 "To understand Heidegger experientially ... is not at all to reduce ontology to psychology, it is the only way to do ontology, as he insists." "Heidegger brought forward a line of development ... the founding of our assertions directly on our living, as we experience." E.Gendlin, "*Befindlichkeit*: Heidegger and the Philosophy of Psychology." pp. 55 & 69.

54 R. Magliola, *Derrida on the Mend.* p. 87. See also D. Loy, "The Deconstruction of Buddhism."

55 G. Lakoff & M.Johnson, *Metaphors We Live By.*

56 C.W. Huntingdon, "The System of Two Truths in the Prasannapadā and the Madhyamakāvatāra."

57 C.W. Huntingdon, *The Emptiness of Emptiness.* p. 136.

58 In Tibetan this branch of learning is known as *blo rigs*. For discussion of this topic see Geshe Rabten, *The Mind & Its Functions.*
59 Until recently dualistic Western science has spoken of five bodily senses and mind as separate. However, it seems that more current research corresponds more closely to the Buddhist view. A very recent study of consciousness stated: "Images and inner speech are truly internally created sensations." B. Baars, *In the Theatre of Consciousness*. p. 62.
60 *Majjima Nikaya*. p. 203. PTS I. 112.
61 The presentation of causes of mistaken sensory perception clearly displays the equal emphasis given to what the West would call subjective and objective poles of perception. There are four causes of deception; those within the object, within the sense organ, within the situation, and within the immediately preceding condition. An example of the last would be disturbance of the mind due to prior emotion such as fear or anger.
62 S. Langer, *Philosophy in a New Key*. p. 72.
63 See Geshe Rabten, *The Mind and its Functions*; H. Guenther, *Mind in Buddhist Psychology*; D.R. Komito, *Nāgārjuna's Seventy Stanzas*. introduction. R. Johannson, *Dynamic Psychology of Early Buddhism*; D. Kalupahana, *Principles of Buddhist Psychology.*
64 See *Lakāvatāra sūtra*, chapter 6.
65 This doctrine in its developed form is to be found mainly in a series of early Mahāyāna sūtras and śāstras, the most important being the *Ratnagotravibhāga* of Maitraya/Asaṅga. Also see Y.S. Hakeda, *The Awakening of Faith*; D.S. Ruegg, *La Théorie du Tathāgatagarbha et du Gotra*.
66 "This is what I described earlier as the mind's fundamental nature, the clear light nature of mind." Dalai Lama, *Mind Science*. p. 21.
67 Aṇguttara Nikāya 1. 9,10. For discussion of this idea in the Pali canon see E. Lamotte's introduction to his translation of the Vimalakīrti-nirdésa.
68 *Suvikrāntavikrāmin* 15 from *Vimalakīrtinirdésasūtra*. trs. E. Lamotte, introduction. p. LXXX
69 The Madhyamaka approach, instantiated particularly by the Tibetan dGe lugs pa, asserts that emptiness which is ultimate may be an object of wisdom. The rDzogs Chen pa assert the ultimate to be Unconditioned Mind, seen more subjectively as applying to the subjective mind rather than the object of wisdom. In either case it affords an opening to the unconditioned which to Western discourse seems problematic, if not impossible. Moreover it is not presented, particularly in dGe lug discourse as mystical, but as attainable through the processes of mind/body attention. First through calming the mind, leading to increasing freedom from personal and cultural dispositions, then through insight and analysis of emptiness leading to special insight which is the combination of both the former, and finally through non-dual, non-cognitive awareness of unconditioned emptiness. For a detailed description of this path, see A.C. Klein, "Mental Concentration and the Unconditioned: A Buddhist Case for Unmediated Experience."

70 "Buddhist psychology is based on the notion that human beings are fundamentally good ... According to the Buddhist perspective there are problems, but they are temporary and superficial defilements that cover one's basic goodness." C. Trungpa, "The Meeting of Buddhist & Western Psychology". p. 4.
71 J. Welwood in interview with the author.

Chapter Four – The Consciousness that Views: Ideas of the Self

1 Nāgārjuna, Mūlamadhyamakakārikā 18. trs. S. Batchelor.
2 J. Hirshfield, from "Lullabye", *Of Gravity & Angels*. p. 69.
3 In a most interesting recent collection of essays on this topic, P. Young-Eisendrath & J.A. Hall (eds.), *The Book of the Self: Person, Pretext & Process*, one contribution alone is dedicated to the terminology of Ego and Self, and that merely amongst Freudians and Jungians.
4 J. Locke, *Essay Concerning Human Understanding*. II 27.9.
5 C. Taylor, *Sources of the Self*. p. 514, citing, in a footnote, Merleau-Ponty, Heidegger, Polanyi and the later writings of Wittgenstein. Taylor himself defines the self by its "orientation to the good", stating that: "My identity is defined by the commitments and identification which provide the frame or horizon within which I can try to determine from case to case what is good or valuable, or what ought to be done, or what I endorse or oppose. In other words, it is the horizon within which I am capable of taking a stand." p. 27.
6 W. James, *Principles of Psychology*. p. 279.
7 *Ibid*. p. 292.
8 J. Bruner, *Actual Minds, Possible Worlds*. p. 61.
9 This view is particularly expressed by Varela, Thompson & Rosch in *The Embodied Mind*, and is designated the enactive approach.
10 J. Bruner, *Acts of Meaning*. p. 138.
11 Varela, Thompson & Rosch, *The Embodied Mind*. p. 80.
12 This translation appears to be used by the more recent and more psychologically-oriented commentators. See R. Johansson, *The Dynamic Psychology of Early Buddhism*; Ñaṇavīra Thera, *Clearing the Path*; Watson, Batchelor & Claxton, (eds.) *The Fly & the Fly Bottle* and S. Hamilton, *Identity and Experience: The Constitution of the Human Being in Early Buddhism*. N.R. Reat in "Some Fundamental Concepts of Buddhist Psychology" suggests that nāma/rūpa denotes the conceptual and apparitional aspects of a given object, which allows for an interpretation of the *pratītya samutpada* formula which "anticipates some modern trends."
13 Reat also emphasises the foundation of *nāma-rūpa* in experience, calling it "an analysis of consciousness as experienced." It refers to the appearance and conceptualisation of objects of consciousness, which is why he translates *rūpa* as "appearance" rather than "substance." This

is in keeping with the idea of Buddhist teachings as experientially oriented from the perspective of the consciousness of a human being.

14 Mikulas writes that although most cognitive-behavioural therapies focus on the products of the mind such as thoughts and images, "cognitions are often late in the chain of events, and thus seldom the optimal point of intervention". He suggests that a more helpful emphasis might be either on overt behaviour in some cases, or in others, on "behaviours of the mind" that precede specific cognitions. He points to concentration, mindfulness and grasping as such fundamental mental behaviours, and to Buddhism as a resource in exploring these. See Mikulas "Mindfulness, Self Control & Personal Growth" in Kwee (ed.) *Psychotherapy, Meditation & Health*. p. 157. I would suggest that it is dispositions that naturally comprise or underlie much mental behaviour, and concentration and mindfulness are the path to recognising and eliminating unhelpful dispositions, clinging and identification.

15 S. Freud, "A Note upon the Mystic Writing Pad." Standard Edition, Vol. XIX.

16 S. Hamilton, "Passionlessness in Buddhism," a paper delivered at Wolfson College, Oxford, March 1994.

17 D. Kalupahana, *The Principles of Buddhist Psychology*. p. 18 on the evidence of *Saṃyutta Nikāya*. III. 87.

18 Udāna 10.8.

19 *Saṃyutta Nikāya*. III. 1–5.

20 W. James, *Principles of Psychology*. p. 379.

21 F. Varela (ed.), *Sleeping, Dreaming & Dying*. p. 20.

22 Watson, Batchelor & Claxton, *The Fly & the Fly Bottle*. p. 13.

23 See above p. 79.

24 Ñāṇananda, *Concept & Reality*. p. 4.

25 *Madhupindika sutta* of the *Majjhma Nikāya in* Ñāṇananda, *Concept & Reality*. p. 5.

26 *Ibid*. p. 6. Kalupahana disputes the impersonality of the process prior to the arising of feelings, arguing that consciousness, and thus also the dispositions which are inseparable from consciousness, have to some extent at least already come into play at this stage. However, with feeling, the dispositions increase in strength and solidify to the extent that they not only individuate a person, but lead to identification with such individuation, producing metaphysical notions of self. D. Kalupahana, *The Principles of Buddhist Psychology*. p. 33.

27 S. Hamilton, *The Constitution of the Human Being in Early Buddhism*. p. 110. She backs up her argument with complementary examples from the *Salāyatana sutta*, *Saṃyutta Nikāya*. IV. 71 and Aṇguttara Nikāya. III. 294, IV. 69, II. 161.

28 MMK trs. Inada, p. 39.

29 M. Sprung, Lucid Exposition of the Middle Way, p. 33. In the glossary of this work Sprung translates prapañca as "the world of named things; the visible manifold." The coming to rest of these, he describes as "the preferred formulation of the 'middle way'; usually interchange-

able with 'dependent origination', 'absence of being in things' and *nirvāṇa.*"

30 *On Knowing Reality. The Tattvārtha Chapter of Asaṇga's Bodhisattvabhūmi.* trs. J. D. Willis.
31 J. Willis, (trs.) *On Knowing Reality.* p. 138.
32 G. Bateson, *Steps to an Ecology of Mind.* p. 302.
33 D. Abram, *The Spell of the Sensuous.* p. 112.
34 M. Donaldson, *Human Minds.* p. 83.
35 *Ibid.* p. 254.
36 Since Donaldson's work was published, Daniel Goleman has produced a best selling work on this subject, writing of the neglect of emotional intelligence, and the htherto under-publicised wrk that has been done, which would seem to make it as important for healthy developmen as intellectural intelligence. See D. Goleman, *Emotional Intelligence.*
37 B. Baars, *In the Theater of Consciousness.* p. 43. Figure 2-1.
38 W. James, *Psychology, the Shorter Course* quoted in Baars, *In The Theater of Consciousness.* p. 142.
39 *Ibid.* p. 153.
40 D. Dennett, quoted by Baars *op. cit.* p. 145. Interestingly from a Buddhist point of view, Baars states that "I" have access to perception, thought, memory and body control., not a very different list from that of the skandhas.
41 B. Baars, *A Cognitive Theory of Consciousness.* p. 328.
42 D. Dennett, *Consciousness Explained.* p. 427.
43 G. Edelman, *Bright Air, Brilliant Fire.* p. 131. Edelman's work will be further discussed in chapter eight from the perspective of embodiment.
44 *Ibid.* p. 150.
45 D. Zohar, *The Quantum Self.* p. 127. I am unqualified to consider the correctness of her description which has been much criticised by Edelman and Claxton among others, but enjoy its resonance with the dependent arising of Buddhism.
46 Watson, Batchelor & Claxton, (eds.), *The Fly & the Fly Bottle.* p. 26.
47 P. Young-Eisendrath & J. Hall, *The Book of the Self.* p. 442.
48 S. Kvale, Introduction to *Psychology & Postmodernism.* p. 14.
49 G. Bennington & J. Derrida, *Jacques Derrida.* p. 143.
50 *Ibid.* p. 28.
51 *Ibid.* p. 84.
52 This relates to the two ways of experiencing body, speech and mind which will be referred to below in chapter eight.
53 Dogen, "Genjokoan" trs. Abe & Waddell p. 133.
54 S. Gans, "Levinas & Pontalis." p. 84.
55 *Ibid.* p. 83. It is important to note that, as with Lacan (see above, chapter 2, no. 23.) "desire" is used to denote a very different concept in the work of Levinas from that current either in Buddhist discourse or the works of Freud. Rather than something to be shunned or a physical drive it points towards the infinite.
56 *Ibid.* p. 84.
57 *Ibid.* p. 85.

58 *Ibid.* p. 89. Dr. Gans and Dr. L. Redler have recently led a seminar entitled "Towards a New Paradigm for Psychotherapy" based on the work of Levinas as the foundation of a psychotherapy grounded in the ethical response of the "face to face."
59 R. Rorty, *Contingency, Irony & Solidarity.* p. 43.
60 D. Loy, *Nonduality.* p. 209.
61 *Ibid.* p. 174.
62 "The most primary of Bakhtinian a prioris is that nothing is anything in itself." M. Holquist, *Dialogism.* p. 38.
63 J. Bruner, *Actual Minds, Possible Worlds.* p. 77.
64 See K. Gergen, "Social understanding and the inscription of the self."
65 G. Lakoff & M. Johnson, *Metaphors We Live By.* p. 233.
66 L.E. Olds, *Metaphors of Interrelatedness.* p. 41. A specific theoretical model, George Kelly's Construct Theory is founded upon the way our constructs structure our selves and our worlds. The goal of his approach is to create alternative and more effective constructs that enable us to predict events more accurately and helpfully. See G.A. Kelly, *A Theory of Personality.*
67 M. Donaldson, *Human Minds.* p. 213.
68 M. Epstein, "Freud & Dr. Buddha" in *Tricycle 1 (3).* 1992 p. 52.
69 *Ibid.* p. 53.
70 M. Epstein, "Beyond the Oceanic Feeling: Psychoanalytic study of Buddhist meditation." p. 162.
71 A critique of this also reveals a general lack of sympathy with such a view: " One source of its weakness as a system is that it makes extensive use of the common human inclination to reify such abstractions as 'the self' and to treat them as tangible structures that can be defective, be subject to direct perception, and be repaired or help to resume growth." F.J. Levine & R. Kravis, "Psychoanalytic Theories of the Self." p. 327.
72 D.W. Winnicott, *Playing & Reality.* p. 53.
73 See M. Kwee, "Relativism as Applied in Cognitive-Behaviour Therapy and Zen Meditation." p. 249.
74 *Ibid.*
75 J.F.T. Bugental, *The Search for Existential Identity.* p. 289.
76 H. Dreyfus, *Being-in-the-world.* p. 127, quoting from M. Heidegger, *Metaphysical Foundations of Logic.* Bloomington, Indiana: Indiana University Press, 1984. p. 140.
77 See *The Carl Rogers Reader.* pp. 240 & 252.
78 C.G. Jung, *Collected Works.* Vol. 9, para 116. Possibly such a statement could be explicated by reference to the Two Truths, the conventional and the absolute; the absolute archetypal God image being compatible to a *gzhan stong* interpretation of Buddha Nature. However it would be open to refutation according to the *dGe lugs pa Madhyamaka* argument.
79 N. Katz, "On the phenomena of the 'Feminine' according to Tantric Hagiographical Texts and Jungian Psychology"; M. Kalff, "The Negation of ego in Tibetan Buddhism & Jungian Psychology"; R. Moacanin, *Jung's Psychology & Tibetan Buddhism.*

80 M. Kalff, *op. cit.* p. 103.
81 J. Engler, "Therapeutic aims in psychotherapy and meditation; Developmental stages in the representation of the self." p. 28.
82 M. Donaldson writes interestingly of the difference between implicit and explicit knowledge, between knowledge and 'acknowledge'. See *Human Minds*. p23.
83 J. Engler, *op. cit.* p. 51.
84 However it has been suggested that this view may lead to misunderstanding. It is not a question of losing something which existed, but of seeing through the *illusion* which we have created by imposing upon a moment to moment working sense of self, a concept of self as a whole, seen as from outside and imbued with characteristics of solidity, permanence and independence.
85 D.M. Levin, *The Body's Recollection of Being*. p. 116. A Buddhist perspective on this topic concerns different types of mental distortions. Inborn mental distortions are those that one is born with, speculative mental distortions are those that one acquires through adopting false views. As the present Dalai Lama writes: "Buddhist practice is aimed not at reverting to an infant-like state of consciousness, but at striving toward an unprecedented state of awakening." H.H. Dalai Lama, *Transcendent Wisdom*. p. 146. no. 2.
86 J. Welwood, "Principles of Inner Work: Psychological & Spiritual." p. 69.
87 M. Washburn, The Ego & the Dynamic Ground.
88 A. Koestler, "Beyond atomism & holism – the concept of the holon." In *Beyond Reductionism*. p. 192.
89 M. Heidegger, "The Age of the World Picture" in *The Question Concerning Technology*. p. 128.
90 *Ibid.* p. 131.
91 *Ibid.* p. 132.
92 Dogen, *Genjokoan*, trs. M. Abe & N. Waddell. p. 133.
93 P. Young-Eisendrath & J. Hall, *The Book of the Self*. p. 6.
94 "Because object relations psychoanalysis has not systematically addressed its basic contradiction – the lack of a unitary self in experience versus the ongoing sense of self-grasping – the open-ended quality that is possible in analysis, though present in all psychoanalysis and particularly in object relations therapy, is limited. Lacanian analysis in Europe may be one exception, and it may have gained some of its power and notoriety because of this quality. A fuller discussion of this fascinating bridge between psychoanalysis and modern cognitive science – and eventually with the meditative traditions – is, however, beyond the scope of this book." Varela, Thompson & Rosch, *Embodied Mind*. p. 110.
95 J. Winterson, *Art Objects*. p. 60.
96 J. Hillman, *We've Had a Hundred Years of Psychotherapy & the World's Getting Worse*. T. Roszak, *The Voice of the Earth* and P. Cushman, *Constructing the Self, Constructing America*.
97 P. Clarkson, *On Psychotherapy*. p. 229.

98 "the deep problem ... with the merely theoretical discovery of mind without self in as powerful and technical a context as late twentieth century science is that it is almost impossible to avoid embracing some form of nihilism." Varela, Thompson & Rosch, *The Embodied Mind.* p. 127.
99 G. Bateson, *Steps to an Ecology of Mind.* p. 440.

Part Two – Path: Preamble

1 Dogen. *Moon in a Dewdrop.* p. 214.
2 In finer detail, a recent paper, "The Origins of Insight Meditation", presented by L.S. Cousins at the Buddhist Forum at SOAS (9.3.94) delineated a comparison of stages of insight according to the Way of the Seven Purifications from the *Visuddimagga* and the Eleven Knowledges and the Eighteen Mahāvipassanā from the *Patisambhidamagga*, showing a similar psychological development which again may be fruitfully compared to stages in psychotherapeutic work. In brief, it delineated stages of definition and comprehension, the achievement of right knowledge, and the seeing of what is true and false, followed by a period of breaking up and dissolving and the destruction of old ways accompanied by wretchedness and disorganisation prior to the achievement of equipoise and reorganisation.

Chapter Five – The Value and Place of Ethics in Psychotherapy

1 Immanuel Kant, *Critique of Practical Reason.* Conclusion.
2 Despite the centrality of ethics within Buddhism, study of this aspect in particular, has been neglected both by tradition and Western scholarship, as Keown has noted. See *The Nature of Buddhist Ethics.* p. 2.
3 W. Rahula, *What the Buddha Taught.* p. 46.
4 Even while writing this, some change may be occurring in this respect. Philip Cushman's work referred to earlier and published in 1995 discusses at length both the importance and the neglect of ethics within psychotherapy.
5 "In the conscious process, current value-free perceptual categorization interacts with value dominant memory. This occurs *before* perceptual events contribute further to the alteration of that memory." G. Edelman, *Bright Air, Brilliant Fire.* p. 121.
6 D. Keown, *The Nature of Buddhist Ethics.* p. 2331.
7 See note 4 above.
8 *Majjhima Nikāya.* p. 537, PTS I, 426.
9 Dīgha Nikāya. Soṇadaṇḍa Sutta p. 131, PTS I. 124.
10 D.J. Kalupahana points out that the Pali term *sammā* prefixed to the eight factors of the path, and usually translated as "right" is not based on the conception of absolute truth, but on that of completeness or

comprehensiveness, as in *sammāsambuddha* the completely or perfectly enlightened. Therefore, he argues that moral conceptions of right and wrong are corollaries of epistemological notions of the true and the confused, rather than absolutist notions of true and false. D.J. Kalupahana, *A History of Buddhist Philosophy*. p. 103.

11 It is interesting to note that the precepts of Buddhism are not the exclusionary commandments of an external authority as in Christianity, but are commitments freely made by the adherent.

12 D. Brown & J. Engler. "Stages of Mindfulness Meditation: A Valuation Study. Part I Study & Results, Part II Discussion" in K.Wilber, J. Engler & D. Brown *Transformation of Consciousness*.

13 *Dīgha Nikāya, Sāmaññphala Sutta*. p. 100, PTS I. 47.

14 See H.H. Dalai Lama, *Worlds in Harmony*. pp. 51–64; D.R. Komito, "Tibetan Buddhism & Psychotherapy: A conversation with the Dalai Lama." p. 8; Thich Nhat Hanh, *Peace is Every Step*. pp. 53–63 and *Transformation & Healing*.

15 G. Edelman, *Bright Fire, Brilliant Air.*

16 D.Keown, *op. cit.* p. 75.

17 "Insight into selflessness and emptiness informs moral activity, while moral activity supports the cultivation of insight." F.E. Reynolds & R. Campany, "Buddhist Ethics" in *The Encyclopaedia of Religion*. (ed. in chief) M. Eliade, New York: Macmillan. 1987.

18 *Māhāyānasaṃghaha*. VI. 1–3.

19 For example: "The fool is careless,
But the master guards his watching
It is his most precious treasure."

20 Śāntideva, *Bodhicaryāvatāra*. trs. S. Batchelor. V, 12.

21 *Ibid.* V, 108.

22 Nāgārjuna. MMK 25 19–20.

23 "Principally I should consider what will be of the most benefit for others.
When this is well understood,
I should always strive for the welfare of others;
The far-seeing Merciful Ones have allowed (a Bodhisattva)
To do some actions that (for others) were forbidden." Śāntideva V 83–84.

24 F. Cook, *Hua-Yen Buddhism*. p. 117.

25 Dōha no. 34 as quoted by B. Misra, *The Development of Buddhist Ethics*. p. 153.

26 D. Keown, *op. cit.* Chapter 4 & p. 157.

27 I. Murdoch. *Metaphysics as a Guide to Morals*. p. 25.

28 Abraham Maslow, who was so instrumental in the foundation of both Humanistic and Transpersonal Psychology, wrote a paper endorsing this argument entitled "The Fusion of Facts and Values.", *American Journal of Psychoanalysis*. 23 (1963).

29 F. Perls, *Gestalt Therapy Verbatim*. p. 4.

30 C. Guignon, "Authenticity, moral values, psychotherapy." p. 236.

31 *Ibid.* throughout. Also P. Cushman, *Constructing the Self, Constructing America*.

32 G. Bateson, *Steps to an Ecology of Mind*. p. 461.

33 Such recontextualisation is also occurring within the earlier therapies. As noted earlier, the idea of narrative has recently become important; the idea of therapy as re-narrativizing a person's life story. And as J. Brunner has noted: "Stories must necessarily related to what is morally valued, morally appropriate, or morally uncertain . . . To tell a story is inescapably to take a moral stance." *Acts of Meaning*. p. 50. See also D. Spence *Narrative Truth & Historical Truth*.
34 E. Levinas & R. Kearney, "Dialogue with Emmanuel Levinas." in *Face to Face with Levinas*. ed. R.A. Cohen. p. 21.
35 *Ibid*. p. 22.
36 *Ibid*. p. 24.
37 E. Levinas, *Totality & Infinity*. p. 38. See above, chapter four, no. 78.
38 *Ibid*.
39 "Dialogue with Emmanuel Levinas." p. 25.
40 *Ibid*. p. 32.
41 E. Levinas, *Totality & Infinity*. p. 79.
42 M.M. Bakhtin, *Toward a Philosophy of the Act*. p. 60 & passim.
43 *Ibid*. p. 75.
44 M. Bakhtin, *Problems of Dostoevsky's Poetics*. p. 324–5.
45 E. Laszlo, *Introduction to Systems Philosophy*. p. 257.
46 See above no. 9.
47 C. Gilligan, *In a Different Voice*.
48 G. Lakoff & M. Johnson, *Metaphors We Live By*; M. Johnson, *The Body in the Mind*.
49 M. Johnson, *Moral Imagination*. p. 253.
50 cf. no. 33 above.
51 M. Johnson, *Moral Imagination*. p. 219.
52 F. Varela, *quel savoir pour l'éthique?*
53 D. Abram, *The Spell of the Sensuous*. p. 69.
54 A. Koestler, "Beyond Atomism & Holism – The Concept of the Holon." In *Beyond Reductionism*. p. 192.
55 C. Gilligan, *In a Different Voice*. p. 74.
56 E. Levinas, "The Paradox of Morality: An Interview with Emmanuel Levinas." In R. Bernasconi & D. Wood. *The Provocation of Levinas*. p. 169.
57 *Ibid*. p. 172.
58 Dogen, *Genjokoan*. trs. N. Waddel & M. Abe.

Chapter Six – Meditation

1 William Least Heat-Moon, *Blue Highways*. p. 17.
2 M. Csikzentmihalyi, Flow: *The psychology of happiness*. p. 2.
3 W. James, *The Principles of Psychology*. p. 401.
4 M. Donaldson, *Human Minds*, chapter. 13.
5 These typologies themselves have been suggested as the basis for psychotherapeutic work. See R.Mann & R. Youd, *Buddhist Character Analysis*.

6 For a fuller discussion of this, see D. Keown, *The Nature of Buddhist Ethics*. p. 78.
7 M. Heidegger, "The Thing." p. 18.
8 "By precise, disciplined mindfulness to every moment, one can interrupt the chain of automatic conditioning – one can not automatically go from craving to grasping and all the rest. Interruption of habitual patterns results in further mindfulness, eventually allowing the practitioner to relax into more open possibilities in awareness and to develop insight into the arising and subsiding of experienced phenomena." Varela, Rosch, & Thompson, *The Embodied Mind*. p. 115.
9 *Majjhima Nikāya* 10 & *Dīgha Nikāya* 20.
10 Trs. Thich Nhat Hanh, see *Transformation & Healing*.
11 *Saṃyutta Nikāya*. XXI, 20. and *Bhaddekaratta Sutta, Majjhima Nikāya*. III, 189.
12 Trs. Thich Nhat Hanh, *Our Appointment with Life*. p. 5.
13 *Udāna* X, 8. & *Saṃyutta Nikāya*. IX, 73.
14 As we have noted earlier there is a difference of presentation of this awareness between dGe lugs pa and rNying ma pa works, see above, chapter 3. n. 69.
15 A.C. Klein, *The Great Bliss Queen*. p. 86.
16 J. Welwood, "On Psychotherapy and Meditation." p. 43. This idea is also central to the Naropa training.
17 J. Welwood, *Awakening the Heart*. p. xiii.
18 Welwood illustrates this with a marvellous quote from the poet Rilke: "Perhaps all the dragons in our lives are princesses who are only waiting to see us act just once, with beauty and courage. Perhaps everything that frightens us is, in its deepest essence, something that feels helpless and needs our love." R.M. Rilke, *Letters to a Young Poet*. trs. S. Mitchell. New York: Random House. 1984 p. 92, quoted by J. Welwood, *Ordinary Magic*. p. 170.
19 W. Dubin, "The Use of Meditative Techniques in Psychotherapy Supervision." p. 65.
20 W. Mikulas, "Mindfulness, Self-Control and Personal Growth." p. 153. A similar statemen is also made in another paper by the same author. See "Buddhism and Behaviour Modification" p. 335.
21 Western psychology is beginning to appreciate the value of widely focussed states of mind in contrast to the narrowly focussed states of deliberative mind. They allow the unconscious processes of the "undermind", and emotional and somatic intelligence to guide us. See G. Claxton *Hare Brain, Tortoise Mind* and D. Goleman, *Emotional Intelligence*.
22 Tarthang Tulku, *Kum Nye Relaxation, Parts I & II*.
23 John Welwood, *Awakening the Heart*. p. xiii.
24 For techniques see K. McDonald, *How to Meditate*, especially pp. 94, 121.
25 See R. Assagioli, *Psychosynthesis*, and for techniques, P. Ferrucci, *What We May Be*.

26 Thus giving rise to the possibility of much confusion concerning transference issues, and the therapeutic relationship.
27 Specific meditation instruction with regard to stress reduction and pain relief has been found to be of value, see J. Kabat-Zinn et. al., "The Clinical Use of Mindfulness Meditation for the Self-regulation of Chronic Pain."
28 See K.K. Wegela, *How to Be a Help and not a Nuisance*. p. 97.
29 Thich Nhat Hanh, *Transformation & Healing*. p. 40.
30 Thich Nhat Hanh, *Transformation & Healing*. p. 86.
31 For a wider discussion of this issue, see J. Welwood, "Meditation and the Unconscious: A new perspective."
32 E. Gendlin, *Focusing*. p. 10.
33 E. Gendlin, "Heidegger & the Philosophy of Psychology." p. 54.
34 See above, p. 53.
35 M. Csikzentmihalyi, *Flow. The Psychology of Optimal Experience.*
36 M. Csikzentmihalyi, *Beyond Boredom and Anxiety.*
37 See above, chapter one, n. 49.
38 M. Boss, *The Foundations of Existential Medicine & Psychiatry.* p. 259.
39 This state is described by a therapist not from a Buddhist background thus: "In this model, there is no such thing as a neutral analyst interpreting drives and defences. There is rather an interpersonal field involving both participants. The observer and the observed form a relational dyad, an interpenetrating, living organism from which a single psychic system can never be clearly extricated." B.S. Sullivan, *Psychotherapy Grounded in the Feminine Principle*. p. 44.
40 M. Sills, "Veils & Seals: A Reflection on Buddhism & Cognitive Science." Unpublished paper.
41 S. Freud, "Analysis of a Phobia in a Five-Year-Old Boy." *Standard Edition*. 10:23 quoted by M. Epstein, *thoughts without a thinker.* p. 114.
42 S. Freud, "Recommendations to physicians practising psychoanalysis." Standard Edition 12:111 noted in Epstein as above, also quoted in Claxton, *Hare Brain, Tortoise Mind*. p. 129.
43 J. Welwood, "Principles of Inner Work." p. 71.
44 C. Tart, "Adapting Eastern Spiritual Techniques to Western Culture. A Discussion with Shinzen Young." p. 163.
45 A.C. Klein, *The Great Bliss Queen*. p. 114.
46 Reported originally in *Cyber*, 40 Milan (November 1992), quoted by E. Laszlo, *The Creative Cosmos*. p. 186.
47 J. Rowan, *The Reality Game*. p. 48.
48 For other descriptions, see M. Lefebure O.P., *Human Experience & the Art of Counselling*.
49 See M. West (ed.), *The Psychology of Meditation*; Wilber, Engler & Brown, *Transformations of Consciousness*.
50 A preponderance of meditation research has been carried out with students of Transcendental Meditation, which is concerned with stabilising or concentrative meditation rather than analytic meditation and mindfulness with which this chapter is more concerned.

51 M. West, "Traditional & Psychological Perspectives in Meditation." p. 22. West suggests that as Buddhist meditation is concerned with self-concept, it is in the field of self-concept and evaluation that further useful research may lie.
52 Śāntideva, *A Guide to the Bodhisattva's Way of Life*. V, 13–14.

Chapter Seven – Goal

1 K. White, "In the great monotony." *Handbook for the Diamond Country*. p. 44.
2 H.H. Dalai Lama, "Tibet's Contribution to the Future."
3 H.H. Dalai Lama, Mind Science. p. 16.
4 D.I. Lauf, *The Secret Doctrines of the Tibetan Books of the Dead*. pp. 215, 217.
5 See P. de Silva, "Meditation and beyond: Buddhism and psychotherapy", "Self-Management Strategies in Early Buddhism: A Behavioural Perspective", and "Buddhism and Behaviour Change: Implications for Therapy."
6 "This process ... is largely a psychological one: understanding the human condition is very much a process of understanding why we don't understand it now: a subjective exploration, so to speak, of one's ignorance in order to bring insight." S. Hamilton, "Passionlessness in Buddhism" p. 3.
7 S. Hamilton points out that the attitude to the body changed during the history of Buddhism. In the Pali suttas the body is approached analytically, negative descriptive values are introduced later in the commentaries. She also criticises some translations from the Pali, suggesting that a sentence reading: "Wherefore, monks, be ye disgusted with the body" should more correctly and less emotively, be translated: "So, monks, be indifferent towards (or disenchanted with) your body." S. Hamilton, *The Constituents of the Human Being* p. 296.
8 T. Scherbatsky, *The Concept of Buddhist Nirvāṇa*. London: Mouton & Co., 1965; G. Wellbon, *Buddhist Nirvāṇa and its Western Interpreters*. Chicago: University of Chicago Press, 1968.
9 *Udāna*. VIII, 11.
10 *Saṃyutta Nikāya*. II, 3, 6. trs. Ñāṇananda.
11 Ñāṇananda, *An Anthology from the Saṃyutta Nikāya*. p. 83.
12 *Majjihma Nikāya*, p. 1087. PTS. III, 245, 26.
13 This point is clearly expressed by Dr. Hamilton in her paper "Passionlessness in Buddhism."
14 Nāgārjuna, *MMK*. XXV 19. trs. S. Batchelor.
15 J. Stambaugh, Impermanence is Buddha Nature. p. ix.
16 Nāgārjuna, *MMK*. XXIV 10. trs. S. Batchelor.
17 Walpola Rahula suggests that this Mahāyāna view of the non-difference of nirvāṇa and saṃsāra developed from Pali texts relating nirvā a to absolute truth, such as the *Dhātuvibhanga sutta* of the

Majjhima Nikāya and *Saṃyutta Nikāya*. See *What the Buddha Taught*. p. 40.

18 "The nature of the transformation is a shift in the quality of consciousness or awareness, rather than a change from living in chaos to participation in a supposed eternal principle or archetype of existence . . . the shift in awareness is one from a bondage derived from assuming that some unchanging essential ultimate reality dominates one's (conditioned) existence to a freedom whereby one has the power and insight to avoid self-debilitating behaviour." F. Streng, "The Process of Ultimate Transformation in Nāgārjuna's Mādhyamika." p. 32. Also, from a Christian, albeit extraordinarily Buddhist-influenced perspective, Don Cupitt suggests: "the way to salvation is not by *escaping* contingency to gain absolute knowledge, but by a radical acceptance of contingency that inwardly transforms the believer." *The Long Legged Fly*. p. 84.

19 Tsong Kha pa, *rtsa she tik chen rigs pa'i rgya mtsho*. p. 401. "*rten cing 'brel bar 'byung ba'i sgra'i don gang yin pa de nyid rang bzhin gyis stong pa'i sgra'i don yin gyi/ don byed nus pa'i dngos po med pa'i don ni stong pa nyid gyi sgra'i don min no/*"

20 "Complete enlightenment is not a heaven or a paradise somewhere else. It is fully realizing the ultimate nature inherent in oneself." Chokyi Nyima Rinpoche, *The Union of Mahamudra & Dzogchen*. p. 98.

21 For a most interesting argument concerning the importance of ascertaining the emptiness of causation for Nāgārjuna's arguments for the relationship of saṃsāra and nirvāṇa, and the interconnection of dependent origination, emptiness and conventional designation in such a way that: "While it might appear that the Mādhyamika argues that nothing really exists except a formless, luminous void, in fact the entire phenomenal world, persons and all, are recovered within that emptiness", see J.L. Garfield, "Dependent Arising and the Emptiness of Emptiness: Why did Nāgārjuna start with Causation?" p. 219.

22 Nishitani Keiji, *Religion and Nothingness*. p. 265. This work will be discussed further in chapter eight.

23 R. Gross, *Buddhism After Patriarchy*. p. 150.

24 Such an approach is supported by another leading Western Buddhist writer Stephen Batchelor as "Agnostic Buddhism", see *Buddhism Without Beliefs*.

25 "Well being is possible only to the degree to which one has overcome one's narcissism; to the degree to which one is open, responsive, sensitive, awake, empty (in the Zen sense). Well being means to be fully related to man and nature affectively to overcome separateness and alienation; to arrive at the experience of oneness with all that exists – and yet to experience *myself* at the same time as the separate entity *I* am, as the individual." E. Fromm, *Psychoanalysis & Zen Buddhism*. p. 36. Cf: "The genuine individuation of the individual, determined by the moment does not mean clinging obstinately to one's own private wishes but being free for the factical possibilities of

current existence." M. Heidegger, *Basic Problems of Phenomenology.* p. 288. Medard Boss also speaks of "the great task that is placed before him as a human being in the world, the task of facing up to everything that addresses him from the open realm of his being-there, and of responding to that call appropriately." *Existential Foundations of Medicine & Psychiatry.* p. 279.

26 "We need to understand, very specifically the inveterate tendency of our experiencing to close and narrow and welcome restriction. We need to understand the tendency to conform to normalize, to secure and control. We need to understand the avoidance of impermanence and the 'constancy' which regulates perception." D.M. Levin, *The Body's Recollection of Being.* p. 74. Similarly Guenther contrasts wisdom and ego-centred cognition as highlighting "the conflict between two major opposing forces in each of us. Through making demands we attempt to impose on and to interfere with all and everything; above all, we tend to cut ourselves off from the possibility of seeing ourselves as unique and whole human beings and, as a consequence, we merely proceed under the aegis of suitability-for-purpose, of making everything no more than a means for our selfish, if not paranoid ends." *Mind in Buddhist Psychology.* p. xxvii.

27 J. Bugental, *Psychotherapy and Process.* p. 133.

28 *Ibid.* pp. 133, 137.

29 H. Guenther, " Buddhist rDzogs-chen Thought and Western 'Daseinsanalyse.'"

30 F. Watts & M. Williams, *The Psychology of Religious Knowing.* p. 152.

31 This prayer has been used in the many Twelve-Step addiction programmes in the United States, and also in a recent form of therapy which calls itself Neo-Cognitive Psychology.

32 "... man is free insofar as he *is*, he is unfree in so far as he conceives himself to be this or that and finds his limits in and by some other this or that." H. Guenther, *Tibetan Buddhism in Western Perspective.* p. 240.

33 Ñāṇananda, *An Anthology from the Saṃyutta Nikāya.* p. 72.

34 These distinctions have been beautifully expressed by A.C. Klein in a discussion of meditation: "Thus, whereas Western psychology takes one to what is most specific and idiosyncratic about one's mind and self, the higher Buddhist stages of practice described here take one to what is considered universal in the human mind. Whereas psychotherapy honors the project of each person fulfilling her or his own unique and creative vision, here the goal is to leave behind the 'personal' for entry into an unconditioned arena where what matters is what is most universally available to Bodhisattvas everywhere." *Path to the Middle*, p. 221, no. 46.

35 See above p. 121.

36 N. Coltart, *Slouching Towards Bethlehem*, p. 167. For the works by Skinner and Welwood cited there, see J. Welwood (ed.) *Awakening the Heart.*

Chapter Eight – Implications

1 H. Guenther, *Creative Vision*. p. 56.
2 Translations used by Hubert Dreyfus in *Being-in-the-world.*
3 G. Samuel, *Mind, Body & Culture*. p. 152.
4 These are the realms of the gods, demi-gods, humans, animals, hungry ghosts and hell beings. These levels have been psychologically interpreted and compared to different ways of relating to the world, see Chogyam Trungpa, *Transcending Madness*. Chapter two and M. Epstein, *thoughts without a thinker*, chapter one.
5 S. Batchelor, *Alone With Others*, chapter six.
6 Yun-Men and Layman P'ang, quoted in N. Wilson Ross (ed.) The World of Zen. pp. 265 & 30.
7 M. Sprung, After Truth. p. viii.
8 Edward Said in a talk entitled "Historical Experience and the Study of Literature" given at SOAS on 7.12.93, exemplified this split by, on the one hand the growth of formalism in twentieth century literary studies, and on the other, a return to experience shown in the increasing valuation of feminine and ethnic viewpoints as expanding and enlarging horizons of experience.
9 M. Shaw, *Passionate Enlightenment*. p. 11.
10 Tsong Kha pa, *rTsa she tik chen rigs pa'i rgya mtsho*. p. 408. quoting from *Madhyamakāvatara*: gnod pa med pa'i dbang po drug rnams kyis/ bzung ba gang shig 'jig rten gyis rtog de/ 'jig rten nyid les bden yin lhag ma ni/ 'jig rten nyid les log par rna par bshag// My translation.
11 *Ibid*: 'phral gyi 'khrul rgyu'i gnod pa med pa'i dbang po drug gi shes pas...
12 Wang-Ch'ug Dor-je, the ninth Karmapa, *The Mahamūdra*. p. 31.
13 *Satipaṭṭāna Sutta in Majjhima Nikāya*. p. 145 PTS. I. 10, *Dīgha Nikāya*. p. 335. PTS, II 22.
14 It is important to note the overlap or interconnection of the three dimensions of body, speech and mind, which was also present in the earlier quotation from Miranda Shaw. Speaking of voice or speech, the commentary to rDzogs chen text notes that in its transformed or esoteric tantric state "voice is not only speech or the sounds produced by our vocal chords, but also all the respiratory energies which supports it, which is itself linked to all our bodily energies." K. Lipman & M. Peterson with Namkhai Norbu, commentary to *You are the Eyes of the World*. p. 68.
15 Thich Nhat Hanh, *Transformation & Healing*. p. 5.
16 Thich Nhat Hanh, *Transformation & Healing*. p. 58.
17 A.C. Klein, *The Great Bliss Queen*. p. 154. Italics of the final line are mine.
18 M. Sprung, "Being and the Middle Way." p. 130.
19 F.D. Cook, *How to Raise an Ox*. p. 102.
20 *Ibid*. p. 112.
21 Dogen, "Bendowa." trs. N.A. Waddel & Masao Abe, *Eastern Buddhist* 4, (1). p. 130.

22 See M. Abe, *A Study of Dogen*, chapter 1.
23 Mention was made in chapter five of the way in which the enactive approach in Cognitive Science and Systems Theory reunite means and ends in a circular interdependent process.
24 F. Cook, "Dogen's View of Authentic Selfhood". p. 139.
25 M. Heidegger, Poetry, *Language & Thought*. p. 181.
26 "For without a phenomenology of the lived body, a hermeneutical phenomenology of experiential perception, there can be no 'grounding' of theory and praxis in experiential meaning." D.M. Levin, *The Listening Self*. p. 174.
27 See above, p. 144.
28 This work was briefly mentioned in relation to Buddhist thought in chapter three, and its relation to ethics in chapter five.
29 M. Johnson, *The Body in the Mind*. p. xiv.
30 One might conjecture the similarity between these cognitive structures and basic dispositions (*samskāras*) prior to their solidification with value-laden grasping. See above pp. 98–9.
31 "Through metaphor, we make use of patterns that obtain in our physical experience to organize our more abstract understanding." *Ibid*. p. xv.
32 *Ibid*. p. xvi.
33 Johnson's non-objectivist approach which he terms cognitive "semantics" employs three key notions; embodiment, imagination and understanding which, I suggest, align with the body, speech and mind model.
34 *Ibid*. p. 102.
35 "It is essential to show that both dualism and monism are false because it is generally supposed that these exhaust the field, leaving no other options." J.R. Searle, *The Rediscovery of the Mind*. p. 2.
36 *Ibid*. p. xii.
37 F. Varela, *quel savoir pour l'ethique?* p. 88.
38 G. Edelman, *Bright Air, Brilliant Fire*. p. 122. cf the ideas of ongoing self and self concept discussed above in chapter four.
39 *Ibid*. p. 152.
40 Varela, Thompson & Rosch, *The Embodied Mind*. p. 27.
41 *Ibid*. p. 31.
42 "The possibilities for total personal re-embodiment inherent in the mindful, open-ended approach to experience that we have been describing may provide the needed framework and tools for implementation of an existential, embodied psychoanalysis. In fact, the relationship between meditation practice, Buddhist teachings and therapy is a topic of great interest and great controversy among Western mindfulness/awareness practitioners.... An adequate discussion of this ferment would lead us too far afield at this point, but we invite the reader to consider what form a reembodying psychoanalysis might take." *Ibid*. p. 180.
43 See above, no. 18 & no. 7.
44 M. Johnson, *The Body in the Mind*. p. 196.

45 E.g. Bioenergetic exercises, Reichian breathing, Hatha Yoga from the Hindu tradition, Chi Kung exercises from the Taoist tradition, and the Tibetan Kum Nye exercises as presented in the West by Tarthang Tulku.
46 Rainer Maria Rilke, from *Ninth Duino Elegy*, author's translation.
47 See S. Batchelor, *Alone With Others*. p. 74. n.4.
48 S. Langer, *Philosophy in a New Key*. p. 26.
49 J. Searle in B. Magee, *Men of Ideas*. p. 184 Perhaps the most extreme views concerning the importance of language in the construction of world come in the work of B. Lee Whorf, *Language, Thought and Reality: Selected Writings*.
50 Terry Eagleton neatly encapsulates both these approaches, while giving his approval to the more radical "enactive" stance, stating: "Language always pre-exists the individual subject, as the very realm in which he or she unfolds; and it contains 'truth' less in the sense that it is an instrument for exchanging accurate information than in the sense that it is the place where reality 'un-conceals' itself, gives itself up to our contemplation." *Literary Theory*, p. 63.
51 C. Gilligan, *In A Different Voice*. p. xvi. Introduction to 1993 edition.
52 C.W. Huntingdon, The Emptiness of Emptiness. p. 54. This is his paraphrase of his own translation of Candrakīrti, *Madhyamakāvatara* 6. 173–6.
53 *Ibid*. p. 59.
54 H. Guenther, Creative Vision. p. xiii.
55 See above no. 50. It is interesting also to compare this with idea of the openness of utterance as expressed by Bakhtin, and Levinas' distinction between Saying and the Said.
56 J.I. Cabezon, *Buddhism & Language*. p. 51.
57 In "Letter on Humanism", repeated in On the way to Language. p. 135.
58 *Ibid*. p. 108.
59 R. Bernasconi, *The Question of Language in Heidegger's History of Being*. p. 62.
60 "*The essential being of language is Saying as showing*. Its showing character is not based on signs of any kind; rather, all signs arise from a showing within whose realm and for whose purpose they can be signs." *On the Way to Language*. p. 123.
61 *Ibid*. p. 135.
62 "Experience is nothing mystical, not an act of illumination, but rather the entry into dwelling in Appropriation. Thus awakening to Appropriation remains indeed something which must be experienced." *Time & Being*. p. 53.
63 "The face speaks. It speaks. It is in this that it renders possible and begins all discourse." E. Levinas. *Ethics & Infinity*. p. 77.
64 E. Levinas, *Totality & Infinity*. p. 39.
65 Simon Critchley in his excellent study of Levinas and Derrida, *The Ethics of Deconstruction*, suggests that Levinas' *Otherwise Than*

Being is an attempt to maintain the ethical Saying within the ontological Said – "a performative enactment of ethical writing." p. 8. This paradox is also found in Buddhism wherein to speak at all of ultimate truth necessitates the use of conventional language.

66 *The Vajracchedika Prajnāpāramitā Sutra.* 23.

67 See C. Gudmunson, *Wittgenstein & Buddhism*; R. Thurman, *Tsong Kha pa's Speech of Gold.* Introduction, esp. p. 103; C.W. Huntingdon, *The Emptiness of Emptiness.* pp. 10–11.

68 L. Wittgenstein, *Tractatus Logico-Philosophicus.* 7. p. 151.

69 L. Wittgenstein, *Prototractatus.* pp. 15 & 16.

70 *Philosophical Investigations.* 309. See also: "The philosopher's treatment of a question is like the treatment of an illness." *Ibid.* 255.

71 "The real discovery is the one that makes me capable of stopping doing philosophy when I want to. – The one that gives philosophy peace, so that it is no longer tormented by questions which bring *itself* in question. *Ibid.* 133.

72 J.F. Peterman, *Philosophy as Therapy.* p. 82.

73 S. Critchley, *The Ethics of Deconstruction.* p. 22.

74 *Ibid.* p. 23.

75 See above p. 88, and for more detailed description, J.I. Cabezon, *Buddhism & Language.* p. 124.

76 For discussion of Derrida and Buddhism, see R. Magliola, *Derrida on the Mend*; H. Coward, "Derrida and Indian Philosophy", and D. Loy, *Nonduality* and "The Deconstruction of Buddhism." Both Magliola and Loy compare Derrida's critique of Western philosophy with Nāgārjuna and Mādhyamika, and critique Derrida for his failure to go far enough, remaining in a halfway house of textuality, while Nāgārjuna points to a transformed way of experiencing the world instantiated in meditative practice which is, as Loy states: "another praxis beside conceptualization." They point out also that Nāgārjuna deconstructs emptiness or difference as well as identity or self-being, whereas Derrida, deconstructing only identity would merely set in motion another swing of the pendulum, from identity to difference. Magliola (as briefly noted above, p. 85), suggests that Nāgārjuna's middle path goes beyond Derrida in that it frequents the "unheard-of thought" and at the same time by its presentation of the two truths allows for reinstatement of the logocentric.

77 G. Claxton, *Noises From the Darkroom.* Parts III & IV. Exploration of this 'undermind' is continued in his subsequent book *Hare Brain, Tortoise Mind.*

78 "Language is based on cognition – that is, on cognitive models that can be understood in terms of bodily functioning. This cognitive basis is constrained by the nature of physical reality and also depends on imagination and social interactions." G. Edelman, *Bright Fire, Brilliant Air.* p. 250.

79 J. Bruner, *Acts of Meaning.* p. 72.

80 D. Abram, *The Spell of the Sensuous.* p. 74.

81 *Ibid.* p. 274.

82 M. Heidegger, *Poetry, Language, Thought*. p. 208.
83 *Ibid*. p. 132.
84 M. Johnson, *The Body in the Mind*. p. 151.
85 J. Locke, *An Essay Concerning Human Understanding*. Vol. 2. p. 5. New York: Dover Books.
86 B. Baars, *In the Theatre of Consciousness*. p. 63.
87 J. Winterson, *Art Objects*. p. 66.
88 R. Rorty, *Essays on Heidegger & Others*. p. 13.
89 The formulas most common are: *OṂ svabhāva-śuddhāḥ-sarva-dharmāh-svabhāva- suddho 'haṃ*; Pure of essence are all events, pure of essence am I, and *OṂ śūnyatā-jñana vajra-svabhāvâtmako 'haṃ*: I am the very self whose essence is the diamond of the knowledge of Emptiness. Translations from S. Beyer, *The Cult of Tara*. p. 33.
90 G. Lakoff & M. Johson. *Metaphors We Live By*. p. 233.
91 S.Batchelor, "A Democracy of the Imagination." p. 6. A version of this text, not containing the above passage appeared in Tricycle, Vol. IV, no. 2. 1994.
92 O.Barfield, Saving the Appearances. p. 147.
93 See R.Avens, Imagination is Reality.
94 "For each time you or I treat images as representations of something else – Penis or Great Mother or Power Drive, or Instinct, or whatever general, abstract concept we prefer – we have smashed the image in favour of the idea behind it. To give to imagination interpretative meanings is to think allegorically and to depotentiate the power of the imagination." J.Hillman, "Peaks & Vales" p. 50.
95 J. Hillman, *Revisioning Psychology*. p. 9.
96 R. Avens, *op. cit*. p. 86.
97 A. Jardine, *Gynesis*. p. 147.
98 "One concept which we already have incorporated into feminist thinking has to do with the intrinsic interrelationship between the external world and the internal psychological world. I could not call a theory woman-based, if it recognized any other relationship than one of complicated interaction between reality and the circumstances in which we live." H. Lerman, *A Mote in Freud's Eye*. p. 176.
99 T.T. Williams, *An Unspoken Hunger*. p. 53.
100 Sherry Ortner, quoted by T. Roszak, *The Voice of the Earth*. p. 235.
101 J. Gyatso, "Down with the Demoness: Reflection on a Feminine Ground in Tibet." p. 40.
102 "Equivocation constitutes the epiphany of the feminine." E. Levinas, *Totality & Infinity*. p. 264.
103 "Perhaps ..., all these allusions to the ontological differences between the masculine and the feminine would appear less archaic if, instead of dividing humanity into two species (or into two genders), they would signify that the participation in the masculine and in the feminine were the attribute of every human being. Could this be the meaning of the enigmatic verse of *Genesis* I.27: 'male and female created He them?'." E. Levinas, *Ethics and Infinity*. p. 68.

104 "I cannot evade the notion (though I hesitate to give it expression) that for women the level of what is ethically normal is different from what it is in men. Their super-ego is never so inexorable, so impersonal, so independent of its emotional origins, as we require it to be in men." S. Freud, "Some Physical Consequences of the Anatomical Structure between the sexes." p. 27.
105 B.S. Sullivan, *Psychotherapy Grounded in the Feminine Principle.*
106 *Ibid.* p. 20.
107 *Ibid.* p. 81.
108 Here I would echo Levinas' statement: "The not-knowing is not to be understood as a privation of knowing." E. Levinas, *Ethics & Infinity.* p. 66.
109 "The feminine defined as lack, is a cultural construct that is necessary for the self-perpetuation of the gender hierarchy because the very illusion of masculine self-sufficiency demands that the devalorized Other be there to serve as a mirror." D. Cornell, *The Philosophy of the Limit*. p. 173.
110 There is an ongoing dialogue now between feminism and Buddhism in the West, which may well influence the form a Western Buddhism will take. Recent works in this field also include M. Shaw, *Passionate Enlightenment*; S. Boucher, *Turning the Wheel* and A.C. Klein, *Meeting the Great Bliss Queen.*
111 "Meaning may well be ultimately undecidable if we view language contemplatively, as a chain of signifiers on a page; it becomes 'decidable' and words like 'truth', 'reality', 'knowledge' and 'certainty' have something of their force restored to them when we think of language rather as something we *do*, as indissolubly interwoven with our practical forms of life." T. Eagleton, *Literary Theory, An Introduction*. p. 146.
112 Thomas Traherne from *Centuries of Meditation.*
113 An outstanding exception is William James, who distinguishes the often ignored 'transitive' moments of consciousness from the substantive moments, i.e. thoughts.
114 This is especially true according to the doctrines of the Yogācāra school.
115 J. Welwood, "Exploring Mind: Form, Emptiness & Beyond." p. 90.
116 H. Guenther, *The Creative Vision*. p. xiv.
117 "...we are through and through compounded of relationships with the world." M. Merleau Ponty, *The Phenomenology of Perception.* p. xiii.
118 *Ibid.*
119 *Ibid.* p. xx.
120 *Ibid.* p. xxi.
121 L. Wittgenstein, *Tractatus Logico-Philosophicus*. 6.44.
122 M. Merleau Ponty, *op. cit.* p. 94.
123 *Ibid.* p. 96.
124 E. Laszlo, *Introduction to Systems Philosophy.* p. 43.
125 G. Edelman, *Bright Air, Brilliant Fire*. p. 224.

126 P. Clarkson, *On Therapy.* p. 229.
127 *Ibid.* p. 230. Her essay ends: "I believe that psychology, counselling, psychotherapy, supervision and organisational work needs also to acknowledge the final mysteries – the end of our knowledge and the beginning of nothingness . . ." p. 231. Perhaps emptiness (śūnyatā) is a doorway to nothingness for the West.
128 Ñāṇavīra Thera, *Clearing the Path.* p. 105.
129 *Ibid.* p. 487.
130 *Udāna* 10. 8 and above, p. 99.
131 Śantideva, *Guide to the Bodhisattva's Way of Life.* VIII 114.
132 *Saṃyutta Nikāya* 116.iv.95. Note "conceiver", as both conception mentally, and the bringing forth of Varela, Thompson & Rosch.
133 G. Claxton, *Noises from the Darkroom.* p. 90.
134 *Ibid.* chapter 10.
135 *Ibid.* p.12.
136 See: "Dialogism functions . . . as a principle of radical otherness or, to use again Bakhtin's own terminology, as a principle of *exotopy*: far from aspiring to the *telos* of a synthesis or a resolution, as could be said to be the case in dialectical systems, the function of dialogism is to sustain and think through the radical exteriority or heterogeneity of one voice with regard to any other, including that of the novelist himself." P. de Man "Dialogue and Dialogism. p. 109. De Man believes that it is by way of exotopy that larger philosophical claims may be made for Bakhtin.
137 See particularly S. Critchley, *The Ethics of Deconstruction*, in which Crichley argues convincingly for a reading of deconstruction according to a Levinasian hermeneutics which reveals the ethical saying of alterity at work within the said of a text. "The ethical moment that motivates deconstruction is this Yes-saying to the unnameable, a moment of unconditional affirmation that is addressed to an alterity than can neither be excluded from nor included within logocentric conceptuality." p. 41, where the unnameable refers to *différance*.
138 E. Levinas, *Totality & Infinity.* p. 260 "The "saying" and not only the said, is equivocal. The equivocal does not play between two meanings of speech, but between speech and the renouncement of speech . . ."
139 M. Heidegger, *On the Way to Language.* p. 72.
140 See above, chapter 1, no. 25.
141 "An interrupted series, a series of interlaced interruptions, a series of *hiatuses (. . .).*" J. Derrida, "En ce moment même dans cet ouvrage me voici" in *Textes pour Emmanuel Levinas.* F. Larnette (ed.). Paris: Jean-Michel Place. 1980 p. 48, quoted by S. Critchley, *The Ethics of Deconstruction.* p. 128., who describes it thus: "The concept of seriature describes the relations between binding and unbinding, between being bound to ontological or logocentric language while at the same moment being unbound to that language."
142 M. Merleau Ponty, *The Visible and the Invisible.*

143 "The Saying shows itself within the Said by interrupting it." S. Critchley, *The Ethics of Deconstruction*. p. 164.
144 *Ibid.* p. 169.
145 *Ibid.* p. 173.
146 Nāgārjuna, *Mūlamadhyamakakārikā,* XXV. 20. "The limits (i.e. realm) of *nirvāṇa* are the limits of *saṃsāra*. Between the two, also, there is not the slightest difference whatsoever." trs. K. Inada.
147 "The personal self, which is both free and yet determined, subjective and objective exists creatively by being the world's expression and yet expressing the world within itself, as the contradictory identity of the transcendent and immanent planes of the conscious act." Nishida Kitaro, *Last Writings*. p. 73.
148 F. Nietzsche, *The Will to Power.* paras 2 & 3 quoted in J. Stambaugh, *The Other Nietzsche*. p. 123.
149 D.M. Levin, *Pathologies of the Modern Self*. p. 44.
150 Taitetso Unno, "Emptiness & Reality in Mahayana Buddhism." p. 315.
151 Nishitani Keiji, *Religion & Nothingness*. p. 47.
152 Cf. G. Claxton's similar argument discussed earlier.
153 Nishitani Keiji, *op. cit.* p. 105.
154 *Ibid.* p. 111.
155 M. Abe, "Nishitani's Challenge to Philosophy and Theology." p. 26.
156 "Emptiness of *śūnyatā* is not an emptiness represented as some 'thing' outside of being – other than being – it is not simply an 'empty nothing', but rather an *absolute emptiness*, emptied even of these representations of emptiness. And for that reason, it is at bottom one with being, even as being is at bottom one with emptiness." Nishitani Keiji, *op. cit.* p.122.
157 "... on a field of emptiness where being is seen as *being-sive-nothingness*, *nothingness-sive*-being, where the *reality* of being at the same time bears the stamp of *illusion*. On this field, a mode of being is constituted wherein things, just as they are in their real suchness are illusory appearances, wherein as things-in-themselves they are phenomena." *Ibid.* p. 147.
158 *Ibid.* p. 150.
159 "All the things that are in the world are linked together, one way or the other." *Ibid.* p. 149.
160 *Ibid.* p. 148.
161 R. Thurman, "Nishitani & the Inner Science of Buddhism." p. 162.
162 Nishitani Keiji, *op. cit.* p. 128.
163 M. Heidegger, *What is Called Thinking*. p. 78.
164 L. Wittgenstein, *On Certainty* quoted in H. Dreyful, *Being-in-the-world. p. 155.*
165 Varela, Thompson & Rosch, *The Embodied Mind*. p. 217.
166 D. Loy, "Avoiding the Void". p. 171.
167 C.W. Huntington, *The Emptiness of Emptiness*. p. 136.

Chapter 9 – Towards an Empty Fullness

1 A. Dillard, *Pilgrim at Tinker Creek*. p. 226.
2 A. Maslow, *The Farther Reaches of Himan Nature*. p. 61.
3 J. Hayward, *Shifting Worlds, Changing Minds*. p. 2.
4 A. Phillips, *On Flirtation*. p. 153.
5 *Ibid*. p. 21.
6 C.W. Huntingdon, *The Emptiness of Emptiness*. p. 162.
7 Amongst others, from Analytic approaches, Fromm, Epstein, Engler, Coltart, Moacanin; from Cognitive-Behavioural perspective, de Silva, Mikulas, Kwee; from Existentialism, Binswanger and Boss, and from the Transpersonal school, Welwood, Wegela, Walsh.
8 Such a goal is shared by other approaches to therapy, cf.: "The answer to the question after the ultimate meaning of human existence can never be given intellectually, but only existentially; not in words, but by our life, by our whole existence." V. Frankl, "Reductionism and Nihilism." p. 408. However it is the contention of this work that a Buddhist framework helps both to underpin such aims with its philosophy, and to actualise them with its practices.
9 J. Hillman & M. Ventura, *We've had a hundred years of psychotherapy and the world is getting worse*. p. 83.
10 Theodore Roszak likens the industrial city to the body armour of our culture, pathologically cutting us off from contact with the natural world from which we evolve. *The Voice of the Earth*. p. 220.
11 C.G. Jung, *Collected Works*. Vol. 7, para 18.
12 K. Kissel Wegela, "Touch and go in clinical practice." p. 7.
13 Sogyal Rinpoche, *The Tibetan book of Living and Dying*. p. 61.
14 Psychosynthesis would also be exempt from this stricture.
15 A.C. Klein, *The Great Bliss Queen*.
16 We have noted earlier the possible influence of feminism also, see chapter eight, no. 110. Although as outlined in my Introduction the process of Buddhism's interaction with psychology began at the turn of the century, any specifically Western form of Buddhism is still, I would suggest, merely embryonic.
17 Hayward & Varela (eds.), *Gentle Bridges*. p. 115.
18 Published in Tricycle Magazine, Vol. III, no. 1, Fall 1993.
19 "... to pretend it to be the Buddhist interpretation would be a degeneration. However, it's all right to make such symbolic interpretations, providing one makes clear that this is one's own view, whether correct or not. That's all right. No problem." D.R. Komito, "Tibetan Buddhism & psychotherapy: A conversation with the Dalai Lama" p. 4.
20 Similarly, Japanese therapies, such as Morita and Nakan, although they have been introduced to the West by David Reynolds, portray desirable attitudes towards parents and elders that are very far from most contemporary western experience.
21 See chapter two, no. 88.

Bibliography

Texts and Translations

Aṅguttara Nikāya E.M. Hare (ed.) *The Book of the Gradual Sayings,* London: Pali Text Society. 1935.

—— An Anthology. trs. Nyanaponika. Kandy: Buddhist Publication Society. 1981.

Bodhicāryāvatāra of Śāntideva, trs. S. Batchelor *A Guide to the Bodhisattva's Way of Life.* Dharamsala: Libarary of Tibetan Works. 1979.

Dhamma-Saṅganī, C.A.F. Rhys Davids (trs.) *A Buddhist Manual of Psychological Ethics.* London: Pali Text Society. 1974.

Dhammapada. T. Byrom (trs.) London: Wildwood House. 1976.

Dīgha Nikāya, M. Walshe (trs.) *The Long Discourses of the Buddha.* Boston: Wisdom. 1995.

The Mahāmudrā Eliminating the Darkness of Ignorance, Wang Ch'ug Dor'je, A. Berzin (trs.) Dharamsala: Library of Tibetan Works. 1978.

Mahāyāna-Saṃgraha of Asaṅga, E. Lamotte (trs.) *La Somme du Grand Véhicule d'Asaṅga,* Louvain: Institut Orientaliste. 1973.

Majjima Nikāya, Ñāṇamoli & Bodhi (trs.) *The Middle Length Discourses of the Buddha.* Boston: Wisdom. 1995.

Mūlamadhyamikakārikā of Nāgārjuna, K. Inada (trs.) Tokyo: Hokkaido Press. 1970.

—— S. Batchelor (trs.) *Intelligence. Poems from the Centre.* unpub.

Sutta-Nipata, E.M. Hare (trs.) *Woven Cadences of Early Buddhists.* London: Oxford University Press. 1947.

Saṃyutta Nikāya, Rhys Davids & Woodward (trs.) *The Book of the Kindred Sayings.* London: PTS. 1918–30.

—— An Anthology. Ireland & Ñānānanda (trs.) Kandy: Buddhist Publication Society. 1981.

Tsong Khapa, *rtsa.she.tik.chen.rigs.pa'i.rgya.mtsho.* Varanasi. nd.

Udāna, F.W. Woodward (trs.) *Minor Anthologies of the Pali Canon II.* London: Pali Text Society. 1934.

Vimalakīrtinirdeśasūtra, E. Lamotte (trs.) Eng. trs. S. Boin, *The Teachings of Vimalakirti,* London: Routledge, Kegan Paul. 1976.

Visuddhimagga, Ñāṇamoli (trs.) *The Path of Purification* Boulder: Shambhala. 1976.

Abe, M. *Zen & Western Thought.* Honolulu: University of Hawai Press. 1985.

—— *A Study of Dogen.* trs. S. Heine. Albany, N.Y: SUNY Press. 1992.

—— "The Oneness of Practice & Attainment" in W.R. LaFleur, (ed.), 1985.

—— "Nishitani's Challenge to Philosophy & Theology" in Unno, (ed.), 1989.

Abram, D. *The Spell of the Sensuous.* New York: Vintage. 1996.

Akong Rinpoche. *Taming the Tiger.* Samye Ling, Scotland: Dzalendara Publishing. 1987.

Allen, R. *Polanyi.* London: The Claridge Press. 1990.

Assagioli, R. *The Act of Will.* London: Wildwood House. 1973.

—— *Psychosynthesis:* Wellingborough, Northants: Turnstone Press. 1975 (first pub. 1965).

Avens, R. *Imagination is Reality.* Dallas: Spring Publications. 1980.

—— *The New Gnosis*. Dallas: Spring Publications. 1984.

Baars, B.J. *A cognitive theory of consciousness.* Cambridge: Cambridge University Press. 1988.

—— In the Theater of Consciousness. Oxford: Oxford University Press. 1997.

Bakhtin, M.M. *The Dialogic Imagination.* trs. C. Emerson & M. Holquist. Austin: University of Texas Press. 1981.

—— *Speech Genres & Other Late Essays.* trs. V.W. McGee. Austin: University of Texas Press. 1986.

—— *Toward a Philosophy of the Act.* trs. V. Liapunov. Austin: University of Texas Press. 1993.

Barfield, O. *Saving the Appearances: a study in idolatry.* London: Faber. 1965.

—— *The Rediscovery of Meaning.* Middletown, Conn.: Wesleyan University Press. 1977.

Barnhart, M.C. "Textualism and Incommensurability" in *Philosophy East & West.* Vol. 44, no. 4. 1995.

Batchelor, S. *A Guide to the Bodhisattva's Way of Life.* Dharmasala: Library of Tibetan Works. 1979.

—— *Alone With Others.* An existential approach to Buddhism: New York: Grove Press. 1983.

—— *The Awakening of the West.* London: Aquarius. 1994.

—— *Buddhism Without Beliefs.* New York: Riverhead Books. 1997.

—— "A Democracy of the Imagination" in *Tricycle* Vol. IV, no. 2. 1994.
Bateson, G. & Bateson, M.C. *Angels Fear.* New York: Macmillan. 1987.
Bateson, G. *Steps to an Ecology of Mind.* London: Granada. 1973.
—— *Mind & Nature.* London: Wildwood House. 1979.
Bennington, G. & Derrida J. *Jacques Derrida.* Chicago: University of Chicago Press. 1993.
Bernasconi, R. & Wood, D. (eds.) *The Provocation of Levinas.* London: Routledge. 1988.
Bernasconi, R. *The Question of Language in Heidegger's History of Being.* Atlantic Highlands, N.J.: Humanities Press. 1985.
Bertalanffy, L. von. *Organismic Psychology & Systems Theory.* Barre, Mass: Clark University Press. 1968.
Betelheim, B. *Freud and Man's Soul.* New York: Vintage Books. 1984.
Betty, L.S. "Nāgārjuna's masterpiece – logical, mystical, both or neither?" in *Philosophy East & West*, Vol. 33, no. 2. 1983.
Beyer, S. *The Cult of Tara.* Berkeley: University of California Press. 1978.
Bhabha, H. *The Location of Culture.* London: Routledge. 1994.
Binswanger, L. *Being-in-the-World.* New York: Basic Books. 1963.
—— "Existential Analysis & Psychotherapy" in Fromm, Reichman & Moreno, (eds.), 1956.
Bishop, P. *Dreams of Power: Tibetan Buddhism & the Western Imagination.* London: Athlone Press. 1993.
Boss, M. *A Psychiatrist Discovers India* London: Oswald Wolff. 1965.
—— *Psychoanalysis & Daseinsanalysis.* New York: Da Capo Press. 1982.
—— *Existential Foundations of Medicine & Psychiatry.* New York: Jason Aronson. 1983.
—— "Martin Heidegger's Zollikon Seminars" in *Review of Existential Psychology and Psychiatry* Vol. 16, nos. 1–3. 1978/9.
—— "Eastern Wisdom & Western Psychotherapy " in Welwood, (ed.), 1979.
Boucher, S. *Turning the Wheel.* Boston: Beacon Press, 1993 (updated).
Bruner, J. *In Search of Mind;* New York: Harper & Row. 1983.
—— *Actual Minds Possible Worlds.* Cambridge, Mass.: Harvard University Press. 1986.
—— *Acts of Meaning.* Cambridge, Mass.: Harvard University Press. 1990.
Bucknell, R.S. & Stuart-Fox, M. *The Twilight Language:* London: Curzon Press. 1986.
Bugental, J.F.T. *Psychotherapy & Process.* New York: Random House. 1978.

—— *The Search for Existential Identity.* San Francisco: Jossey Bass. 1984.

—— *The Art of the Psychotherapist.* New York: W.W. Norton & Co. 1987.

Buswell, R.E. & Gimello, R.M. (eds.) *Paths to Liberation.* Honolulu: University of Hawai Press. 1992.

Cabezon, J.I. *Buddhism & Language.* Albany, N.Y: SUNY Press. 1994.

Campbell, J. *Myths To Live By.* London: Granada Publishing. 1985.

—— *The Inner Reaches of Outer Space.* New York: Alfred Van Der Marck Editions. 1986.

—— *The Power of Myth.* New York: Doubleday. 1988.

—— *The Flight of the Wild Gander.* New York: Harper. 1990. (reprint).

—— (ed). *In All Her Names.* San Francisco: Harper. 1991.

Capra, F. *The Tao of Physics.* London: Fontana. 1976.

Casper, M. "Space Therapy & the Maitri Project" in *Journal of Transpersonal Psychology,* Vol. 6, no. 1. 1974.

Chokyi Nyima, *The Union of Mahamudra & Dzogchen.* Kathmandu: Rangjung Yeshe Publications. 1989.

Clarkson, P. *On Psychotherapy.* London: Whurr Publishers. 1993.

Claxton. G. *Wholly Human.* London: Routledge. 1981.

—— *Noises from the Darkroom,* London: Aquarian. 1994.

—— *Hare Brain, Tortoise Mind.* London: Fourth Estate. 1997.

—— (ed.) *Beyond Therapy.* London: Wisdom. 1986.

Clifford, T. *Tibetan Medicine & Psychiatry: The Diamond Healing.* Northants: Aquarian Press. 1984.

Cohen, R. (ed.) *Face to Face with Levinas.* Albany, N.Y: SUNY Press. 1986.

Collins, S. *Selfless Persons* Cambridge: Cambridge University Press. 1982.

Coltart, N. *Slouching Towards Bethlehem ... and further psychoanalytic explorations.* London: Free Association Books. 1992.

Conze, E. *Selected Sayings from the Perfection of Wisdom.* London: The Buddhist Society. 1955. (reprint 1975).

—— *Buddhist Meditation.* London: George Allen & Unwin. 1956.

Cook, F.H. *Hua Yen Buddhism: The Jewel Net of Indra.* Pennsylvania State University Press. 1977.

—— "Dogen's Views of Authentic Selfhood & its Socio-ethical Implications." in W.R. LaFleur, (ed.), 1985.

Corey, G. *Theory & Practice of Counselling & Psychotherapy.* Belmont, Ca: Brooks Cole Publishing. 1991 (4th edition.).

Cornell, D. *The Philosophy of the Limit.* London: Routledge. 1992.

Coward, H. & Fosshay, T. (eds.) *Derrida & Negative Theology.* Albany: SUNY Press. 1992.

Coward, H. (ed.) *Derrida and Asian Thought*. Albany: SUNY Press. 1990.

Critchley, S. *The Ethics of Deconstruction*. Oxford: Blackwell. 1992.

Crook, J.H. & Rabgyas T. "The Essential Insight: A central theme in the philosophical training of Mahayanist monks" in A.C. Paranjpe, (ed.), 1988.

Crook, J.H. *The Evolution of Human Consciousness*. Oxford: Clarendon Press. 1980.

Crook, J.H. & Fontana, D. (eds.) *Space in Mind: East-West Psychology and Contemporary Buddhism*. Shaftesbury, Dorset: Element. 1990.

Csikzentmihalyi, M. *Beyond Boredom & Anxiety*. San Francisco: Jossey-Bass. 1975.

—— *Flow. The Psychology of Optimal Experience*. New York: Harper. 1990.

Cupitt, D. *The Long-Legged Fly*. London: SCM Press. 1987.

—— *What is a Story?* London: SCM Press. 1991.

—— *The Time Being*. London: SCM Press. 1992.

—— *The Last Philosophy*. London: SCM Press. 1995.

Cushman, P. *Constructing the Self, Cnstructing America. A Cultural History of Psychotherapy*. Reading, Mass: Addison Wesley. 1995.

De Silva, P. *An Introduction to Buddhist Psychology*. London: Macmillan. 1973.

De Silva, P. "Buddhism & Behaviour Change: Implications for Therapy" in Claxton, (ed.), 1986.

—— "Self-Management Strategies in Early Buddhism: A Behavioural Perspective." in Crook & Fontana, (eds.), 1990.

—— "Meditation and beyond: Buddhism and psychotherapy." in Kwee, (ed.), 1990.

Dalai Lama, H.H. *Four Essential Buddhist Commentaries*. Dharamsala: Library of Tibetan Works & Archives. 1987.

—— *Transcendent Wisdom*. A Commentary on the Ninth Chapter of Shantideva's Guide to the Bodhisattva Way of Life. Ithaca, New York: Snow Lion Publications. 1988.

—— *Worlds in Harmony*. Berkeley: Parallax Press. 1992.

—— *Tibet's Contribution to the Future*. London: The Office of Tibet. 1992.

—— *The Meaning of Life from a Buddhist Perspective*. Boston: Wisdom Publications. 1992.

De Man, P. "Dialogue & Dialogism" in Moorsom & Emerson, (eds.), 1987.

De Martino, R. "The Human Situation & Zen Buddhism" in Fromm, Suzuki & De Martino, (eds.), 1960 & Katz, (ed.), 1983.

De Wit, H. *Contemplative Psychology.* Pittsburgh, Penn: Duquesne University Press. 1991.

Dennett, D. *Consciousness Explained.* London: Penguin 1993.

Derrida, D. 1982 *Margins of Philosophy.* trs. A. Bass. Chicago: University of Chicago Press. 1982.

—— *Aporias,* trs. T. Tutort. Stanford, Ca.: Stanford University Press. 1993.

Derrida, D. & Bennington, G. *Jacques Derrida.* Chicago: University of Chicago Press. 1993.

Dethlefsen, T. & Dahlke, R. *The Healing Power of Illness.* Shaftesbury, Dorset: Element. 1983.

Dillard, A. *Pilgrim at Tinker Creek.* London: Picador. 1976.

Dilworth, D. "The initial formations of 'pure experience' in Nishida Kitaro and William James." in *Monumenta Nipponica.* XXIV. 1969.

Dogen, *Shobogenzo.* trs. T. Cleary. Honolulu: University of Hawai Press. 1986.

—— *Moon in a Dewdrop.* ed. Kazuaki Tanahashi. Shaftesbury, Dorset: Element. 1988.

—— "Genjokoan" trs. M. Abe, N. Waddell in *Eastern Buddhist* Vol. 5, no. 2. 1972.

Donaldson, M. *Human Minds.* London: Allen Lane. 1992.

Dowman, K. *The Flight of the Garuda.* Boston: Wisdom. 1993.

Dreyfus, H.L. *Being-in-the-world.* A commentary on Heidegger's Being and Time, Division 1. Cambridge, Mass: MIT Press. 1991.

Dubin, W. 1991 "The use of meditation techniques in Psychotherapy supervision" in *Journal of Transpersonal Psychology.* Vol. 23, no. 1. 1991.

Dumoulin, H. *Zen Buddhism in the Twentieth Century.* New York: Weatherhill. 1992.

Eagleton, T. *Literary Theory.* Oxford: Blackwell. 1983.

Edelman, G. *Bright Air, Brilliant Fire.* London: Allen Lane. 1992.

Eisler, R. *The Chalice & the Blade.* London: Unwin. 1990.

—— "The Goddess of Nature & Spirituality. An Ecomanifesto" in J. Campbell, (ed.), 1991.

Eliot, T.S. *Collected Poems 1909–1962.* London: Faber & Faber. 1963.

Elliot, P. *From Mastery to Analysis.* Ithaca & London: Cornell University Press. 1991.

Engler, J. "Therapeutic Aims in Psychotherapy & Meditation: Developmental stages in the representation of self". in *Journal of Transpersonal Psychology* Vol. 16, no. 1. 1984.

Epstein, M. *Thoughts without a thinker.* New York: Basic Books. 1995.

—— "The deconstruction of the self; ego & 'egolessness' in Buddhist insight meditation" in *Journal of Transpersonal Psychology*, Vol. 20, no. 1. 1988.

—— "Forms of Emptiness: Psychodynamic, meditative and clinical perspectives" in *Journal of Transpersonal Psychology*, Vol. 21, no. 1. 1989.

—— "Beyond the Oceanic Feeling: Psychoanalytic Study of Buddhist Meditation" in *International Review of Psycho-analysis*. Vol. 17. 1990.

—— "The Psychodynamics of Meditation: Pitfalls on the spiritual path". in *Journal of Transpersonal Psychology*, Vol. 22, no. 1. 1990.

—— "Freud & Dr. Buddha: The search for selflessness." in *Tricycle* Vol. 1, no. 3. 1992.

Erikson, E. *Childhood & Society*. London: Penguin. 1967.

Ferrucci, P. *What We May Be*. Wellingborough, Northants: Turnstone Press. 1982.

Franck, F. (ed.) *The Buddha Eye*. New York: Crossroad. 1991.

Frankl, V.E. *Psychotherapy & Existentialism*. London: Penguin Books. 1967.

—— *Man's Search for Meaning*. London: Hodder & Stoughton. 1987.

—— "Reductionism & Nihilism" in Koestler & Smythies, (eds.), 1969.

Freud, S. *The Ego & The Id* trs. J. Strachey London: The Hogarth Press & The Institute of Psycho-analysis. 1923.

—— *The Future of an Illusion*. trs. J. Strachey London: The Hogarth Press & The Institute of Psycho-analysis. 1962.

—— *An Outline of Pscho-Analysis*. trs. J. Strachey London: The Hogarth Press & The Institute of Psycho-analysis. 1963. (6th impression).

—— "A Note upon the Mystic Writing Pad." in *The Standard Edition of the Complete Psychological Works* Vol. XIX. trs. J. Strachey. London: The Hogarth Press & Institute of Psycho-analysis. 1961.

Fromm, E. *Psycho-analysis & Zen*. London: Unwin. 1960.

Fromm, E., Suzuki, D.T. & de Martino, R. *Zen Buddhism & Psychoanalysis*, New York: Harper & Row. 1960.

Fromm, E., Reichman A. & Moreno, J. (eds.) *Progress in Psychiatry*, New York: Grune & Stratton. 1956.

Fryba, M. *The Art of Happiness. Teachings of Buddhist Psychology*. Boston: Shambhala. 1989.

Gablik, S. *The Reenchantment of Art*. London: Thames & Hudson. 1991.

Gans, S. "Levinas & Pontalis: Meeting the Other as in a Dream" in Bernasconi & Wood, (eds.), 1988.

Garfield, J.L. "Dependent Arising and the Emptiness of Emptiness: Why did Nāgārjuna start with Causation?" in *Philosophy East & West*. Vol. 44, no. 2. 1994.

Geertz, G. *The Interpretation of Cultures*. New York: Basic Books. 1973.

Gendlin, E. *Focusing*. Toronto: Bantam. 1981.

—— *Focusing-Oriented Psychotherapy*. New York: The Guildford Press. 1996.

—— "Heidegger & the Philosophy of Psychology" in *Review of Existential Psychology & Psychiatry*. Vol. 16, nos. 1–3. 1978/79.

—— "On Emotion in Therapy." to be published in J.D. Safron & L.S. Greenberg (eds.). *Emotions & The Process of Therapeutic Change*. New York: Academic Press.

Gergen, K. "Social understanding and the inscription of self" in Stigler, Shweder & Herdt, (eds.), 1990.

—— "Toward a postmodern psychology" in Kvale, (ed.), 1992.

Goleman, D. & Thurman, R. (eds.) *MindScience. An East-West Dialogue*. Boston: Wisdom. 1991.

Goleman, D. *The Meditative Mind*. Los Angeles: Jeremy P. Tarcher Inc. 1988.

—— *Emotional Intelligence*. London: Bloomsbury. 1996.

—— "A Map for Inner Space" in Walsh & Vaughan, (eds.), 1980.

Gombrich, R. *How Buddhism Began*. London: Athlone Press. 1996.

—— "How Buddhism Began: The Conditioned Genesis of the Early Teachings." The Louis H. Jordan Lectures in Comparative Religion, SOAS. 1994. (typescript).

Grof, S. *Beyond the Brain. Birth, Death & Transcendence in Psychotherapy*. Albany, N.Y: SUNY Press. 1985.

Gudmunson, C. *Wittgenstein & Buddhism*. London: Macmillan. 1977.

Guenther, H. & Kawamura, L.S. *Mind in Buddhist Psychology*. California: Dharma Publishing. 1975.

Guenther, H.V. *Philosophy & Psychology in the Abhidharma*. Delhi: Motilal Banarsidas. 1973.

—— *The Creative Vision*. Novato, Ca: Lotsawa. 1987.

—— *Tibetan Buddhism in Western Perspective*. Berkeley: Dharma Publishing. 1989.

—— *From Reductionism to Creativity*. Boston: Shambhala. 1989.

—— "Buddhist rDzogs-chen Thought and Western 'Daseinsanalyse'" in Katz, (ed.), 1983.

Guignon, C. (ed.)*The Cambridge Companion to Heidegger*. Cambridge: Cambridge University Press. 1993.

—— "Authenticity, moral values and psychotherapy" in Guignon, (ed.), 1993.

Guntrip, H. *Psychoanalytic Theory, Therapy & the Self*. London: Maresfield Library. 1985.

Gyatso, J. "Down with the Demoness: Reflections on a Feminine Ground in Tibet" in Willis, (ed.), 1987.

Hakeda, Y.S. *The Awakening of Faith*. New York: Columbia University Press. 1967.

—— *Kukai : Major Works*. New York: Columbia University Press. 1972.

Hamilton, S. *The Constitution of the Human Being According to Early Buddhism*. Phd Thesis, Oxford. 1992 published as.

—— *Identity and Experience*. London: Luzac Oriental. 1996.

—— "Annatta, a different approach" in *The Middle Way*. Vol. 70, no. 1. 1995.

—— "Passionlessness in Buddhism." (typescript) 1994.

Hampden-Turner, C. *Maps of the Mind*. London: Mitchell Beazley. 1981.

Hardy, J. *Psychology with a Soul*. London: Routledge. 1987.

Hayward, J. & Varela, F. (eds.) *Gentle Bridges: Conversations with the Dalai Lama on the Sciences of Mind*. Boston: Shambhala. 1992.

Hayward, J.W. *Shifting Worlds Changing Minds*. Boston: Shambhala. 1987.

Heidegger, M. *Existence and Being*. trs. various. London: Vision Press. 1968. (3rd. edition).

—— *What is Called Thinking*. trs. J.G. Gray & F. Wieck. New York: Harper & Row. 1968.

—— *On the Way to Language*. trs. P.D. Hertz. San Francisco: Harper. 1971.

—— *Poetry, Language, Thought*. trs. A. Hofstadter. New York: Harper. 1971.

—— *The Question Concerning Technology and other Essays*. trs. W. Lovitt. New York: Harper. 1977.

—— *Basic Problems of Phenomenology*. trs. A. Hofstadter. Bloomington: Indiana University Press. 1982.

—— *Early Greek Thinking*. trs. D.F. Krell & F.A. Capuzzi. San Francisco: Harper. 1984.

—— *Basic Writings*. ed. D.F. Krell. London: Routledge & Kegan Paul. 1984.

Heine, S. *Existential & Ontological Dimensions of Time in Heidegger & Dogen*. Albany: SUNY Press. 1988.

Hillman, J. *Insearch. Psychology & Religion*. Dallas: Spring Publications. 1967.

—— *Revisioning Psychology*. New York: Harper & Row. 1975.

—— *Archetypal Psychology*. Dallas: Spring Publications. 1985.

—— *A Blue Fire*. London: Routledge. 1990.

Hillman, J. & Ventura, M. *We've Had a Hundred Years of Psychotherapy and the World's Getting Worse*. San Francisco: Harper Collins. 1992.

Hirshfield, J. *Of Gravity and Angels*. Middletown, Conn.: Wesleyan University Press. 1988.

Holquist, M. *Dialogism. Bakhtin & his world*. London: Routledge. 1990.

Hookham, S. *The Buddha Within*. Albany: SUNY Press. 1991.

—— "The Practical Implications of the Doctrine of Buddha-Nature: in Skorupski, (ed.), 1991.

Hookham, S. & Tsultrim Gyamtso, Khenpo. *Progressive Stages of Meditation on Emptiness*. Oxford: Lonchen Foundation. 1986.

Hopkins, G.M. *Poems and Prose of Gerard Manley Hopkins*. London: Penguin. 1953.

Hopkins, J. *Meditation on Emptiness*. London: Wisdom Publications. 1983.

Huntingdon, C.W. *The Emptiness of Emptiness*. Honolulu: University of Hawai Press. 1989.

—— "A non-referential view of language and conceptual thought in the work of Tsong-kha-pa" in Philosophy East & West. Vol. 33, no. 4. 1983.

—— "The System of the Two Truths in the Prasannapada and the Madhyamakāvatara" in *Journal of Indian Philosophy*. Vol. 11. 1983.

Inada, K. & Jacobson, N.P. *Buddhism & American Thinkers*. Albany: SUNY Press. 1984.

Irigary, L. *je, tu, nous Toward a Culture of Difference*. New York: Routledge. 1993.

Jaffe, A. *The Myth of Meaning*. trs. R.F.C. Hull. London: Hodder & Stoughton. 1970.

James, W. 1981 *The Principles of Psychology*. Cambridge, Mass: Harvard University Press. 1981.

—— *Varieties of Religious Experience*. London: Penguin. 1982.

—— *The Essential Writings*. ed. B.W. Wilshire. Albany: SUNY Press. 1984.

—— *The Writings of William James*. ed. J.J. McDermott, New York: Modern Library. 1986.

Jardine, A.A. *Gynesis. Configurations of Woman & Modernity*. Ithaca, N.Y: Cornell University Press. 1985.

Jaynes, J. *The Origin of Consciousness in the Breakdown of the Bicameral Mind*. Boston: Houghton Mifflin. 1990.

Johansson, R.E.A. *The Dynamic Psychology of Early Buddhism*. London: Curzon Press. 1985.

Johnson, M. *The Body in the Mind*. Chicago: The University of Chicago Press. 1987.

—— *Moral Imagination*. Chicago: The University of Chicago Press. 1993.

Jung, C.G. *Collected Works Vol. 9. I The Archetypes and The Collective Unconscious*. London: Routledge. (2nd edition) 1969.

—— *Collected Works Vol 9. II Aion*. London: Routledge. (2nd edition) 1968.

—— *Collected Works Vol. 11. Psychology & Religion: West & East*. London: Routledge. 1958.

Kabat-Zinn, J., Lipworth, L. & Burney, R. "The Clinical Use of Mindfulness Meditation for the Self-Regulating of Chronic pain" in *Journal of Behavioural Medicine*. Vol. 8, no. 2. 1985.

Kalff, M. "The Negation of the ego in Tibetan Buddhism and Jungian Psychology" in *Journal of Transpersonal Psychology*. Vol. 15, no. 2. 1983.

Kalupahana, D.J. *The Principles of Buddhist Psychology*. Albany, SUNY Press. 1987.

—— *A History of Buddhist Philosophy. Continuities & Discontinuities*. Honolulu: University of Hawai Press. 1992.

Kasulis, T. & Ames, R.T. & Dissanayake, W. (eds.) *Self as Body in Asian Theory & Practice*. Albany: SUNY Press. 1993.

Katz, N. "Nagarjuna & Wittgenstein on Error" in Katz, (ed.), 1983 (ed.) *Buddhist & Western Psychology*. Boulder, Colorado: Prajna Press. 1983.

Kelly, G.A. *A Theory of Personality*. New York: W.W. Norton. 1963.

Keown, D. *The Nature of Buddhist Ethics*. London: Macmillan. 1992.

Klein, A.C. *Knowledge and Liberation*. Ithaca, N.Y: Snow Lion. 1986.

—— *Path to the Middle*. Albany, N.Y: SUNY Press. 1994.

—— *Meeting the Great Bliss Queen*. Boston: Beacon Press. 1995.

—— "Mental Concentration and the Unconditioned" in Buswell & Gimello, (eds.), 1992.

Koestler, A & Smythies, J.R., (eds.) *Beyond Reductionism. The Alpbach Symposium*. London: Hutchinson. 1969.

Koestler, A. "Beyond atomism and holism – the concept of the holon" in Koestler & Smythies, (eds.), 1969.

Kohut, H. *The Restoration of the Self*. Madison, Conn: International Universities Press. 1977.

—— *Self Psychology & the Humanities*. New York: W.W. Norton & Co. 1985.

Komito, D.R. *Nāgārjuna's Seventy Stanzas*. Ithaca: Snow Lion. 1987.

—— "Tibetan Buddhism & Psychotherapy: a conversation with the Dalai Lama" in *Journal of Transpersonal Psychology* Vol. 15, no. 1. 1983.

—— "Tibetan Buddhism & Psychotherapy: further conversations with the Dalai Lama" in *Journal of Transpersonal Psychology*. Vol. 16, no. 1. 1984.

Kosko, B. *Fuzzy Thinking*. London: Flamingo. 1994.

Kristeva, J. *The Kristeva Reader*. ed. T. Moi, Oxford: Basil Blackwell. 1986.

—— *In the Beginning was Love; Psychoanalysis & Faith*. New York: Columbia University. 1987.

Kuhn, T. *The Structure of Scientific Revolutions*. Chicago: University of Chicago Press. 1970.

Kurtz, R. *Body-Centered Psychotherapy: The Hakomi Method*. Mendocino, Ca.: Life Rhythms. 1990.

Kvale, S. "Introduction: From the Archaeology of the Psyche to the Architecture of Cultural Landscape" in Kvale, (ed.), 1992.

—— "Postmodern Psychology: A Contradiction in Terms?" in Kvale, (ed.), 1992.

—— (ed.) *Psychology & Postmodernism*. London: Sage Publications. 1992.

Kwee, M.G.T. (ed.) *Psychotherapy, Meditation & Health*. London, The Hague: East/West Publications. 1990.

—— Relativism as applied in cognitive-behaviour therapy and Zen-meditation. in Kwee, (ed.), 1990.

La Fleur, W. *The Karma of Words*. Berkeley: University of California Press. 1986.

—— (ed.) *Dogen Studies*. Honolulu: University of Hawai Press. 1985.

Lacan, J. *Écrits*. trs. A. Sheridan. New York: Norton. 1977.

—— *The Four Fundamental Concepts of Psycho-Analysis*. trs. A. Sheridan. London: Penguin Books. 1979.

Laing, R.D. *The Politics of Experience*. London: Penguin. 1967.

—— *Knots*. London: Tavistock. 1970.

Lakoff, G. & Johnson, M. *Metaphors We Live By*. Chicago: Chicago University Press. 1980.

Lamotte, E. *History of Indian Buddhism*. trs. S. Boin-Webb. Louvain: Publications de l'Institut Orientaliste de Louvain-le-Neuve. 1988.

Langer, M.M. *Merleau-Ponty's Phenomenology of Perception*. London: Macmillan. 1989.

Langer, S. *Philosophy in a New Key*. Cambridge, Mass.: Harvard University Press. 1942.

—— *Philosophical Sketches*. Baltimore: John Hopkins Press. 1962.

Laszlo, E. *Introduction to Systems Philosophy*. New York: Gordon Breach Publishers. 1972.

—— *The Creative Cosmos*. Edinburgh: Floris Books. 1994.

Lauf, D.I. *Secret Doctrine of the Tibetan Book of the Dead.* Boston: Shambhala. 1977.

Least Heat Moon, W. *Blue Highways.* London: Picador. 1984.

Lefebure, M. *Human Experience & the Art of Counselling.* Edinburgh: T. & T. Clark. 1985.

Lerman, H. *A Mote in Freud's Eye. From Psychoanalysis to the Psychology of Women.* New York: Springer. 1986.

Levin, D.M. *The Body's Recollection of Being.* London: Routledge & Kegan Paul. 1985.

—— *The Opening of Vision.* London: Routledge. 1988.

—— *The Listening Self.* London: Routledge. 1989.

—— (ed.) *Pathologies of the Modern Self.* New York: New York University Press. 1987.

—— "Mudra as Thinking: Developing Our Wisdom-Being in Gesture and Movement" in G. Parkes, (ed.), 1987.

Levinas, E. *Existence & Existents.* trs. A. Lingis. Dordrecht: Kluwer Academic Publishers. 1978.

—— *Totality & Infinity.* trs. A. Lingis. Dordrecht: Kluwer Academic Publishers. 1991.

—— *Ethics and Infinity. Conversations with Philippe Nemo.* trs. R.A. Cohen. Pittsburgh: Duquesne University Press. 1985.

Levine, F.J. & Kravis, R. "Psychoanalytical Theories of the Self" in Young-Eisendrath & Hall, (eds.), 1989.

Lindtner, C. *Nagarjuniana.* Delhi: Motilal Banarsidas. 1987.

Lopez, D. *Buddhist Hermeneutics.* Honolulu: University of Hawai Press. 1988.

Loy, D. *NonDuality a study in comparative philosophy.* New Haven: Yale University Press. 1988.

—— "How not to criticize Nagarjuna: A response to L. Stafford Betty" in *Philosophy East & West.* Vol. 34, no. 4. 1984.

—— "The Nonduality of Life & Death. A Buddhist View of Repression" in *Philosophy East & West.* Vol. 40, no. 2. 1990.

—— "Avoiding the void: The *lack* of self in psychotherapy and Buddhism" in *Journal of Transpersonal Psychology.* Vol. 24, no. 2. 1993.

Luce, G.G. "Tibetan Buddhism meets Western Psychology" in *Chrystal Mirror* III. (see Tarthang Tulku.) 1974.

Lyotard, J-F. *The Postmodern Condition.* trs. G. Bennington & B. Massumi. Manchester: Manchester University Press. 1986.

Macy, J. *Mutual Causality in Buddhism and General Systems Theory.* Albany: SUNY Press. 1991.

Magee, B. *Men of Ideas.* London: BBC. 1978.

—— *The Philosophy of Schopenhauer.* Oxford: Clarendon Press. 1983.

—— *The Great Philosophers*. London: BBC. 1987.
Magliola, R. *Derrida On the Mend.* West Layfayette, Indiana: Purdue University Press. 1984.
—— "Nagarjuna/Derrida/Kyoto School: How traces denegate both silence (pace Harold Coward) & paradox (pace Masao Abe)." (typescript).
Mann, R. & Youd, R. *Buddhist Character Analysis.* Bradford-on-Avon: Aukana. 1992.
Maslow, A. *Towards a Psychology of Being.* Princetown, N.J.: Van Nostrand. 1962. (revised edition 1968).
—— *The Farther Reaches of Human Nature.* London: Penguin. 1971.
Mathur, D.C. "The historical Buddha (Gautama), Hume, and James on the self: comparisons and evaluations" in *Philosophy East & West.* Vol. 28, no. 3. 1978.
Maturana, H.R. & Varela, F.J. *The Tree of Knowledge.* Boston: Shambhala. 1992. (Revised edition).
May, R. *The Discovery of Being.* New York: Norton. 1983.
—— *The Cry for Myth.* New York: Delta. 1991.
—— "The Origins & Significance of the Existential Movement in Psychology" in May, Angel & Ellenberger, (eds.), 1958.
May, R., Angel E. & Ellenberger H. (eds.) *Existence: A New Dimension of Psychology.* New York: Basic Books. 1958.
McDonald, K. *How to Meditate.* London: Wisdom Publications. 1984.
Merleau-Ponty, M. *Phenomenology of Perception.* trs. C. Smith. London: Routledge & Kegan Paul. 1986.
—— *The Visible & the Invisible.* trs. A. Lingis. Evanston, Ill: Northwestern University Press. 1992.
Mikulas, W. "Four Noble Truths of Buddhism Related to Behaviour Therapy" in *The Psychological Record.* Vol. 28. 1978.
—— "Buddhism & Behaviour Modification." in *The Psychological Record.* Vol. 31. 1981.
—— "Mindfulness, self-control, and personal growth." in Kwee, (ed.), 1990.
Milner, M. *A Life of One's Own.* London: Virago. 1986.
Minoru Kyota (ed.). *Mahayana Buddhist Meditation: Theory & Practice.* Honolulu: University of Hawai Press. 1976.
Misra, G.S.P. *Development of Buddhist Ethics.* New Delhi: Munshiram Manoharlal Publishers. 1984.
Moacanin, R. *Jung's Psychology and Tibetan Buddhism.* London: Wisdom. 1986.
Moorsom, G.S. & Emerson, C. (eds.) *Rethinking Bakhtin.* Evanston, Illinois: Northwestern University Press. 1987.
Mora, G. "Recent American Psychiatric Developments" in *American Handbook of Psychiatry.* New York: Basic Books. 1960.

Mumford, S. *Himalayan Dialogue*. Madison: University of Wisconsin Press. 1989.

Murdoch, I. *Metaphysics as a Guide to Morals*. London: Penguin. 1993.

Murti, T.V.R. *The Central Philosophy of Buddhism*. London: George Allen & Unwin. 1955.

Nagao, G. *The Foundational Standpoint of Mādhyamika Philosophy*. Albany, N.Y: SUNY Press. 1989.

—— *Mādhyamika and Yogācāra*. Albany, N.Y: SUNY Press. 1991.

Ñāṇananda, Bhikku.*Concept & Reality in Early Buddhist Thought*. Kandy: BPS. 1971.

Napper, E. *Dependent-Arising and Emptiness*. Boston: Wisdom. 1989.

Napper, E. & Lati Rinbochay. *Mind In Tibetan Buddhism*. Ithaca: Snow Lion. 1980.

Naranjo, C. & Ornstein, R.E. *On the Psychology of Meditation*. New York: Penguin. 1976.

Nhat Hanh, T. *The Heart of Understanding*. Berkeley: Parallax Press. 1988.

—— *The Sutra on the Full Awareness of Breathing*. Berkeley: Parallax Press. 1988.

—— *Our Appointment with Life*. Berkeley: Parallax Press. 1990.

—— *Transformation and Healing*. Berkeley: Parallax Press. 1990.

Nishida, K. *Last Writings. Nothingness and the Religious Worldview*. Honolulu: University of Hawai Press. 1987.

Nishitani, K. *Religion & Nothingness*. trs. J. van Bragt. Berkeley: University of California Press. 1982.

Norcross, J. (ed.) *Handbook of Eclectic Psychotherapy*. New York: Brunner/Mazel. 1986.

Nyanaponika, Thera. *Abhidamma Studies*. Kandy: BPS. 1985.

Odin, S. *Process Metaphysics and Hua-Yen Buddhism*. Albany, N.Y: SUNY Press. 1982.

Olds, L.E. *Metaphors of Interrelatedness*. Albany, N.Y.: SUNY Press. 1992.

Paranjpe, A.C., Ho, D.Y.F. & Reiber, R.W. (eds.) *Asian Contributions to Psychology*. New York: Praeger. 1988.

Parkes, G. (ed.) *Heidegger & Asian Thought*. Chicago: University of Chicago Press. 1987.

—— (ed.) *Nietzsche & Asian Thought*. Honolulu: University of Hawai Press. 1991.

Peperzak, A. *To the Other. An Introduction to the Philosophy of Emmanuel Levinas*. West Lafayette, Indiana: Purdue University Press. 1993.

Perls, F.S. *Gestalt Therapy Verbatim*. Lafayette, Ca.: Real People Press. 1969.

Peterman, J.F. *Philosophy as Therapy.* Albany, N.Y: SUNY Press. 1992.
Philadelphia Association. *Thresholds between Philosophy and Psychoanalysis.* London: Free Association Books. 1989.
Phillips, A. *On Kissing, Tickling and Being Bored.* London: Faber & Faber. 1993.
—— *On Flirtation.* London: Faber & Faber. 1994.
Piaget, J. & Inhelder, B. *The Psychology of the Child.* trs. H. Weaver. London: Routledge Kegan Paul. 1969.
Pickering, J. "Buddhism and Cognitivism: a postmodern appraisal." in *Asian Philosophy.* Vol. 5. no. 1, 1995.
Podvoll, E. *The Seduction of Madness.* London: Century. 1990.
Polanyi, M. *The Tacit Dimension.* Garden City, New York: Doubleday. 1966.
Polanyi, M. & Prosch, H. *Meaning.* Chicago: University of Chicago Press. 1975.
Polkinghorne, D. "Postmodern Epistemology of Practice" in Kvale, (ed.), 1992.
Pontalis, J.B. *Frontiers in Psychoanalysis. Between the Dream & Psychic Pain.* trs. C. & P. Cullen. London: Hogarth Press & Institute of Psychoanalysis. 1981.
Rabin, B. & Walker, R. "A Contemplative Approach to Clinical Supervision" in *Journal of Contemplative Psychotherapy.* Vol. IV. Boulder, Col.: Naropa Institute. 1987.
Rabten, G. *Echoes of Voidness.* London: Wisdom. 1983.
—— *The Song of the Profound View.* London: Wisdom. 1989.
Rabten, G. & Batchelor S. *The Mind & Its Functions.* Switzerland: Tharpa Choeling. 1978.
Reat, N.R. "Some Fundamental Concepts of Buddhist Psychology" in *Religion.* Vol. 17. 1987.
Redfearn, J.W.T. "Terminology of Ego and Self" in Young-Eistendrath & Hall, (eds.), 1987.
Reynolds, D. *The Quiet Therapies.* Honolulu: University of Hawai. 1980.
—— *Playing Ball on Running Water.* London: Sheldon Press. 1985.
Rilke, R.M. "Worpswede" in *Rodin & Other Pieces.* trs. G.C. Houston. London Quarto. 1986.
Rogers, C. *The Carl Rogers Reader.* (eds.) H. Kirschenbaum & V.L. Henderson. London: Constable. 1990.
—— *Carl Rogers Dialogues.* London: Constable. 1990.
Rorty, R. *Philosophy & the Mirror of Nature.* Oxford: Blackwell. 1980.
—— *Contingency, irony and solidarity.* Cambridge: Cambridge University Press. 1989.

—— *Essays on Heidegger & Others.* Cambridge: Cambridge University Press. 1991.
—— *Consequences of Pragmatism.* New York: Harvester Wheatsheaf. 1991.
Ross, N. Wilson, The World of Zen. London: Collins. 1962.
Roszak, T. *The Voice of the Earth. An Exploration of Ecopsychology.* New York: Touchstone. 1993.
Rowan, J. *The Reality Game.* London: Routledge. 1983.
Ruegg, D.S. *La Théorie du tathagatagarbha et du gotra.* Paris: A. Maisonneuve. 1969.
—— *The Literature of the Madhyamaka School of Philosophy in India.* Wiesbaden: Otto Harrassowitz. 1981.
—— *Buddha Nature, Mind and the Problem of Gradualism in a Comparative Perspective.* London: SOAS. 1989.
—— "The Jo nan pa: A School of Buddhist Ontologists" in *Journal of the American Oriental Society.* 1963.
—— "On the Knowability and Expressibility of Absolute Reality in Buddhism" in *Journal of Indian & Buddhist Studies.* 1971.
Russell, R. *Report on Effective Psychotherapy & Legislative Testimony.* Lake Placid, N.Y.: Hilgarth Press. 1981.
Sacks, O. *Seeing Voices.* Berkeley: University of California Press. 1989.
Samuel, G. 1990 *Mind, Body and Culture.* Cambridge: Cambridge University Press. 1990.
—— *Civilised Shamans: Buddhism in Tibetan Societies.* Washington: Smithsonian Institute Press. 1993.
Sarup, M. *Jacques Lacan.* New York: Harvester Wheatsheaf. 1992.
—— *Post-Structuralism & Postmodernism.* New York: Harvester Wheatsheaf. 1993.
Searle, J. *The Rediscovery of the Mind.* Cambridge, Mass: M.I.T Press. 1992.
Shaner, D.E. *The BodyMind Experience in Japanese Buddhism.* Albany: SUNY Press. 1985.
Shaw, M. *Passionate Enlightenment. Women in Tantric Buddhism.* Princeton, N.J: Princeton University Press. 1994.
—— "William James & Yogacara Philosophy: A comparative inquiry" in *Philosophy East & West.* Vol. 37, no. 3. 1987.
Simmer-Brown, J. "Pratityasamutpada: Seeing the Dependent Origin of Suffering as the Key to Liberation" in *Journal of Contemplative Psychotherapy,* Vol. IV. Boulder, Col: Naropa Institute. 1987.
Skinner, R. "Psychotherapy & Spiritual Tradition" in Welwood, (ed.), 1983.
Skorupski, T. (ed.) *The Buddhist Forum.* Vol II. London: S.O.A.S. 1991.
Smith, E.W.L. *The Body in Psychotherapy.* Jefferson, N. Carolina & London: McFarland & Co. 1985.

Sogyal Rinpoche. *The Tibetan Book of Living and Dying*. London: Rider. 1992.

Southwold, M. *Buddhism in Life*. Manchester University Press. 1985.

Spence, D. *Narrative Truth & Historical Truth*. New York. W.W. Norton. 1982.

—— "Turning Happenings into Meanings: The Central Role of the Self" in Young-Eisendrath & Hall, (eds.), 1987.

Sprung, M. *Lucid Exposition of the Middle Way*. London: Routledge & Kegan Paul. 1979.

—— *After Truth. Explorations in Life Sense*. Albany, N.Y: SUNY Press. 1994.

—— (ed.) *The Question of Being*. University Park & London: Pennsylvania State University Press. 1978.

—— "Being and the Middle Way" in Sprung, (ed.), 1978.

Stambaugh, J. *Impermanence Is Buddha-nature. Dogen's Understanding of Temporality*. Honolulu: University of Hawai. 1990.

—— *The Other Nietzsche*. Albany, N.Y: SUNY Press. 1994.

Stcherbatsky, T. *The Central Conception of Buddhism*. Delhi: Motilal Banarsidas. 1988 (first edition 1922).

Steinbeck, J. *The Log from the Sea of Cortez*. London: Penguin. 1977.

Steiner, G. *Real Presences*. London: Faber & Faber. 1989.

Stevens Sullivan, B. *Psychotherapy Grounded in the Feminine Principle*. Wilmette, Illinois: Chiron Press. 1989.

Stigler, J.W., Shweder, R.A., & Herdt., G. (eds.) *Cultural Psychology*. Cambridge: Cambridge University Press. 1990.

Stiles, W.B., Shapiro, D.A. & Elliot, R. "Are All Psychotherapies Equal?" in *The American Psychologist*. February 1986.

Streng, F. *Emptiness. A Study in Religious Meaning*. Nashville: Abingdon Press. 1968.

Suzuki, D.T. *The Essentials of Zen Buddhism*. ed. B. Phillips. London: Rider. 1963.

Sweet, M.J. & Johnson C.R. "Enhancing Empathy: The Interpersonal Implications of a Buddhist Meditation Technique" in *Psychotherapy*. Vol. 27. Spring 1990.

Tart, C. "Adapting Eastern Spiritual Techniques to Western Culture. A discussion with Shinzen Young" in *Journal of Transpersonal Psychology*. Vol. 22, no. 2. 1990.

Tarthang Tulku. *Time Space & Knowledge*. Emeryville, Ca.: Dharma Publishing. 1977.

—— *Kum Nye Relaxation*. Vols. I & II. Emeryville, Ca.: Dharma Publishing. 1978.

—— *Knowlege of Freedom*. Emeryville, Ca.: Dharma Publishing. 1984.

—— *Knowledge of Time & Space*. Emeryville, Ca.: Dharma Publishing. 1990.

—— (ed.). *Chrystal Mirror* III. Emeryville, Ca.: Dharma Publishing. 1974.

—— (ed.). *Reflections of Mind*. Emeryville, Ca.: Dharma Publishing. 1975.

—— "The self-image" in *Journal of Transpersonal Psychology*. Vol. 6, no. 2. 1974.

Taylor, C. *Sources of the Self*. Cambridge, Mass. Harvard University Press. 1989.

Thurman, R. *Tsong Khapa's Speech of Gold in the Essence of True Eloquence*. Princeton, New Jersey: Princeton University Press. 1984.

—— "Philosophical nonegocentricism in Wittgenstein & Candrakirti in their treatment of the private language problem" in *Philosophy East & West*. Vol. 30, no. 3. 1980.

—— "Nishitani and the Inner Science of Buddhism" in Unno, (ed.), 1989.

Todorov, T. *Mikhail Bakhtin. The Dialogical Principle*. trs. W. Godzich. Minneapolis: University of Michigan Press. 1984.

Trungpa, C. *Transcending Madness*. Boston: Shambhala. 1992.

—— "The Meeting of Buddhist & Western Psychology" in N. Katz, (ed.), 1983.

Tuck, A. *Comparative Philosophy and the Philosophy of Scholarship*. New York: Oxford University Press. 1990.

Turner, V. *Dramas, Fields, and Metaphors*. Ithaca: Cornell University Press. 1974.

Unno, T. (ed.). *The Religious Philosophy of Nishitani Keiji*. Berkeley: Asian Humanities Press. 1989.

Varela, F *quel savoir pour l'éthique?* Paris: Éditions La Découverte. 1996.

—— (ed.) *Sleeping, Dreaming and Dying*. Boston: Wisdom Publications. 1997.

Varela, F., Thompson, E. & Rosch, E. *The Embodied Mind*. Cambridge, Mass.: MIT Press. 1991.

Vaughan, F. *The Inward Arc*. Boston: Shambhala. 1986.

Von Bertalanffy, L. *Organismic Psychology & Systems Theory*. Barre, Mass: Clark University Press. 1966. Heinz Werner Lecture Series. 1968.

—— *General Systems Theory*. London: Penguin. 1971.

Wallace, B.A. *Choosing Reality*. Boston: Shambhala. 1989.

Walsh, R. "The Transpersonal Movement" in *Journal of Transpersonal Psychology*. Vol. 25, no. 2. 1993.

Walsh, R. & Vaughan, F. (eds.) *Beyond Ego. Transpersonal Dimensions in Psychology.* Los Angeles: Tarcher. 1980.

—— (eds.) *Paths Beyond Ego. The Transpersonal Vision.* Los Angeles: J.P. Tarcher. 1993.

—— "The art of transcendence: An introduction to common elements of transpersonal practices" in *Journal of Transpersonal Psychology.* Vol. 25, no. 1. 1993.

—— "On Transpersonal Definitions" in *Journal of Transpersonal Psychology.* Vol. 25, no. 2. 1993.

Washburn, M. *The Ego & the Dynamic Gound.* Albany, N.Y: SUNY Press. 1988.

Watson, G., Batchelor, S. & Claxton, G. (eds.) *The Fly & The Fly Bottle. Buddhism & Cognitive Science.* Ashprington, Devon: Sharpham Trust. 1992.

Watts, A. *Psychotherapy East & West.* New York: Pantheon Books. 1961.

Watts, F. & Williams, M. *The Psychology of Religious Knowing.* Cambridge: Cambridge University Press. 1988.

Wegela, K.K *How to Be a Help and Not a Nuisance.* Boston: Shambhala. 1996.

—— "'Touch & Go' in Clinical Practice: Some Implications of the View of Intrinsic Health for Psychotherapy" in *Journal of Contemplative Psychotherapy* Vol. V. Boulder, Col.: Naropa Institute. 1988.

—— "Contemplative Psychotherapy: A Path of Uncovering Brilliant Sanity" in *Journal of Contemplative Psychotherapy* Vol. IX. Boulder, Col.: Naropa Institute. 1994.

Welwood, J. *Journey of the Heart.* New York: Harper Collins. 1990.

—— (ed.) *The Meeting of the Ways. Explorations in East/West Psychology.* New York: Schocken. 1978.

—— (ed.) *Awakening the Heart. East/West Approaches to Psychotherapy and the Healing Relationship.* Boston: Shambhala. 1983.

—— (ed.) *Ordinary Magic.* Boston: Shambhala. 1992.

—— "Meditation & the Unconscious: a new perspective" in *Journal of Transpersonal Psychology.* Vol. 9, no. 1. 1977.

—— "Exploring Mind: Form, Emptiness, and Beyond" in Welwood. (ed.). 1978.

—— "Principles of Inner Work: Psychological & Spiritual" in *Journal of Transpersonal Psychology.* Vol. 16, no. 1. 1984.

West, M.A. "Traditional and psychological perspectives on meditation." in West, (ed.), 1987.

—— (ed.) *The Psychology of Meditation.* Oxford: Clarendon Press. 1987.

White, K. *Handbook for the Diamond Country.* Edinburgh: Mainstream Publishing. 1990.
Whorf, B.L. *Language, Thought and Reality. Selected Writings.* New York: Wiley. 1956. (reprint 1981).
Wilber, K. & Welwood J. "Ego structure and egolessness" in Welwood, (ed.), 1978.
Wilber, K. *The Spectrum of Consciousness.* Wheaton, Ill: Theosophical Publishing House. 1977.
—— *No Boundary.* Boston: Shambhala. 1979.
—— "Psychologia Perennis: The Spectrum of Consciousness" in Vaughan & Walsh, (eds.), 1980.
Wilber, K., Engler, J. & Brown, D. (eds.) *Transformations of Consciousness.* Boston: Shambhala. 1986.
Williams, P. *Mahayana Buddhism.* London: Routledge. 1989.
Williams, T.T. *An Unspoken Hunger.* New York: Pantheon Books. 1994.
Willis, J.D. *On Knowing Reality. The Tattvartha Chapter of Asanga's Bodhisattvabhumi.* New York: Columbia University Press. 1979.
—— (ed.) *Feminine Ground.* Ithaca: Snow Lion. 1987.
Winnicott, D. *Human Nature.* London: Free Association Books. 1988.
—— *Playing & Reality.* London: Routledge. (reprint). 1991.
Winterson, J. *Art Objects.* London: Jonathan Cape. 1995.
Wittgenstein, L. *Tractatus Logico-Philosophicus.* trs. D.F. Pears & B.F. McGuinness. London: Routledge, Kegan Paul. 1969 (4th edition).
—— *Philosophical Investigations.* trs. G.E.M. Anscombe. Oxford: Blackwell. 1968 (3rd edition).
Wright, D.S. "Rethinking Transcendence: The Role of Language in Zen Experience" in *Philosophy East & West.* Vol. 42. 1992.
Young-Eisendrath, P. & Hall, J.A. (eds.) *The Book of the Self. Person, Pretext & Process.* New York: New York University Press. 1987.
Yuasa, Y. *The Body. Towards an Eastern Mind/Body Theory.* Albany: SUNY Press. 1987.
—— *The Body, Self-Cultivation and Ki Energy.* trs. Shigenori Nagatomo & M.S. Hull. Albany, N.Y: SUNY Press. 1993.
Zohar, D. *The Quantum Self.* London: Flamingo. 1991.

Index